Money with a [
Volume

Managing the Social Performance of Microfinance

Money with a Mission
Volume 2

Managing the Social Performance of Microfinance

Edited by

Alyson Brody, Martin Greeley and Katie Wright-Revolledo

ITDG PUBLISHING

Published by ITDG Publishing
Schumacher Centre for Technology and Development
Bourton Hall, Bourton-on-Dunsmore, Warwickshire CV23 9QZ, UK
www.itdgpublishing.org.uk

© Institute of Development Studies 2005

First published 2005

ISBN 1 85339 615 X

All rights reserved. No part of this publication may be reprinted
or reproduced or utilized in any form or by any electronic, mechanical,
or other means, now known or hereafter invented, including photocopying
and recording, or in any information storage or retrieval system,
without the written permission of the publishers.

A catalogue record for this book is available from the British Library.

The contributors have asserted their rights under the Copyright Designs and
Patents Act 1988 to be identified as authors of their respective contributions.

ITDG Publishing is the publishing arm of the Intermediate Technology
Development Group Ltd. Our mission is to build the skills and capacity of
people in developing countries through the dissemination of information
in all forms, enabling them to improve the quality of their lives and that
of future generations.

Typeset by RefineCatch Limited, Bungay, Suffolk
Printed in India by Replika Press

Contents

Acknowledgements	ix
List of figures	xii
List of tables	xiii
List of abbreviations and acronyms	xiv
Contributors	xvi

1 From service providers to learning organizations: microfinance practitioners' experiences of social performance management — 1

Alyson Brody, James Copestake and Martin Greeley

Introduction	1
Scope of the book	3
Summary of case studies	4
Managing a participatory approach	8
Lessons and general guidelines for SPM of microfinance	10
General guidelines for social performance management	11

2 Delivering inclusive microfinance with a poverty focus: the experience of the Bangladesh Rural Advancement Committee (BRAC) — 15

Imran Matin

Introduction	15
BRAC's microfinance canvas	17
Building opportunity ladders for the extreme poor: designing grants that build livelihoods	19
What does it take? Lessons from BRAC's experience	22
Conclusion	25

3 Institutionalizing a social performance management system at Lift Above Poverty Organization (LAPO), Nigeria 26

Stanley Aifuwa Garuba

Introduction	26
Microfinance in Nigeria	26
LAPO's social performance monitoring system	27
Development of LAPO's SPM system	28
Conclusion	38

4 Cost-effective impact management: the case of the Small Enterprise Foundation (SEF), South Africa 40

Ted Baumann

Introduction	40
The Small Enterprise Foundation	40
Impact management of SEF	41
Lessons	46
Conclusion	53

5 Methodological and organizational lessons from impact assessment studies: the case of SHARE, India 55

Marie Jo A. Cortijo and Naila Kabeer

Introduction	55
Analyzing outreach: reconciling different approaches to poverty measurement	58
Analyzing impacts on poverty	60
Controlling for dual membership: an analysis of wider impacts	64
Conclusion	65

6 The challenge of sustainability in India's poorest state: the case of the Centre for Youth and Social Development (CYSD) 68

Anup Dash and Naila Kabeer

Introduction	68
The challenge of working in India's poorest state	69
CYSD: its programme and mission	70
Imp-Act assessment of CYSD's programme in Koraput	74
Learning from the *Imp-Act* study	81
Conclusion	82

7 Institutionalizing internal learning systems: experiences from Professional Assistance for Development Action (PRADAN), India 83

D. Narendranath

Introduction	83
Background	83
Approach to impact assessment	86
Institutionalization of the internal learning system	88
The field test	91
Use of the ILS	93
Conclusion	97

8 Measuring and managing change in Bosnia-Herzegovina: Prizma's steps to deepen outreach and improve impact 98

Sean Kline

Introduction	98
Understanding context for social performance	100
Measuring social performance	105
Managing social performance	110
Conclusion	112

9 Achieving the double bottom line: a case study of Sinapi Aba Trust's (SAT) client impact monitoring system, Ghana 114

Lydia Opoku

Introduction	114
Background	114
CIMS design process	115
Process and lessons learned in developing the CIMS	120
Key lessons	124
Conclusion	126

10 Institutionalizing feedback from clients using credit association meetings: the experience of FOCCAS, Uganda 127

Regina Nakayenga and Susan Johnson

Introduction	127
Starting out: how satisfied are the clients?	128
Crisis and coping: understanding and responding	129
Institutionalizing feedback: credit association management meetings	133
Lessons learned	135
Conclusion	136

11 Microfinance networks and the evaluation of social performance: the case of FINRURAL, Bolivia   138

Irina Aliaga, Reynaldo Marconi and Paul Mosley

Introduction	138
Conceptual framework for impact assessment activities	138
The FINRURAL impact assessment service	140
Conclusion	144

12 The potential of regional networks to stimulate innovation in microfinance: lessons from the Microfinance Centre (MFC) in Eastern Europe   147

Katarzyna Pawlak

Introduction	147
MFC's involvement in regional innovation processes in CEE and the NIS	148
The innovation scaling-up model	150
Conclusion	154

13 Client assessment lessons learned from the Small Enterprise Education and Promotion (SEEP) Network, USA   157

Gary Woller

Introduction	157
What is client assessment?	160
Obstacles to client assessment	161
Lessons learned	164
Good practice in client assessment	167
Conclusion	170

Notes	172
References	178
Index	183

Acknowledgements

This book is the work of a large group of people over five years. Our shared goal was nothing less than to rethink and reshape the way we thought about microfinance, and to do so in an open, collaborative way that would have a practical effect on the way microfinance is managed and could contribute to global poverty reduction. This involved forming a global network (*Imp-Act*) to facilitate exchange of ideas and coordinate research carried out by more than thirty microfinance organizations across four continents. The network included not only staff of these organizations, but a large number of consultants and collaborators, members of supporting and umbrella organizations, and staff in three UK universities. Particular thanks for getting this book to print are due to Kathryn O'Neill for diligent and flexible sub-editing, to Malcolm Harper for providing detailed comments on the entire draft, and to the staff of ITDG Publications. We would also like to acknowledge and thank the contribution of the following individuals for their contributions to the work of the *Imp-Act* programme on which the book is based. No such list can ever be definitive and our thanks go to others we have missed, as well as to the many users and non-users of financial services who responded positively to requests for information.

Irina Aliaga Romero (FINRURAL, Bolivia), Elena Alexeeva (FORA, Russia), Aniceta R. Alip (CARD, Philippines), Jaime Aristotle B. Alip (CARD, Philippines), María Alvarado Vásquez (PROMUC, Peru), Ted Baumann (Community Microfinance Network, South Africa), Brian Beard (Opportunity International, USA), Demecia Benique Mamani (ProMujer-Peru, Peru), Jorge Bernedo Alvarado (Consultant, Peru), Georgina Blanco-Mancilla (Translator), Antoinette B. Bolaños (Asian Institute of Management, Philippines), Deborah Caro (Cultural Practice, LLC, USA), Miriam Cherogony (K-Rep Development Agency, Kenya), Augustine Cheruiyot (K-Rep Development Agency, Kenya), Ronald Chua (Asian Institute of Management, Philippines), Monique Cohen (Microfinance Opportunities, USA), James Copestake (University of Bath), Marie Jo Cortijo (Consultant), Patrick Crompton (FINCA International, USA), Anup Dash (CYSD, India), Peter Dawson (University of Bath, UK), Stephen Devereux (IDS, UK), Chris Dunford (Freedom From Hunger, USA),

x ACKNOWLEDGEMENTS

Ever Egusquiza Canta (Copeme, Peru), Godwin Ehigiamusoe (LAPO, Nigeria), Mark Ellison (University of Bath, UK), Laura Foose (ACT, USA), Grzegorz Galusek (MFC, Poland), Carter Garber (IDEAS, USA), Mateo Garcia Cabello (Translator), John Gaventa (IDS, UK), Stanley Garuba (LAPO, Nigeria), Laura Elena Garza Bueno (Colegio de Postgraduados, Mexico), Frank de Giovanni (Ford Foundation, USA), Maja Gizdic (Prizma, Bosnia-Herzegovinia), Jennifer Grant (Translator), Martin Greeley (IDS), Shantana R. Halder (BRAC, Bangladesh), Syed Hashemi (CGAP, USA), John Hatch (FINCA International, USA), Dirk van Hook (Cerudeb, Uganda), Alfredo Hubard (CAME, Mexico), Uwa Izekor (LAPO, Nigeria), Biljana Jahic (BosVita, Bosnia-Herzegovinia), Susan Johnson (University of Bath, UK), Lalaine M. Joyas (Microfinance Council of the Philippines), Naila Kabeer (IDS), Dana de Kanter (SEEP, USA), Ana Klincic (DEMOS, Croatia), Sean Kline (Freedom From Hunger, USA), Katherine E. Knotts (Secretariat), Olga Kostukova (FORA, Russia), M. Udaia Kumar (SHARE, India), Jean-Paul Lacoste (Ford Foundation, Chile), Marie Jennifer de Leon (Microfinance Council of the Philippines), José Andrés Loayza Pacheco (PROMUC, Peru), Reynaldo Ojeda Marconi (FINRURAL, Bolivia), Kalipe Mashaba (SEF, South Africa), Imran Matin (BRAC, Bangladesh), Michal Matul (MFC, Poland), Julian May (University Natal, South Africa), Zanele Mbeki (WDB, South Africa), Jamie McDade (CERUDEB), J. Allister McGregor (University of Bath, UK), Delores McLaughlin (PLAN International, USA), Gustavo Medeiros Urioste (FINRURAL, Bolivia), Rekha Mehra (Ford Foundation, India), Anibal Montoya Rodriguez (Covelo, Honduras), Juan Pedro Mora Sono (Consultant, Peru), Paul Mosley (University of Sheffield, UK), George Muruka (K-Rep Development Agency, Kenya), Leonard Mutesasira (*MicroSave*, Uganda), David Myhre (Ford Foundation, Mexico), Regina Nakayenga (FOCCAS, Uganda), Richard Nalela (CERUDEB, Uganda), D. Narendranath (PRADAN, India), Miguel Navarro (ODEF, Honduras), Lizbeth Navas-Aleman (Translator), Max Nino-Zarazua (Translator), Ben Nkuna (SEF, South Africa), Candace Nelson (Editor), Jamee Newland (Secretariat), Helzi Noponen (Consultant, India), Daniela Olejarova (Integra, Romania), Kathryn O'Neill (Editor), Lydia Opoku (Sinapi Aba Trust, Ghana), Ana Ortiz Monasterio (Translator), Katarzyna Pawlak (MFC, Poland), Anna Portisch (Secretariat), Pedro Pablo Ramirez Moreno (Colegio de Postgraduados, Mexico), Isabel Ramos (CAME, Mexico), Camelia Reyes Emba (CAME, Mexico), Kate Roper (SEF, South Africa), Catherine van de Ruit (University of Natal, South Africa), Suzy Salib-Bauer (Opportunity International, USA), Raul Sanchez (Katalyis, Honduras), Rodney Schuster (UMU, Uganda), Alla Serova (FORA, Russia), Namrata Sharma (CMF, Nepal), Shalik Ram Sharma (CMF, Nepal), Roshan Shrestha (CMF, Nepal), Anton Simanowitz (Secretariat), Frances Sinha (EDA, India), Sonthi Somayajulu (SHARE, India), Julius Ssegirinya (CERUDEB, Uganda), Moses Ssimwogerere (UMU, Uganda), Sonya Sultan (BRAC, Bangladesh), Ruomei Sun (FPC, China), Nelson Tasenga (FOCCAS, Uganda), Chizoba Unaeze (SEF, South Africa), Iris Villalobos Barahona (Katalysis, Honduras), Alice Walter (Consultant, France), Andrew Watson (Ford Foundation, China),

John de Wit (SEF, South Africa), Gary Woller (SEEP, USA), Graham A. N. Wright (*MicroSave*, Kenya), Katie Wright-Revolledo (University of Bath, UK), Hugo Yanque Martinez (PROMUC, Peru), and Emma Zapata (Colegio de Postgraduados, Mexico).

Finally, we would like to extend a sincere note of appreciation to the Ford Foundation Development Finance Affinity Group for initiating, funding, and actively contributing to the *Imp-Act* programme as it developed. Their good faith, toleration and flexibility set a model for us all. It was a lively, challenging, often messy and sometimes fraught experience: one that none of us will forget or would have missed.

Figures

Figure 3.1	LAPO's revised poverty means test	31
Figure 3.2	LAPO's client impact learning system	34
Figure 5.1	Poverty status of new and mature clients	62
Figure 8.1	Poverty scorecard	107
Figure 8.2	Poverty outreach and percentage of Prizma clients by branch	109
Figure 8.3	Prizma's mission statement	110
Figure 8.4	Annual team incentive sheet	112
Figure 9.1	Main reasons for leaving	119
Figure 9.2	Components of the Sinapi Aba client impact monitoring system	120
Figure 11.1	Conceptual framework for evaluation of the financial and social performance of MFIs	139
Figure 12.1	Regional microfinance industry landscape	149

Tables

Table 2.1	BRAC's inclusive microfinance with a poverty focus	17
Table 2.2	Reaching deeper: TUP and VGD members	22
Table 2.3	Comparing the 'selected' and 'not selected' ultra-poor over time	23
Table 3.1	Comparison of the distribution of LAPO's clients in poverty categories	32
Table 3.2	Use of instruments	37
Table 5.1	Share of clients in each poverty tercile	59
Table 9.1	Sample by type of client and by tool	117
Table 9.2	Means test point of mature and non-clients	117
Table 10.1	FOCCAS – key performance indicators	127
Table 10.2	Summary of changes to loan product	133
Table 11.1	FINRURAL initiatives in the assessment of MFIs' social and financial performance	140
Table 11.2	Characteristics of FINRURAL's impact assessment service	141
Table 11.3	Timeframe of activities planned and executed	144
Table 13.1	CAWG research partners	159

Acronyms and abbreviations

ABC	activity-based costing
AIMS	Assessing the Impact of Microenterprise Services
AP	Andhra Pradesh
BRAC	Bangladesh Rural Advancement Committee
CA	credit association
CAMM	credit association management meeting
CAWG	Client Assessment Working Group
CEE and NIS	Central and Eastern Europe and the Newly Independent States
CFPR/TUP	Challenging the Frontiers of Poverty Reduction: Targeting the Ultra Poor
CGAP	Consultative Group to Assist the Poor
CIMS	Client Impact Monitoring System
CYSD	Centre for Youth and Social Development
DWCRA	Development of Women and Children in Rural Areas
FFH	Freedom From Hunger International
FGD	focus group discussion
FINRURAL	Association of Financial Institutions for Rural Development
FOCCAS	Foundation for Credit and Community Assistance
HYV	high yield variety
IA	impact assessment
IAS	impact assessment service
IFPRI	International Food Policy Research Institute
IGVGD	Income Generation for Vulnerable Groups Development
ILS	Internal Learning System
ISM	innovation scaling-up model
JFRP	Jamalpur Flood Rehabilitation Project
LAPO	Lift Above Poverty Organization
LSMS	Living Standards Measurement Survey
MCP	Microcredit Programme
MDGs	Millennium Development Goals
MFC	Microfinance Centre

MFI	microfinance institution
MIS	management information system
MR	market research
NFHS	National Family Health Survey
OI	Opportunity International
PAR	portfolio-at-risk
PAT	Poverty Assessment Tool
PLA	Participatory Learning and Action
PRA	Participatory Rural Assessment
PRADAN	Professional Assistance for Development Action
PWR	participatory wealth ranking
SAT	Sinapi Aba Trust
SEEP	Small Enterprise Education and Promotion Network
SEF	Small Enterprise Foundation
SHARE	Society for Helping Awaken Rural Poor through Education
SHG	self-help group
SML	SHARE Microfin Ltd
SPM	social performance management
TA	technical assistance
TCP	Tšhomišano Credit Programme
UNDP	United Nations Development Programme
VGD	Vulnerable Group Development Programme
WFP	World Food Programme

Contributors

Ted Baumann is a South African political economist and development activist based in Cape Town. He is currently director of Bay Research & Consultancy Services (www.brcs.co.za), offering services on microfinance, housing, and development policy. Through BRCS Ted has worked extensively in African microfinance issues, concentrating on Eastern and Southern Africa. He has worked directly with institutions in Kenya, Tanzania, Zimbabwe, Mozambique, and Namibia, and indirectly with many more.

Marie Jo A. Cortijo is an independent consultant in microfinance. She graduated from IDS Sussex with a PhD in Economics.

Anup Dash is Professor of Sociology at Utkal University in India. He held the Ambedkar Chair as Professor at the National Institute of Social Work and Social Sciences, Bhubaneswar during 1994–1995. This Chair was created by the Government of India. His publications include: *The Political Elite In A Developing Society* (Delhi: Academic Foundation, 1994).

Stanley Garuba is Head of Planning and Research for LAPO (Lift Above Poverty Organization), a leading microfinance and development non-governmental organization in Benin City, Nigeria. He has significant experience in research, impact assessment, monitoring and evaluation work with LAPO.

Susan Johnson is lecturer in International Development at the University of Bath. She formerly worked for Action-Aid. She co-authored *Microfinance and Poverty Reduction* which was published in 1997, and since then has researched and written on impact assessment in microfinance, mainly in Africa.

Naila Kabeer is Professorial Fellow at the Institute of Development Studies. She has been engaged in research, training and advisory work on issues related to gender, poverty and social policy. Her most recent book is *Gender Mainstreaming in Poverty Eradication and the Millennium Development Goals: a Handbook for Policymakers and concerned stakeholders* which was published by the Commonwealth Secretariat and the International Development Research Centre, Canada.

Sean Kline is Senior Microfinance Technical Advisor for Freedom from Hunger. He founded and led a poverty-focused microfinance institution to full financial self-sufficiency, and has published on microfinance.

Imran Matin is a development researcher and has been working on various aspects of microfinance and its impacts on poverty for the last ten years. His doctoral thesis explores joint liability and group dynamics of group-based microlending. Dr Matin is currently the Director of BRAC's Research and Evaluation Division.

Paul Mosley is Head of the Department of Economics at the University of Sheffield. He is author (with David Hulme) of *Finance against Poverty* (1996) and other publications on political economy, finance and development.

D. Narendranath has worked for Professional Assistance for Development Action (PRADAN) India, on microfinance and livelihoods promotion for the rural poor for the past 13 years. He heads the Research and Resource Centre for PRADAN.

Reynaldo Marconi Ojeda has been the head of FINRURAL for over ten years. He is also a board member for the Latin American Rural Finance Forum (FORO LAC). He is the author of various publications on microfinance.

Lydia Opoku currently works with Sinapi Aba Trust (SAT), a leading microfinance organisation in Ghana overseeing all of SAT's Microfinance research projects. Her work includes conducting market surveys and research on a variety of issues, impact evaluation, product development and training of staff and other MFIs on impact assessment.

Katarzyna Pawlak is Deputy Director and Research Manager of the Microfinance Centre for Central and Eastern Europe and the Newly Independent States (MFC). She has written extensively on microfinance in Eastern Europe, especially for MFC.

Gary Woller is President of Woller & Associates, an international development consulting firm. His clients include, among others, the World Bank, USAID, DFID, UNDP, OECD, and numerous NGOs throughout the development world. Gary has published widely on international development and microfinance in academic and practitioner journals. He is the co-founder and former editor of the Journal of Microfinance.

CHAPTER ONE
From service providers to learning organizations: microfinance practitioners' experiences of social performance management

Alyson Brody, James Copestake and Martin Greeley

Introduction

Specialist providers of microfinance (referred to in this book as microfinance institutions or MFIs) have become preoccupied with demonstrating that the services they provide can be sustainable, and that they can operate on a sufficient scale to make a significant impact on development. The drive to be sustainable requires MFIs to measure, monitor and manage their financial performance carefully in terms of profit/loss and subsidy dependence. But few MFIs are interested in profit for its own sake. Most have an explicit social mission. This varies from MFI to MFI but common goals include reaching people excluded from regulated financial services or exploited by informal services, poverty reduction, the empowerment of women, and promotion of community solidarity. As with financial goals, it is likely that MFIs will be more successful in achieving these goals if they can measure, monitor and manage their progress towards them.

The central theme of the book examines the extent to which (and how) MFIs can improve their contribution to development by assessing and managing their social performance as systematically as is usually done for their financial performance. For those that are dependent on external funds, there is also external pressure to demonstrate that they are making a positive difference to clients' lives. For those who are, or are expecting to become, financially self-sufficient, the pressure is to improve the financial health of the organization without 'mission creep' (that is, unduly compromising their social mission goals). When the MFI clients are poor households the trade-offs can be acute because costs per dollar lent are higher. Mission creep is a real risk when the commercially-driven incentives to grow are strong.

As microfinance addresses the challenge of increasing its positive impact, an important approach is to understand and respond more directly to the specific needs of the clients it serves. Recent years have seen the beginnings of a fundamental shift in microfinance from a supply-led industry, inspired by a number of blue-print models of how access to financial services might be improved, to a more client-focused and demand-led approach (Sebstad and Cohen, 2001). The early growth of a new generation of MFIs responded to the success of a small number of pioneering organizations, including BancoSol in Bolivia, BRI in Indonesia, and Grameen Bank and BRAC in Bangladesh. This phase of growth saw the replication of successful models of microfinance in a range of new countries and contexts. It was also characterized by a rapid growth in the number of organizations and clients served, and in the value of funds managed. However, doubts also grew about the basis of this growth. In the rush for growth and financial sustainability, new MFIs risked failing to adequately adapt their initial blue-prints to different contexts and clients.

One set of doubts about their performance arose from weaker than expected financial performance. Many MFIs remained heavily dependent upon subsidies. Also, the growth of microfinance has been not been as fast as many had hoped. Moreover, much of the global growth in numbers of clients has been achieved by a relatively small number of 'high performers' in a few Asian countries (Morduch, 1999). Yet growth is also becoming harder to achieve. MFIs have increasingly found themselves competing head-to-head with each other, as well as facing high client exit and turnover rates (Rhyne, 2001). These problems have served as a wake-up call, prompting many MFIs to review and redesign their services. The most fundamental lesson has been for MFIs to become more market-oriented through design and delivery of services that are better matched to the specific conditions, needs and preferences of clients.

A more market-led approach represents an important step forward for microfinance, but the issue does not end there. As markets have become more competitive, so have doubts grown concerning MFI performance on their social mission. The impacts of many MFIs have been assessed but these assessments have been largely driven by an external donor agenda and conducted by someone from outside the organization. Reputable research is often complex and expensive. Moreover, the information is of limited use to address areas of organizational weakness because it is not produced with the MFI's own needs and concerns mainly in mind. High quality impact assessment studies, while contributing importantly to public policy debate, were increasingly seen to be too time consuming, costly and complex to be routinely useful to practitioners (Hulme, 2000).

Growing use of the concept of social performance reflects a shift in thinking away from set-piece social impact assessment studies, towards ways of institutionalizing assessment of outreach and impact on clients within routine operations of MFIs. During the late 1990s, a number of initiatives began to point this way, particularly the USAID-funded AIMS (Assessing the Impact of Microenterprise Services project) (Cohen, 2002). However, it became clear that designing new and more practitioner-friendly impact or client assessment tools was only part of the issue; the bigger challenge was to integrate new tools and systems into MFIs' decision-making practices, both at operational and strategic levels (Copestake, 2000; Simanowitz, 2001). To be effective, decision-makers would need to understand the usefulness of information about clients – beyond their loan repayment performance – in improving operations and achieving goals. They would have to be receptive to collecting the information and using it to make systematic changes in products and organizational processes. This is what the term 'social performance management' (SPM) means. SPM complements financial management and provides the basis for an MFI-developed double bottom line assessing both social and financial performance.

Scope of the book

This book is one product of a four-year programme called '*Imp-Act*, improving the impact of microfinance on poverty: an action-research programme'.[1] In commissioning this programme, the Ford Foundation had in mind three concerns and one conviction.[2] The first concern was with a lack of transparency about the social costs and benefits of microfinance, revealed in part by a certain amount of naïve and often self-serving optimism about what it could achieve on its own. The second concern was that the social mission of microfinance might be lost in the drive to commercialize. The third was that mainstream donor approaches to evaluation and impact assessment of microfinance did not attach much value to practitioners' own views and priorities, or indeed reveal much respect for them. The conviction was that specialist MFIs needed space to build and retain a capacity for internal learning and innovation, taking into account both social and financial goals.

A synthesis of findings from the *Imp-Act* programme is being published in parallel with this book (Copestake *et al*, 2005), and a third volume (*Imp-Act*/MFC, 2005) presents detailed guidelines, derived from the programme, on how MFIs can reach their social goals more effectively. The purpose of this volume is to provide additional space for some of the MFIs themselves, and those who worked closely with them, to describe their experiences in a way that reflects more fully their distinctive character and operating environment.

The *Imp-Act* programme was launched in the belief that innovation would result from allowing MFIs a greater opportunity to develop and manage their own projects and systems for generating information about outreach and impact. It also seemed appropriate to give them as much opportunity as possible to describe what they did themselves – hence this book. The book describes the organizational learning processes involved in trying to establish new ways of assessing progress in achieving social goals. As the title suggests, it is concerned with financial service providers and their efforts to strengthen themselves as learning organizations on social performance.

This book is made up of twelve case studies, each focusing on a different organization that actively participated in the *Imp-Act* programme. These include supporting NGOs and networks that do not directly provide services themselves, but support MFIs or grass-roots organizations that do. But it is neither a complete nor a representative record of the experience of thirty organizations that contractually formed part of the *Imp-Act* network. All participants were required to write a final report and a short summary of their experiences.[3] They were additionally encouraged, and in several cases received additional support, to go further and produce a more detailed account. The case studies presented here are the result. They were all written either by staff of the organization concerned or by researchers who worked closely with them. Although this book is intended for anyone with an interest in microfinance, it is aimed primarily at microfinance practitioners that share the aspirations and concerns of the *Imp-Act* participants to more systematically monitor progress and improve performance on their social goals.

Summary of case studies

The first nine case studies all focus on specific organizations directly involved in providing financial services, either themselves or through user groups. A second set of three case studies document the experience of microfinance networks.

Reaching and serving poor people through microfinance: three approaches

1. Reaching poor and very poor people without geographical targeting
In the first group are organizations that seek to work directly with households in absolute poverty. However, given that there are also less poor people in their programme areas, the organizations use poverty targeting tools, such as the Poverty Wealth Ranking used by SEF (Small Enterprise Foundation) in South Africa, to ensure that they do not experience mission drift.[4] These organizations chose to use their time with *Imp-Act* for improving methods of assessing poverty outreach, as well as for developing ways to monitor changes in clients' lives and levels of client satisfaction as a precursor to making services more client-focused and driven.

The first case study focuses on the work of BRAC (Bangladesh Rural Advancement Committee) (Chapter Two), whose dual mission is alleviation of poverty and empowerment, and which works in all 64 districts of Bangladesh, with 3.73 million members. BRAC offers an insightful example of how extremely poor people can be reached with microfinance initiatives, provided they are part of a creative, dynamic strategy that responds to the complex needs of these people. The chapter outlines an approach that combines microfinance with parallel programmes on health, education and other aspects of welfare. One of BRAC's main strengths is its commitment to innovate constantly and to evaluate and improve its impacts. These strategies enable BRAC to work with very poor households while maintaining microfinance as a key component of its activities.

LAPO (Lift Above Poverty Organization) (Chapter Three) operates in six states of Nigeria using a group lending methodology and has a membership of over 25,000. LAPO's work under *Imp-Act* aimed to ensure that the organization was reaching its very poor target group, in addition to understanding more about the impacts of its microfinance services on clients. Rather than devise new technologies for assessing poverty targeting, LAPO adapted an existing poverty means test, which was already an element of its client intake instrument – the participation form. The lengthy eight-indicator questionnaire was replaced with a five-indicator poverty assessment tool that can be quickly and easily administered. LAPO also wished to develop a comprehensive system to track changes in client status, yet when impact information was collected on existing clients, the data in fact revealed minimum impact. As a result of this discovery, LAPO has become more committed to assessing client impacts on an ongoing basis and to following up information on trends with qualitative research. This latter process has revealed a more nuanced picture of impact, which the simple indicators were unable to capture.

SEF (Small Enterprise Foundation) (Chapter Four) in South Africa, is an MFI operating in the country's poorest region of Tzaneen Province. SEF serves both poor and very poor people, while maintaining financial sustainability. The chapter is an assessment of SEF's existing monitoring system that was refined under *Imp-Act*. It stresses the centrality of SEF's impact management system to its success as an MFI, both socially and financially, enabling it to balance the priorities of the non-poor targeted Microcredit Programme (MCP) and the poverty-targeted Tšhomišano Credit Programme (TCP). The system is concerned primarily with monitoring the activities and impacts of the TCP on an ongoing basis, so as to identify potential problems early and to continually improve impacts on poverty. It has been invaluable in arresting client dropout rates, which in turn has led to increased financial stability for SEF, resulting in a situation where the costs of monitoring have been offset by savings incurred. These savings occur by avoiding having to constantly recruit new clients to replace dropouts.

SHARE (Society for Helping Awaken Rural Poor through Education) (Chapter Five) is one of the largest and fastest-growing MFIs in India, with an excellent repayment record. Its mission is to alleviate poverty 'among the poorest of the poor, especially women' through credit and savings programmes. SHARE commissioned three comprehensive studies under *Imp-Act*, all led by external consultants, but involving SHARE staff. One was a poverty outreach study and two were impact assessments, of which one had a specific focus on wider impacts of microfinance, including political awareness and social cohesion. The chapter on SHARE explores the implications of these studies, both in terms of methodology and lessons for the organization. Some of the caveats entailed in conducting such studies are highlighted; these include issues around attribution of impacts to a single microfinance programme and the ways in which levels of poverty outreach are affected by whether absolute or relative measures of poverty are used.

2. Reaching very poor people through geographical targeting

Among the case studies of organizations directly involved in providing financial services is a second group of organizations that can claim to reach the poorest people because they target geographical areas with high concentrations of extreme poverty. However, these organizations usually have no systematic way of monitoring or assessing the impacts they have, which is important information to convince donors and other stakeholders of their significance in poverty reduction. Thus, the emphasis of CYSD (Centre for Youth and Social Development) and PRADAN (Professional Assistance for Development Action) in India was on identifying and chronicling changes in clients' lives as a result of their interventions. The ways in which each organization chose to implement these studies were fundamentally different. CYSD (Chapter Six) has tailored its services to the harsh realities of remote tribal livelihoods in rural Orissa, promoting a self-help group (SHG)[5] approach to microfinance, which is the cornerstone of a broader livelihoods and empowerment agenda. CYSD chose to conduct a large-scale impact study under *Imp-Act*, with some external assistance. That its particular approach to poverty reduction has been successful is reflected in the findings of the study, which are the focus of the chapter.

PRADAN (Chapter Seven) is an NGO working in seven of the poorest states in India, focusing on livelihoods promotion and capacity-building strategies. Microfinance is an important component of its mission, following an SHG model. PRADAN's approach to managing social performance reflects a commitment to facilitating self-sufficiency and building capacities for poor people. In the *Imp-Act* programme, PRADAN wished to introduce and pilot a highly participative method of assessment that would eventually be integrated into its organizational practices. An underlying aim was to develop a system that would be useful for SHG members themselves. PRADAN has therefore invested in adapting and piloting the Internal Learning System (ILS), which is based on pictorial 'learning diaries' that enable members to track and reflect on their own progress. The chapter details the intense and participatory process of design and feedback.

3. Focus on service and product design

A third group of direct service-provider organizations does not target in the ways outlined above, but prioritizes service and product design in their strategies to reach poor and very poor clients. Prizma (Chapter Eight) in Bosnia-Herzegovina, assists poor and low-income clients in achieving sustainable livelihoods and basic needs. Its work under *Imp-Act* involved conducting research into the specific conditions of poverty in the region and reviewing not only existing products, but also organizational culture in response to the findings. The analysis revealed a disjuncture between particular elements of organizational structure and the needs of poor people in the region, which was leading to self-exclusion and exclusion of poor clients. As a consequence, the practice of rewarding field staff for achieving 100 per cent loan repayment rates within a fixed period has been replaced by an incentive system that reflects attention to the organization's social goals. In addition, fundamental aspects of Prizma's loan policy have been revised, such as introducing a more flexible approach to default.

In Ghana, SAT (Sinapi Aba Trust) (Chapter Nine) has also developed an ongoing client monitoring system that will enable managers to make immediate, short-term decisions based on knowledge of changes in client status and levels of client satisfaction, known as the Client Impact Monitoring System (CIMS). These aims were prompted by a desire to meet mission goals, to provide donors with proof of impact and to increase SAT's credibility amongst growing competition. SAT implemented a two-phase programme under *Imp-Act*. The first phase focused on identifying gaps in SAT's knowledge of impacts and client needs. Phase two comprised SAT's development of the CIMS. The initial pilot stage of the CIMS revealed its usefulness; staff and management reported better understanding of clients and made preliminary changes to its products and services, such as the introduction of an asset loan and training to enhance women's empowerment.

FOCCAS (Foundation for Credit and Community Assistance) (Chapter Ten) in Uganda, aimed initially to implement a comprehensive 'progress tracking system', addressing questions about poverty outreach, the impacts of its Credit with Education approach and levels of client satisfaction. In practice, FOCCAS found that a comprehensive study of client satisfaction occupied all of its resources for client and organizational assessment, but was nonetheless an extremely revealing tool. The research period focused on issues of specific local relevance, such as the effects of seasonality on clients and their coping strategies. As a consequence of the research, efforts have been made to tailor services to these particular conditions.

Challenging the culture of microfinance assessment through networks

Six of the *Imp-Act* partners were microfinance networks, operating at national, regional and global levels and this book includes case studies from three of them: FINRURAL (Association of Financial Institutions for Rural Development) (Chapter Eleven), a Bolivian organization that provides support to 14 microfinance organizations; MFC (Microfinance Centre) for Eastern Europe and the New Independent States (Chapter Twelve), a network that provides support to 86 member organizations across 26 countries; and SEEP (Small Enterprise Education and Promotion Network) (Chapter Thirteen), which is a network of over 50 MFIs in developing countries. As the case studies show, these networks have been in a position to promote and implement good practice around social performance management (SPM) by offering training in client assessment tools and designing SPM processes for use in the region.

There can be tensions between achieving a useful model of SPM that can be applied by a network across a region and ensuring that it is appropriate for the diverse range and needs of organizations in the same region. FINRURAL chose to focus on the development of a generic model for impact assessment (IA), which is offered as a service to participating MFIs. Two important benefits have arisen from this process. First, a direct benefit for MFIs involved has been the environment of mutual support and sharing created as a result of the IA studies. The 'network model of impact evaluation' has provided them with a platform for exchanging ideas on how to improve their services. Second, for FINRURAL, a flexible, relatively low-cost research mechanism has been developed, which permits comparisons across a range of institutions, is able to respond more effectively to specific local conditions than a ready-made impact assessment package, and provides rigorous baseline information for future studies.

The Eastern European network, MFC, based in Poland, has used its links to organizations across the region for conducting client and organizational assessments in a similar way to FINRURAL. Under *Imp-Act*, it has furthered the development of a common SPM methodology, known as the 'innovation scaling-up model' (ISM) through a complex action-research and piloting process. Yet, there is an important departure from FINRURAL's centralized methods: the ways in which MFC's solutions are implemented depend on the organizations themselves, and the ultimate aim is for the MFIs to become self-sufficient in their application of the packages so that their SPM is effective, relatively low-cost and sustainable. Hence, the ISM eliminates the costly stage of SPM system development for resource-poor MFIs, but enables them to conduct their own assessments and monitoring as a precursor to improving their services.

SEEP services include training programmes, workshops and publications to improve the functioning of MFIs and their impacts on poverty. The chapter reports on a series of studies conducted by their Client Assessment Working Group (CAWG), which aimed to capture participating SEEP members' experiences of, and responses to, the introduction of client assessment components into their work. Some of these SEEP members were also *Imp-Act* partners. The chapter presents lessons learned through the organizations' active engagement with client assessment and offers practical suggestions for the successful design of client assessment frameworks as well as their implementation and institutionalization into organizational practices. Notably, a longitudinal view of decision-making processes around priorities for client assessment is provided, which demonstrates a shift from the desire to *prove* impacts to donors, to the desire to use information for *improving* practice.

Managing a participatory approach

As already emphasized, *Imp-Act* started from the premise that SPM systems should not simply be imposed on organizations, but should evolve in an organic way out of the perspectives, needs, ideas and situations of each MFI and its clients. This approach is rooted in the reality that no two MFIs are the same; they have different missions, client bases and socio-cultural foundations, and the systems they employ to assess the effectiveness of their interventions must be tailored to these specific contexts, as should the services and products they offer. More than this, the programme aimed to be participatory, employing an action-research methodology. The goal was to empower staff of MFIs to develop and implement their own SPM systems and to initiate more detailed studies into impacts of their services. At the core of this methodology was a desire to respect and build on the local knowledge of MFIs – to take their experience as a basis for investigation and new strategies, rather than imposing an external 'expert' approach, with its 'unavoidable paternalism' (Chambers, 1983).

In principle this meant that the priorities of each individual organization and network would drive *Imp-Act*'s research agenda. Members of a core academic team would offer technical assistance to the MFIs, but these academics would also be learning from the processes undergone by each organization, whether positive or negative. This lack of a prescriptive agenda led to a variety of ways in which organizations decided the *Imp-Act* work would be useful to them, and to varying degrees of success in implementation and utility. Several organizations chose to conduct impact or poverty assessment studies, or both, but were also concerned with developing or modifying ongoing systems that would be incorporated into their routine work (Prizma in Bosnia-Herzegovina is a good example of this).

Some organizations (such as FOCCAS, LAPO, SAT and PRADAN) were developing such systems for the first time, while others (CYSD and SHARE) chose to conduct full-scale impact assessments in order to demonstrate the effectiveness of their approaches to external stakeholders. The assessments were facilitated to varying degrees by consultants, but involved staff within the organizations where possible, and therefore constituted an important learning process and provided a model for future studies. For the impact assessment components, many of the organizations used existing assessment tools, such as AIMS-SEEP,[6] the Consultative Group to Assist the Poor (CGAP) Poverty Assessment Tool[7] (PAT) and the *MicroSave* Tools,[8] adapted to the specific needs and conditions of each organization. Similarly, the six networks that were *Imp-Act* partners interpreted the challenge of promoting SPM in ways that reflected the priorities and interests of each network. Collectively, the process has resulted in a diversity of approaches but a common commitment to direct organizational learning towards improvement in social performance.

Learning through action-research is never simple and often messy; it is full of dead ends, unanswered questions and is beset by logistical issues. These usual complications were heightened by the complex and, at times, unwieldy nature of the programme. During the period of hands-on engagement with MFIs, the programme posed several challenges, ranging from frequent turnover of MFI staff working directly with *Imp-Act*, to communication gaps, differences in interpretation and problems with email.

In practice, it was realized that a balance needed to be reached between the 'intellectual autonomy' of action research and the central guidance and support of the UK academic team in order to ensure that the programme objectives did not go off track. While the aims of the programme remained constant, its findings and messages were frequently revisited and revised through dynamic, iterative processes of discussion and debate. These discussions were shaped through meetings at the level of the UK academic team and steering committee and at regional and global levels, as well as being continued through informal email exchanges. Such meetings and discussions also offered the MFI practitioners involved a unique opportunity to exchange ideas and learn from others working in completely different environments.

These learning processes were extremely valuable for the management and staff of MFIs directly involved in *Imp-Act*. A survey conducted at the end of the action research phase[9] yielded mostly positive feedback. The majority of partners reported a very constructive experience and felt they had benefited from the action-research process itself. One partner noted that 'the flexibility and autonomy the programme allowed is really to be appreciated'. Survey responses indicated that the 'organizational champions' leading the SPM process for each partner had, for the most part, succeeded in creating or strengthening a learning culture within their organizations; in revitalizing concerns for meeting mission objectives; and in communicating the importance of listening to both clients and staff members.

Lessons and general guidelines for SPM of microfinance

Institutionalizing social performance management

While each social performance management system is unique in its design or adaptation to a particular context, there are core considerations that all MFIs need to address. The most significant of these is the need to ensure that an SPM is institutionalized. This entails eliciting long-term support and commitment at all levels of the organization – from clients to the MFI board. The case study organizations included here have all recognized that the systems would fail if staff did not see their value, and therefore invested in processes to ensure this 'buy-in'.

For example, SAT and FOCCAS have both invested time in making sure that policy changes are properly communicated to staff so that they can see how they will facilitate their own work, as well as improving impacts on clients. They have held staff training in interview techniques, in particular to ensure they understand the intent behind the questions. Efforts are being made to keep the interviews short and focused and to incorporate them into existing systems as much as possible so as to avoid placing an added burden on staff. This increases staff support of the client assessment process, in addition to improving the quality of the interviews and information gathered. In the case of LAPO, management was particularly conscious of the need to garner support of its board members in identifying SPM as an important step towards enabling LAPO to meet its mission objectives.

In PRADAN, field staff were initially resistant to the introduction of the learning diaries, seeing them as an addition to their already heavy workload. PRADAN tackled this scepticism by implementing an extremely participatory approach to the development of the Internal Learning System (ILS), involving staff and clients in its fundamental design and testing. Care was taken in training staff in the purpose and administration of the workbooks, and their use of the ILS was closely monitored. In the case of SEEP, members also stressed the importance of securing buy-in from both staff and management, chiefly by demonstrating the connection between client assessment and organizational performance and involving them in assessment processes from the start.

Other partners have made it their mission to reach extremely poor people who are often left out of microfinance programmes because they are considered 'high risk' or too difficult to reach and serve effectively. As noted above, and as the cases of BRAC and CYSD exemplify, building capacity to reach these groups involves creative responses based on a deep understanding of the conditions faced by very poor people. As the examples of SEF and Prizma clearly demonstrate, attracting and maintaining these groups also requires institutional mechanisms that highlight potential problems before they become damaging for the organization.

General guidelines for social performance management

The main goal of the *Imp-Act* programme was to draw upon experience of a wide range of microfinance organizations, including those described in the book, in order to produce more coherent guidelines for the wider industry on how social performance can be more effectively assessed and managed. It is clear from the examples included that there is no single blueprint for improved social performance management of microfinance that can be applied to all organizations. A key ingredient is the creativity and commitment of practitioners to design and implement systems that are suited to their own organizations and environments. But this is not, of course, the same as saying that 'anything goes' or that MFIs cannot learn from each other's experiences. There is a common framework.[10]

The starting point for the common framework is the lesson that having a mission and turning it into a workable strategy is not enough. It is also necessary to build systems for routinely monitoring who intended clients are, their needs, how effectively they are being reached, whether services provided bring the expected benefits and at what cost. In their absence, social performance will not improve as fast as it could and mission drift is more likely. This perspective is summarized in the six questions below. Effective SPM requires an MFI to have clear answers to all these questions or be committed to developing such answers.

1. What are your social goals, and how do you seek to achieve them?
2. How do you monitor who uses and who is excluded from using your services?

3. How do you monitor and assess why some clients leave or become inactive?
4. How do you assess the effect of your services on loyal and active clients?
5. How do you use/expect to use the information you collect?
6. How do you maintain and improve the quality of the systems and processes through which you answer these questions, including making them more cost-effective?

The following paragraphs elaborate on the six questions.

Goals, strategy and ownership

SPM should be linked to specific organizational goals and a clear strategy for how to achieve them. The strategy may be minimalist (for example, to provide a safe and sustainable savings facility to as many people as possible) or it may be broader (for example, to empower women through group-based savings, credit and adult education). It may yield unexpected negative side-effects and it may need revision, but that is no excuse for lack of clarity of intent. More specifically, a key argument of the book is that poverty reduction and other impacts through provision of microfinance services do not happen by accident; they require clear intent and careful planning. Statements of intent are meaningful only if the most powerful actors within an MFI – its board and senior management – are fully committed to them.

Client status monitoring

To assess impact on clients it is necessary to know the social and economic characteristics of clients and how these are changing over time. This may seem obvious but much investment in impact assessment has nevertheless failed for lack of a sound monitoring foundation. The literature on this aspect of SPM has mostly been concerned with choice of indicators. However, whatever indicators are selected, the critical point is that the data is routinely and effectively summarized and reported so that differences (for example, between branches and different categories of client) and trends over time can be systematically reviewed.

It is better to have routine, disaggregated and reliable information on a few indicators than to drown in a sea of indicators. A particular challenge for many MFIs has also been to ensure that such monitoring systems clearly explain the extent to which the status of clients is changing due to new entry, exit and changed status of loyal clients (Woller *et al*, 2004). It is also important to ensure that routine status monitoring (for example, of poverty) and explicit targeting are not conflated in a way that create incentives for data distortion.

Exit monitoring and assessment

Knowing how many clients are leaving is an integral part of any client status monitoring system, as discussed above. When clients leave because they graduate to other financial services providers (for example, those who offer bigger loans), it probably reflects well on the MFI. But in other cases exit data may have additional significance for programmes. If the act of leaving (or of allowing a savings account to become dormant) reveals clients' assessment of the poor quality of the services they receive it may suggest specific needs for product changes or other programme improvements. One caveat to this is that it is necessary to find a simple and routine way of checking how far incidental factors, such as variation in mobility and morbidity, also explain variation in exit rates. Quantitative analysis of these different reasons for dropouts can be a means for programme changes that improve profitability.

Impact assessment

The very act of remaining an active user of an MFI's services generally suggests their impact is positive. However, all clients are not equally well informed and their experience of 'value added' is very variable; both an MFI's social and financial performance goals can benefit from better understanding why. There are three broad approaches to doing so.

The first favours statistical analysis of predetermined quantitative survey data about a representative sample of clients and non-clients. This approach is important for public policy analysis but is generally too complex, time consuming and expensive for MFIs to use routinely, even to inform long-term strategic planning. Large quantitative impact surveys are 'methodologically indivisible': reliable results can be obtained only from analysis of data from one or more rounds of hundreds of interviews. More modest 'mid-range' impact surveys can be useful in conjunction with other methods, particularly to monitor change in a small number of key indicators. But close and experienced supervision is needed to avoid time and cost over-runs, and to avoid biased interpretation of findings.

A second approach is to rely on collection, analysis and expert interpretation of more open-ended (qualitative) data from a range of sources, including key informants, in-depth interviews and focus groups. Insights can be rich and unexpected, but this can also be expensive and time consuming. Encouragingly, recent experience with the Qualitative Individual In-depth Interview Protocol (QUIP) suggests that in-depth interviews can be conducted more cost-effectively than has often been the case in the past (*Imp-Act*, 2004).

The third approach is to rely on more applied methods of market research and participatory appraisal, including the use of satisfaction surveys and focus groups. On their own these tools may be less rigorous. But reliability can be enhanced both by repeated use and through cross-checking results from a variety of different sources including feedback from staff and routine reports on trends in client-level indicators. The metaphor of triangulation applies: it is better to take bearings from several points and to see where they cross, rather than to concentrate on trying to get a very precise bearing from one point. It is also better to do this as frequently as possible so as to be able to monitor how impact is changing over time. While each source will be imperfect, a complementary mix can be adequate.

Use of social performance data

The key test of social performance management, emphasized by the ideas of the feedback loop, is that data is used for organizational learning (*Imp-Act*, 2003). Decisions may be strategic, relate to product development, quality of service enhancement or routine operations. In each case, we start by considering what we already know and what gaps remain. For some MFIs within the programme, this required an initial investment of resources in needs assessment; others started off with priority issues and sought to augment their systems gradually. In many cases the most urgent question was *not* impact (Question 4), but either knowing more about whom clients were (Question 2) or why they were leaving (Question 3). By directing often scarce resources at the most pressing questions, those responsible for SPM were able to develop credibility and trust within their organization, thereby generating internal support for more ambitious and longer term investment in SPM.

System improvement

There is no blueprint for SPM. The balance between monitoring and assessment is needs and performance driven. The client status monitoring system should be routine, comprehensive and generate simple, standardized data. Where statistics diverge or change unexpectedly then this should trigger further investigation. MFIs need the capacity to respond by finding out in more detail what is happening to particular groups of clients and why, and acting on these findings. The approach to SPM should also be capable of growing and changing in line with the MFI itself. Thus, SPM should incorporate means for reviewing the appropriateness of the information collected in response to changing organizational needs and priorities.

CHAPTER TWO

Delivering inclusive microfinance with a poverty focus: the experience of the Bangladesh Rural Advancement Committee (BRAC)

Imran Matin

Introduction

Reading discourses in the right way is important. The discourse around microfinance has been and is being shaped by the interplay of ideas and forces, and it is important that we understand these dynamics and their implications for a poverty and social performance-centric microfinance future.

The rhetoric of 'inclusive microfinance' (CGAP, 2003) that is employed by global microfinance discourse power centres, such as CGAP, is interesting and we need to read it right. It allows the debate on poverty and microfinance – especially depth of poverty outreach, trade-offs, impact and social performance – to be absorbed within a wider discourse of inclusiveness. Does this matter for the future of poverty and social performance-centric discussions about microfinance? Apparently the language and spirit of inclusiveness should bode well for those who come to microfinance from a poverty perspective. However, a closer reading suggests that the framework on inclusiveness will not necessarily advance the agenda of a more poverty-focused microfinance future.

There are two core elements that describe what CGAP means by inclusiveness in microfinance. First, promoting institutional diversity, and second, promoting diverse financial services to a broad range of clients (CGAP, 2003). The question of how such diversity contributes to poverty alleviation is not an explicit element of the inclusive microfinance agenda. This has real implications for debates and conversations that are important and relevant for developing a more poverty-focused microfinance future. For instance, 'mission drift' (providers veering away from their mission of serving the poor and the poorest), an important issue in terms of keeping a microfinance focus on the poor, can easily be seen as a non-issue. After all, it should not matter as long as providers are 'diversifying' their client base, which is, according to the new inclusive microfinance agenda, an end in itself.

Similarly, financial product innovation and diversification will themselves be important, irrespective of their focus on deepening poverty outreach. Initiatives to serve poorer market segments become no more important than initiatives to go upmarket. The search for supporting market segments that create greater poverty-alleviating effects becomes as important as strategizing upmarket interventions with no poverty focus. The progress of the sector will be measured in terms of increases in the range of providers and products, and client pool; there is no weighting scheme to prioritize the many different ways of attaining inclusiveness. It is interesting to note that the rephrasing of CGAP's acronym from Consultative Group to Assist the *Poorest* to Consultative Group to Assist the *Poor*, and the language of inclusiveness as the centrepiece of its microfinance and global discourses, followed one another.

Yet the concept of inclusiveness, if framed through a poverty and social performance lens, could have been very powerful. Framing inclusiveness from such a perspective would not, by definition, preclude serving non-poor market segments, or ask every microfinance provider directly to target the poor and the poorest. It would also, by definition, neither delimit microfinance provision to certain types of providers such as NGOs, nor stifle new financial product innovation.

The only constraint that inclusiveness from a poverty and social performance perspective would involve is an explicit recognition that whatever microfinance does, ultimately it should have a poverty alleviation argument at its core. This would mean that the proof of poverty outreach would not only lie with microfinance providers claiming to reach the poor, but providers serving non-poor market segments would also have to think carefully about, and develop strategies to monitor and demonstrate, how their services are delivering on poverty alleviation, however indirectly. This would have been very powerful because the strength of a range of diverse players, from donors to commercial investors, from NGOs to banks, could all have been harnessed towards supporting microfinance as a poverty alleviation tool that works. These players could have been inclusive in ways that matter for poverty alleviation promoting a real inclusiveness with an overarching vision, as opposed to an inclusiveness that is merely a strategy without a meaningful end.

This chapter is a case study on how microfinance institutions can deliver on inclusive microfinance with a focus on poverty alleviation. It is based on how the Bangladesh Rural Advancement Committee (BRAC), a large development NGO in Bangladesh, has managed to serve the poorest, poor and non-poor market segments with microfinance, but always having at the core of its approach a poverty-focused argument, thinking, strategizing and monitoring. There have been challenges and things have not always gone as expected. The important point, however, is that these challenges and unanticipated consequences are identified and very much part of the 'organizational discomfort' that provides the fodder, language and arguments for new innovations. The aim here is to elaborate on how such challenges and fissures are made to count within an organizational culture.

BRAC's microfinance canvas

The poor are a heterogeneous group with diverse livelihoods, needs and potential that change over time due to life cycle, new opportunities and external shocks. This diverse and dynamic reality of poor people's lives forms the canvas upon which BRAC conceptualizes and designs its repertoire of development programmes, of which microfinance is a core element. In this section, we first provide a glimpse of BRAC's microfinance canvas and then focus on how it has challenged itself to deliver on including the poorest in its operational as well as conceptual focus of microfinance.

A number of points emerge from Table 2.1. First, the poor and the poorest constitute over 97 per cent of BRAC's microfinance clients. Interestingly, almost 26 per cent of BRAC's microfinance clients are the poorest and join its core microfinance programme, *Dabi*, through the Income Generation for Vulnerable Groups Development (IGVGD) programme. Second, expansion of BRAC's microfinance programmes for the 'non-poor', called Progoti and Unnati, is much faster for the agricultural credit programme (Unnati) than it is for the non-agricultural credit programme (Progoti). This suggests the wisdom

Table 2.1 BRAC's inclusive microfinance with a poverty focus

Programme name	Started from	Main arguments	Target group	Product summary	Total no. of clients (December 2003)
IGVGD	1985	The poorest need grant-based entry points into microfinance	Poorest women receiving food aid under the Government of Bangladesh/WFP Vulnerable Group Development Programme	• Monthly food aid for 2 years • Social awareness and income-generating activities training • Health support • Savings • Microcredit (av. 1st loan Tk2,000 (US$31))	1,085,114
Dabi (continued)	1974	Poor women can successfully use and repay loans	Moderate poor women from households owning no more than 50 decimals of land	• Loan repayable in 46 equal weekly instalments • 1st loan Tk5,000 (US$78)	2,984,886

Table 2.1—*continued*

Programme name	Started from	Main arguments	Target group	Product summary	Total no. of clients (December 2003)
Progoti	1996	Micro-entrepreneurs face major credit constraints in expanding their business. Expansion of microenterprises can generate employment and local economic growth	Micro-entrepreneurs in rural and peri-urban areas	• Collateralized loan repayable in monthly instalments • 24-month, 36-month and 48-month loans • Interest rebate in case of early repayment • 1st loan size from Tk20,000 (US$310)	41,633
Unnati	2001	Small farmers face major credit constraints in diversifying into cash crop and non-crop sectors. Expansion of employment opportunities for the poor and a boost to agricultural production	Small farmers (owning 3 acres or more) involved	• Collateralized year-long loan repayable in weekly instalments • 1st loan size Tk12,000 (US$186)	64,534

a focus on supporting the agricultural sector for more robust local economic growth, which has been argued in the literature to have far stronger poverty-alleviating effects. Third, the interlinkage between the various microfinance programmes is worth mentioning. For instance, about 70 per cent of the IGVGD clients who come from the poorest segment of the population graduate to BRAC's Dabi microfinance programme; over 13 per cent and 40 per cent of our Progoti and Unnati programme clients respectively are 'graduates' from the Dabi programme.

The range of BRAC's microfinance programmes is designed to serve various market segments, but the focus is very much on supporting sectors that have greater poverty-alleviating effects. More importantly, programmes have a strong element of supporting various levels of graduation. In the rest of this chapter, we focus on the experience of BRAC's programmes for the poorest, of which microfinance is a core component of the programmatic strategy.

Building opportunity ladders for the extreme poor: designing grants that build livelihoods

BRAC had long realized the difficulties of reaching and addressing the needs of the extreme poor using conventional microfinance. However, the organization's challenge was to develop mechanisms through which the extreme poor could be included within its microfinance programmes using the window of opportunity provided by grants to build sustainable livelihoods in such a way as to be cost-effective and go beyond the grants.

IGVGD programme: including those left out

In 1985 BRAC approached the World Food Programme (WFP), which was already providing a time-bound food assistance scheme to the extreme poor under its Vulnerable Group Development (VGD) programme, with a view to implementing a new linkage and sustainable model for the vulnerable group. The IGVGD programme was thus designed to link extremely vulnerable women to mainstream development activities. Under this initiative, extremely poor women were organized into groups and provided with skill development training in sectors such as poultry, where many opportunities for self-employment can be created. During the programme period these extremely poor women received food transfers, a savings scheme was developed and later, small amounts of programme credit were also provided so that the training they received could be more meaningfully used for more secure livelihoods.

The whole programme was focused on developing a systematic approach to take advantage of the window of opportunity in the lives of these extremely poor women while they received the food transfers, which represented short-term security. It provided support so that the women could stand on more solid ground once the transfer period was over. An independent study by WFP found that through this strategic linkage, more than three quarters of those who received the VGD card in every cycle ended up becoming regular clients of BRAC's microfinance programme.

A study by Hashemi (2001) found that the subsidy per VGD woman was about US$135, which 'represents a small subsidy, given the overwhelming majority of IGVGD women who graduate out of a need for continuous handouts'. Needless to say, the greater the proportion of the VGD women who graduate to BRAC's microfinance programme and the better the quality of graduation, the greater the possibility that over a period of time the subsidy is recouped.

Building more solid opportunity ladders

BRAC's IGVGD experiences demonstrated the possibility of creating opportunity ladders from safety nets for those who are left behind by conventional microfinance. This made BRAC even bolder in carrying out further experiments with this concept. BRAC noticed that although, for a great majority, the IGVGD approach led to an increased ability to benefit from regular microfinance programmes, for a significant minority this was not happening. More worryingly, those that failed to 'make it' were among the poorest and most vulnerable (Sattar *et al*, 1999).

There were several reasons for this. BRAC was at times dissatisfied with the targeting carried out by the *upazilla* (village administrative unit) representatives, who sometimes selected participants based on political and other motives. More importantly, the VGD women often failed to get the full benefits of the window of opportunity provided by the food transfer. This is because one VGD card was often unofficially shared between two or more people. Sometimes, VGD cards had to be 'bought' and more often than not, this would mean advance selling of the cards to wheat dealers to raise the money for the 'payment'. BRAC felt the need for a programme where it could have more control over the processes, and where the window of opportunity would be specifically designed to build solid ground from which the extreme poor could move forward.

The Jamalpur Flood Rehabilitation Project

An opportunity arose when BRAC was approached by the European Commission (EC) to design an asset grant-based support scheme for the poorest flood victims in Jamalpur, a very poor district of the country, as a part of its 1998 flood rehabilitation support.[1] This project was known as the Jamalpur Flood Rehabilitation Project (JFRP) and had a two-year duration from 1999 to 2001. A set of targeting indicators was developed for reaching the poorest, based on a review of poverty profile literature of rural Bangladesh. A range of assets, in which BRAC had prior technical support experiences, such as cage rearing of HYV (high yield variety) poultry, livestock (cows and goats) and nursery plants, were provided as one-off grants to the poorest flood victims. In addition, all associated inputs needed, such as poultry feed, cattle fodder, seed and fertilizer for the nursery plants, were provided for free during the first cycle of these enterprises. A monthly food ration was also given to ensure food security before the enterprises started generating income. Intensive income-generation training and monitoring of the enterprises were carried out.

In 2001 an assessment of the JFRP found that over 60 per cent of those supported by the project had already started taking micro-loans from BRAC and joined its village organizations. Those that did not take a loan had socio-demographic structures that made it difficult for them to take loans and use them well.[2] The study also found that although the targeting methodology used was quite effective, because it relied only on an indicator-based methodology it sometimes failed to include the poorest, who lived in interior parts of the village and/or lived in households that could be missed out. More importantly, the community did not have a sense of ownership over the targeting because they were not involved. This led to hostility between those selected and those who were not, which adversely affected the overall aim of the project. Poor health, which was not adequately addressed, was also found to be an important reason for those who failed to do as well as expected (Matin and Begum, 2002).

Putting lessons learnt into practice
These lessons were incorporated in a new experimental programme to meet the apparent challenges. BRAC set up Challenging the Frontiers of Poverty Reduction: Targeting the Ultra Poor (CFPR/TUP), or TUP for short, in January 2002 with support from the BRAC donor consortium.[3] There are two broad strategies in the TUP programme: one 'pushing down' and the other 'pushing out'. First, the programme seeks to 'push down' the reach of development programmes through specific targeting of the ultra-poor, by using a careful targeting methodology that combines participatory approaches with simple survey-based tools. The selected ultra-poor are then brought under a special investment programme that involves asset transfer, intensive social awareness and enterprise training, and healthcare services for a period of two years.[4]

Second, TUP seeks to 'push out' the domain within which existing poverty alleviation programmes operate, by addressing dimensions of poverty that many conventional approaches fail to address. Specifically, this involves a shift away from the conventional service delivery mode of development programming to focusing on human capital and the structures and processes that disempower the poor, especially women, and constrain their livelihoods. It is an approach that puts social development, specifically a rights-based approach to health and socio-political empowerment, at the heart of the agenda. The five-year programme aims to cover 100,000 ultra-poor women from some of the poorest districts of the country.[5]

The whole idea behind the TUP approach is to enable the ultra-poor to develop new and better options for sustainable livelihoods. This requires a combination of approaches, namely promotional, such as asset grants and skills training, and protective, such as stipends and healthcare services. It also requires addressing constraints not just at the household level, but also within the wider environment of institutions, structures and policies. The TUP approach challenges itself to deliver on all these fronts and the hope is that the initial subsidy that this approach entails, which is heavier than the IGVGD, will reap benefits by building a more solid and comprehensive base for the extreme poor to participate in mainstream development programmes, such as microfinance.

Table 2.2 compares the profile of the TUP members with VGD members, clearly showing that the TUP programme is indeed targeting a group of the

Table 2.2 Reaching deeper: TUP and VGD members

Variables	TUP	VGD
Average land ownership (in decimals)	2	5
% of landless households	93	87
% of households not owning homestead land	54	43
% of households having outstanding loan from any source	2	36
% of households reporting that they can manage two meals a day regularly	12	61
% of households reporting that their economic condition deteriorated over the last year	44	35

Source: BRAC (2004b)

poorest, who are on average significantly poorer than those served by BRAC's IGVGD programme. This is the group who either do not get VGD cards or who dropout from the IGVGD programme within a year or so of the end of the food aid period.

Currently the first entrants into the TUP programme have gone through the special investment phase and been organized into separate village groups. They are being offered the full range of BRAC's development services, including microfinance. One lesson from our previous experience of working with the poorest population is that forcing them to take on microcredit can backfire. This is the reason for BRAC's flexible approach: taking on microcredit is seen as a choice by the members rather than an institutional goal-setting exercise to 'prove' graduation. At the time of writing, about 70 per cent of the first entrants into the programme had taken their first loan, averaging Tk2,000 (US$31), and were repaying regularly. BRAC was also planning pilots to develop the most appropriate microfinance products for this group, as its experiences suggested that for many of the poorest, the regular microfinance product and regime may not be the most appropriate.

As shown in Table 2.3, early assessments of change suggest that on average, the food intake levels of the TUP programme participants have increased and become more diversified, with less reliance on cereal. Perceived levels of food security and health status have registered significant positive changes that are also reflected in more direct measures of health-seeking behaviour and anthropometric measures.[6]

What does it take? Lessons from BRAC's experience

In 1985, when BRAC approached WFP to pilot the idea of IGVGD that later became a nationwide programme, BRAC's microfinance work was at a stage where it was gradually becoming more professionalized. Yet, even during such early stages, BRAC realized that the types of efficiency-enhancing measures that would be needed to serve a large number of poor people would also create

Table 2.3 Comparing the 'selected' and 'not selected' ultra-poor over time

	Selected Ultra-Poor		Not Selected Ultra-Poor	
	2002	2004	2002	2004
% of households who reported to be ...				
Always in deficit	62	2	41	25
Occasionally in deficit	35	21	51	50
Never in deficit	3	77	8	25
% of adult women who reported that their overall heath status was ...				
Good	43	55	45	47
Fair	36	27	35	31
Not good/bad	20	18	20	22
% of adult women who reported that their overall health condition over the last year has ...				
Improved	25	51	24	24
Remained the same	26	25	27	36
Deteriorated	50	24	49	40
Total food intake in gm (mean)	759	998	795	807
Total energy intake in kcal (mean)	1911	2093	2017	1820
Cereal as % of total energy	88	78	87	83

Source: Ahmed et al (2004)

structures and incentives that may not be the most suitable for the poorest. This is the reason why BRAC, while taking steps to scale up its regular microfinance, also looked for opportunities that would allow it to experiment and develop mechanisms through which even the poorest could benefit from microfinance services.

Throughout most of the 1990s, but especially during the middle of the decade, both IGVGD and BRAC's microfinance operations grew exponentially. Various internal and external research studies suggested that such rapid growth was leading to the poorest being further excluded. As the IGVGD approach relied on its linkages with microfinance after the food aid period was over, the efficiency-equity trade-off in microfinance started adversely affecting the poorest of the IGVGD members and many of them dropped out or were inactive after the food aid period was over (Chowdhury, 2000; Matin, 2002; Webb et al, 2001). Moreover, as the IGVGD was a partnership programme, due to various types of bureaucratic constraints, it became difficult for BRAC to provide the training and credit to all who needed it during the period in which food aid was being provided, leading to reduced overall impact of the programme.[7]

These findings, and extensive discussions within BRAC, led again to further research to better understand the unique constraints faced by the poorest in participating in and benefiting from existing development approaches (Halder and Husain, 2001). The JFRP pilot followed, along with extensive scoping studies in several of the poorest districts of the country, all contributing towards the proposal for CFPR/TUP that BRAC began preparing in 1999–2000 and which was finally approved in 2001.

As this phase of the CFPR/TUP programme reaches its third year, with two more years remaining, based on research and field-level experiences BRAC is already preparing to take several steps to make the model more efficient and pilot some new ideas that will address gaps. This will enable BRAC, before the current phase of CFPR/TUP is over, not only to develop new ideas and have real ground-level experience of how to make the current model more effective and efficient, but also have experience of piloting new ideas for further expansion. The next phase of the CFPR/TUP will be a comprehensive business plan to attain the Millennium Development Goals for the extreme poor in Bangladesh.

Is microfinance the best means of reaching extremely poor people?

The basis upon which BRAC approached the question of including the poorest in microfinance is an interesting and a strategic one. Broadly, there are two schools of thought. One argues that sustainable microfinance, especially microcredit, cannot and should not attempt to serve the poorest who, according to Marguerite Robinson, a leading proponent of this view, need 'poverty programmes for such purposes as food and water, medicine and nutrition, employment generation, skills training, and relocation' before they can use microfinance (Robinson, 2001). The other school of thought suggests that the main constraint is product design: if we can find ways to design and deliver more appropriate financial products that are more suited to the circumstances of poorer clients in a cost-effective way, then even they can be served (Rutherford, 1999). This latter school of thought, however, does not present a counter view to the first one. While the former argument is about absolute measures of poverty and the extreme poor, the second view is more about deepening poverty outreach rather than serving the poorest with microfinance in an absolute sense. The former embraces product innovation as a way to deepen poverty outreach, while maintaining the view that the poorest in an absolute sense are best left to be dealt with through 'poverty programmes' rather than microfinance.

BRAC has taken a middle position based on an understanding that the poorest people need some key interventions before they can use microfinance, but that these interventions alone will not suffice in helping to build sustainable livelihoods for them unless the link between those interventions and microfinance is made part of an overall strategy of including the poorest. BRAC agrees that new financial products will help, but not without first addressing the key constraints faced by the poorest people.

Conclusion

It is this intelligent and practical positioning within the debates set out above, grounded in its experience of piloting alternative solutions, that allows BRAC to mobilize the intellectual support and resources needed to scale up unconventional ideas. The process goes from contributing to debates, to piloting, to improving effectiveness, to improving efficiency and finally to scaling up these initiatives.

In 1975 when BRAC was operating in only a few districts, it set up its own independent research and evaluation division entrusted with the core task of evaluating the effectiveness of its programmes and looking ahead to identify emerging areas that require attention. This twin focus on improving existing practices and maintaining its relevance as a development organization is the key to BRAC's ability to manage the pressures of scaling up ideas that work, as well as search for new ones. This has allowed BRAC's microfinance services to develop its canvas in a way that is inclusive but also firmly rooted in its focus on poverty alleviation, where new ways of including the poorest are not perceived as beside the point for microfinance but very much at the heart of it.

CHAPTER THREE
Institutionalizing a social performance management system at Lift Above Poverty Organization (LAPO), Nigeria

Stanley Aifuwa Garuba

Introduction

Lift Above Poverty Organization (LAPO) is well known for its commitment to microfinance and innovative social development services targeted at poor households. It has recently developed and institutionalized a simple cost-effective social performance management (SPM) system to measure and monitor progress towards achieving organizational goals and to facilitate internal learning to improve practices and impact. LAPO is keen to prevent mission drift so that it stays focused on its organizational goals. This paper details the context and objectives of LAPO's SPM system, its development based on different tools, the way the different tools are used to realize the objectives of the system, its cost-effectiveness and the commitment of the LAPO board to the use of the SPM system.

Microfinance in Nigeria

The development realities in Nigeria clearly demonstrate the weak income-earning capacity of the poor. The current economic reforms, which emphasize liberalization, have not brought wealth to poor people. There is gross neglect of rural communities in terms of distribution of amenities. Existing credit programmes have not reached poor farmers, especially women farmers.[1] Women have also not fared any better with other institutional credit schemes.

Nigerian society remains a patriarchal one, with low status ascribed to women. This status is sustained by a series of customs and traditional practices that constrain women's potential. Though enlightenment programmes are being implemented to discourage some of these practices, women, especially in rural communities, are still denied access to major assets.

In most communities, long-standing social arrangements pool and distribute financial resources to individuals in need. These credit and savings schemes are known as *osusu* and *adashi* in the south and north respectively. However, modern microfinance practice was launched in the 1980s by NGOs operating as microfinance institutions (MFIs). These non-profit organizations focus on women and rural dwellers. There are currently about 12 active MFIs operating largely in the south, south-west and south-east regions of Nigeria,[2] though a few of the MFIs have started spreading their operations to the north-central region.

LAPO started its operations with just three clients in 1988 in Delta and Edo states in the southern region, where the incidence of poverty, as in other regions, was fast on the increase – from 38 per cent in 1985–86 to over 78 per cent in 1997. Fifteen years on, LAPO has emerged as a leading MFI in Nigeria, having essential features of the Grameen Bank approach that targets poor owners of microenterprises.[3] As of December 2004 it had 29,812 active clients and a total of 244 staff,[4] with value of gross loan outstanding of about US$1,885,414, total financial revenue of about US$1,002,679 and profits of US$222,850. LAPO's sources of funds include interest revenue, fee revenue, members' savings, loan repayments and donor funding. LAPO's mission is to achieve economic empowerment of its target group – mostly poor women within the bottom 50 per cent of socio-economic strata – through access to affordable financial services delivered in a cost-effective and innovative manner.

This paper focuses on five key areas. First, it considers the context and objectives of LAPO's SPM system as well as its design and institutionalization. Second, it discusses in detail the various components of the SPM system, including poverty targeting, poverty monitoring, exit monitoring and the client/staff learning system. The ongoing integration of LAPO's impact monitoring system into the management information system (MIS) is also described. Third, the paper demonstrates how the impact monitoring tools are used by LAPO to realize the objectives of its SPM system. Fourth, the paper looks at the cost-effectiveness of the SPM system. Finally, the paper relates the commitment of the board of LAPO to the SPM system. It concludes with some key lessons learnt from LAPO's experience of developing and institutionalizing the SPM system.

LAPO's social performance management system

Context of the SPM system

LAPO's SPM system was initiated through *Imp-Act*. The primary objective was to generate data on the impact of LAPO's services on clients' poverty status in order to monitor progress towards achieving organizational goals, and to facilitate internal learning to improve impact and practice. As a poverty-focused development organization, its interest has always been in been in tracking changes in clients' poverty status, to understand how those changes occur and to monitor trends of impact on clients.

The system has been designed in such a way that it continually develops throughout the various processes. A simple poverty assessment tool has been developed, which is used to generate data on the trends of impact on clients' poverty status. This data is then used as a basis for further investigation through qualitative research to find explanations for the apparent trends of impact on clients.

LAPO's SPM system utilizes simple formats that contain just a few basic indicators. The system has been well integrated into LAPO's regular processes with simple methods of application. LAPO's regular poverty monitoring system is built on the collection of reliable poverty data, which gives a longitudinal view of changes in clients' poverty status. For LAPO, the challenge is to understand the reality of the pattern of changes that might be observed, to find plausible explanations for such changes and to use the information to continually improve its services and impact.

Objectives of the SPM system

There are two main objectives of the SPM system. First, to monitor progress towards achieving organizational goals. To achieve this objective LAPO monitors poverty to measure improvements in clients' poverty status. The aim is to carry out periodic evaluations of changes in clients' poverty status so that LAPO can know the impact of its services on clients and determine whether it is on track in terms of its overall goal of reducing poverty among its target group.

The second goal is to improve institutional learning and practices. In accordance with this objective LAPO has also developed its poverty monitoring system to enhance knowledge of impact among its staff and clients. It assesses the usefulness of LAPO's services in relation to clients' reasons for participation in the programme and expected changes in their living conditions. The monitoring system was developed to enable staff to identify where changes have occurred and to understand whether those changes are due to clients' participation in LAPO's programme.

Development of LAPO's SPM system

The SPM system includes a poverty targeting system, a regular poverty monitoring system, a client/staff learning system, a client exit monitoring system, integration of poverty monitoring into the management information system and follow-up qualitative research.

Poverty targeting system

LAPO's poverty targeting system is based on the application of its poverty means test, which is incorporated into the participation form used for client intake. LAPO has long used its participation form for poverty assessment, for selection of eligible applicants for its services and for capturing baseline information on clients. The participation form has been modified several times, depending on the need for information. During its participation in the *Imp-Act* programme, the participation form was redesigned with three key sections for different functions. The contents of the revised participation form include demographic information, poverty assessment indicators and impact information.

Poverty assessment indicators were incorporated into LAPO's poverty means test, which is used particularly for selection of eligible applicants for its microfinance services. During the second year of *Imp-Act*, LAPO seized the opportunity to verify the effectiveness of the means test as a tool for its poverty targeting and monitoring. The indicators contained in the means test were consequently tested against the Consultative Group to Assist the Poor Poverty Assessment Tool (CGAP PAT).[5]

LAPO's means test compared to the CGAP poverty assessment tool
The CGAP PAT is a standardized tool to measure the relative poverty of microfinance clients. The CGAP operational tool was designed through a year-long collaboration between CGAP and the International Food Policy Research Institute (IFPRI). It is a simple, low-cost operational tool measuring the poverty level of MFI clients relative to non-clients. The tool involves a survey of 200 randomly selected clients and 300 non-clients. It provides transparency on the depth of poverty outreach of MFIs. It also provides rigorous data on the levels of poverty of clients relative to people within the same community through the construction of a multidimensional poverty index that allows for comparisons between national MFIs, as well as between countries.

LAPO's existing indicators in the means test were tested against the results of the CGAP PAT by comparing data on these indicators for the same 200 clients. The results from the analysis indicate a very high degree of accuracy (97 per cent), with a very small number of placement errors when compared to the CGAP PAT. Analysis of LAPO's poverty assessment data based on the CGAP PAT also produced conclusions about the absolute as well as the relative poverty of LAPO's clients, which means that poverty assessment data from LAPO's simple means test can be linked to international measures of poverty.

LAPO's poverty means test
Prior to the work carried out under the *Imp-Act* evaluation, LAPO's poverty means test contained eight questions, as follows:

1. What is your marital status?
2. May I ask about your approximate level of education?
3. What is your occupation?
4. What is the interior and exterior walls/flooring condition of your dwelling house?
5. What is the sleeping arrangement in your household?
6. How steady is your total household income?
7. How regular are daily meals in your household?
8. How often do you cook special food for your household?

These questions were used as both a screening tool to assess applicants' poverty status, consistent with LAPO's institutional objective to target the poor, and as an impact monitoring tool to track changes in status over time. Each question had five possible responses with point values ranging from 1 to 20. LAPO selected these indicators based on a number of factors, including the results of field research, experience in the field and informed judgements about factors related to poverty in Nigeria.

Prior to the evaluation, the basis for assigning weights to the different indicators was largely subjective, as was selection of the poverty cut-off points. LAPO established 100 points as the total possible in the means test and assigned 20 points to each of its five poverty categories: 1) very poor; 2) poor; 3) average poor; 4) less poor; and 5) least poor. Higher means test scores indicated higher levels of poverty and vice versa and only those applicants with a score of 41 or higher were admitted to the programme.

Adopting a new rapid poverty assessment tool

A revised five-indicator tool

The refinement of LAPO's means test into an effective and reliable poverty screening and monitoring tool is an important success. This process started with the review of LAPO's organizational mission, clarification of its concept of poverty and the selection of basic poverty indicators, which were integrated into the participation form. The final outcome is the recommendation and adoption of a five-indicator poverty assessment tool that can be implemented in 5–10 minutes by field staff. The five indicators, in order of their strength of correlation with the CGAP PAT, are: 1) steadiness of household income; 2) regularity of daily feeding; 3) dwelling conditions; 4) frequency of cooking special foods; and 5) sleeping arrangements.

The rationale for selecting a five-indicator means test that did not include occupation, marital status or level of education was based on an examination of simple correlation coefficients between the means test indicators and the PAT poverty scores. Of the eight means test indicators, occupation was the most weakly correlated and was the sole indicator that was statistically insignificant or inversely related to the PAT poverty score. Marital status was the second least correlated with the PAT poverty score, although only slightly less correlated than educational level. The ability of the means test to produce accurate poverty scores was rigorously examined by testing the sensitivity of the indicators, the weighted value of each question and their susceptibility to errors. The final five-indicator means test is illustrated in Figure 3.1.

Assessing movement between poverty categories

LAPO uses five poverty categories based on its assumption that such classification will enable easier analysis of changes using the monitoring data. Relevant poverty cut-off points for the poverty categories were considered based on poverty survey data for Nigeria. Armed with this data, LAPO has been able

Poverty Assessment Indicators	Scores
1	How steady is your total household income from month to month?	
	Steady (Make up to maximum money to take care of household) = 4	
	Somewhat steady (Sometimes do not have maximum money to take care of household) = 8	
	Somewhat unsteady (Have just minimum money to take care of household) = 12	
	Unsteady (Often do not have minimum money to take care of household) = 16	
	Very unsteady (Generally do not have minimum money to take care of household) = 20	
2	How regular is the daily feeding of your household?	
	Regular (3 meals per day of good quality) = 4	
	Somewhat regular (3 meals per day, but basic) = 8	
	Somewhat irregular (Occasionally miss a meal) = 12	
	Irregular (Often miss a meal) = 16	
	Very irregular (Generally do not have enough food) = 20	
3	How often do you cook special food for your household?	
	When I want = 4	
	Once in four days = 8	
	Once in a week = 12	
	Occasionally = 16	
	Rarely = 20	
4	What is the interior & exterior walls/flooring condition of your dwelling house?	
	Floored with additional covering like ceramic tiles and rug = 4	
	Floored with carpet and walls plastered/painted = 8	
	Floored with cement and walls plastered = 12	
	Floored with cement but walls not plastered = 16	
	Not cemented/plastered = 20	
5	What is the sleeping arrangement in your household?	
	One person to room = 4	
	Two persons to room = 8	
	Husband, wife in each room but children sleep in one room = 12	
	Husband and wife in one room but children sleep in one room = 16	
	All household members in one room only = 20	
Total Poverty Score (0–100)	

Figure 3.1 LAPO's revised poverty means text

to set reasonable cut-off points relative to its five poverty categories. Only those applicants who score 46 or higher are now admitted into the programme.

Ongoing poverty monitoring system

LAPO's main goal of contributing to poverty alleviation among its clients and target group has informed its emphasis on strengthening its poverty-targeting tool. The effectiveness of this tool in the selection and mobilization of the target group increases the need not only to ensure their adequate inclusion, but also to track the resultant changes in clients' poverty status. LAPO expects that as clients continue to participate in the programme, their poverty status will improve. Similarly, these improvements are expected to be significant over time.

Although no one can be certain of the length of time needed for significant improvements in clients' poverty status to materialize, changes are expected to occur. Nevertheless, the extent to which these changes can be attributed to the intervention of LAPO should not be overstated. The key benefit for the MFI might come from analyzing trends over a period of time. Attention may be shifted to explaining the degree of significant change. Where change is found to be indicative of negative impact, the process might lead to modification of practices to improve impact. However, if the change observed signifies positive impact, a reinforcement of strategy might be encouraged.

The essence of the monitoring system may be inferred from LAPO's client impact survey data analysis conducted in 2004 (Nwabuzor and Garuba, 2004) using the five-indicator poverty means test. From the results it was found that LAPO was experiencing some mission drift and that its targeting system for ensuring deeper level of poverty outreach was not being used as effectively as it might be. Table 3.1 reveals the results of the survey.

Table 3.1 Comparison of the distribution of LAPO's clients in poverty categories

Poverty group	Sample clients (%)			LAPO Profile
	Pipeline	Mature	Total	(%)
Very Poor	4.5	6.7	5.8	17.0
Poor	34.0	36.9	35.7	22.5
Average Poor	41.5	29.5	34.6	28.0
Less Poor	17.0	17.9	17.5	19.4
Least Poor	3.0	9.0	6.4	13.0
Total	**100.0**	**100.0**	**100.0**	**100.0**

Source: Omohan and Omorogbe (2004)

LAPO's means test has also been integrated with the regular loan application process. The loan application is completed with clients for all loans every eight months. During this process, credit officers assess a sample (one-tenth) of their clients who are renewing loans, using the poverty means test. Documentation of the data is done at the branch offices, where information can be coded from the formats and processed on a quarterly basis by the research department. Plans to introduce a computerized system for regularly assessing poverty monitoring data across branches, and thus reduce the amount of time spent on this documentation, are about to be implemented. Some relevant operational data will be imported from the portfolio management package to merge with the impact monitoring data in order to conduct some comparative data analysis. Key expected outputs include strengthening LAPO's focus on empowering its clients and preventing mission drift. In addition, data from the minimal poverty monitoring system will be supported by follow-up qualitative research to gain specific knowledge of impact and to generate issues that may be of value to senior management.

Client/staff learning system

LAPO's client/staff learning system involves interaction between clients and their loan officers. The process provides an opportunity for both loan officers and clients to identify and discuss impact trends over a period of time. The basic tool is a form illustrated with pictures, which appears on the first page of the membership booklet (see Figure 3.2).

The process of filling out the form is facilitated with each client so that she can rank her feelings/mood on the condition of her household income, nutrition, dwelling, education of children and her participation in family affairs. Credit officers use the tool with clients once at any time in each loan cycle, preferably on an individual client basis. Responses are coded directly on the page of the passbook normally kept by clients. Ideally, the initial application with clients sets the basis for comparative analysis during subsequent applications. Updating the information for each loan cycle allows clients and credit officers to develop a longitudinal understanding of changes in the client's condition of living over time.

This mid-range participatory system has been developed to strengthen the usual follow-up visits of credit officers to their clients. Interested clients may seize the opportunity to relate pertinent issues about their business and their everyday lives to the credit officer. Some experienced credit officers may offer useful advice to assist clients to cope with various situations. Credit officers are not officially required to report on these procedures to the office and are not expected to formally analyze this information for the MFI, but use it to gain greater knowledge of the programme's impact on clients. However, some credit officers might use the knowledge they have gained from this process to make useful suggestions to management regarding the needs of clients.

Poverty score at entry in LAPO: _____;   Poverty group at entry in LAPO: _____

FORMAT *(To be applied at every loan cycle)*

INDICATORS	Income	Dwelling Place	Food	Children's Education	Participation
LOAN STAGES ☺					
😐					
☹					
😞					

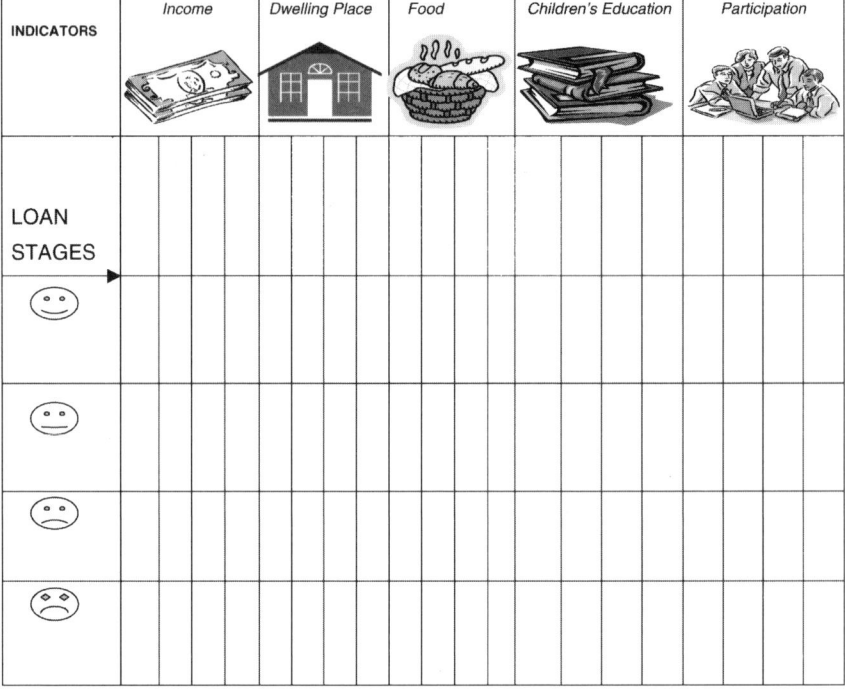

Figure 3.2 LAPO's client impact learning system

Client exit monitoring system

Understanding the reasons for client exit

The increasing incidence of client exit from LAPO's programme shows the importance of a system to track clients' reasons for leaving, especially if the target group clients leave due to negative factors arising from the MFI's policies and practices. LAPO defines exiting clients as those who have stopped accessing loans and have withdrawn their mandatory savings. Exit may occur for several reasons. LAPO's attempt to understand this problem started in 2002, when a study of client exit was conducted under the *Imp-Act* programme.

The study revealed that 47 per cent of clients who left the programme found loan sizes to be inadequate. However, the results also indicated that many of these clients were average to non-poor and were living in urban areas. By contrast, very few poor rural clients were leaving the programme. A deeper analysis of the exit survey results showed that the majority of exits were clients who would not actually have been included in the programme, had the targeting been effective. The demand for larger loan sizes came from a particular group of clients who found that the LAPO loan product was inappropriate for their needs. Furthermore, a significant number of exiting clients reported difficulties in making repayments (36 per cent), a decline in their business (24 per cent) or complained about having to repay for other members (30 per cent). Poorer clients were less likely to be concerned that loan sizes were too small. The leavers were mostly the non-poor.

Changing LAPO's policies and practices in response to exit study results
These findings provoked lively discussion about mission drift – particularly inattention to reaching target groups – created by the realities of the organizational drive for increasing client numbers, targets for loan disbursement, repayment rates and other operational factors. It was also noted that in the past, the problem of client exit was not viewed on an organization-wide level, and therefore the seriousness of the problem was not appreciated.

One of the key areas of concern relates to the problem of lending in rural areas, where business opportunities are scarce. The concern is reflected in LAPO's strengthening of its farming loan product, as encouraged by the findings of the exit study. However, the findings also led to a reorientation towards a greater focus on urban and semi-urban clients. The attention of management has also been drawn to the use of the client selection system to ensure that those who are not part of the preferred target group are excluded from the programme. In addition, it was agreed that a more informed understanding of the broader economic environment would provide guidance on appropriate loan sizes for less poor clients.

The fact that the information provided by the exit study was deemed to be so useful has led to the development of a regular client exit monitoring system. This involves recording the three most important reasons why each client leaves the programme. The system has been integrated with the client withdrawal format and procedure. The format captures basic operational information, including the client's initial poverty score, and lists common client exit reasons, which have been adopted from the AIMS-SEEP client exit survey tool.[6]

Analysis of data is a responsibility of the research staff at LAPO head office, because of the skills required. The process focuses on the categories of clients leaving the programme and the general reasons for their leaving. This is backed up with a qualitative investigation to find the key reasons why clients decide to leave LAPO. The client exit monitoring system provides a useful tool to control the exits of preferred targeted clients due to negative impact arising from involvement in LAPO's programme.

Management information system (MIS)
LAPO has just completed the first phase of the computerization of its portfolio management system. It is currently fine-tuning the link from this system to the accounting package and data consolidation procedure at the head office level. The completion of these processes will lead to the integration of

the means test into the computerized MIS. This will represent a significant achievement for LAPO. The system will track the poverty outreach of LAPO and changes in clients' poverty status.

The monitoring format integrates baseline information (age, sex, education, marital status, business type and initial poverty score), operational variables (branch, location, credit officer, loan stage, loan size) and impact data (current poverty score). This combination will allow LAPO to look for trends such as changes in poverty score from one loan stage to another; nature of change in the different poverty categories; and comparative analysis of trends between branches, business type, location, poverty categories and age groups. Data relevant to the monitoring format can then be exported and analyzed in detail using a statistical package.

Findings from this level of analysis will be investigated through qualitative follow-up research to give reliable conclusions and generate more detailed investigation of relevant information that might be generated from both the simple quantitative monitoring formats and wider-scale surveys. It might be used, for example, to find specific explanations for significant negative or positive change in the average poverty score from one loan cycle to another, considering factors such as location of clients, branches, difference in the degree of change among the different poverty categories or actual impact. Using simple qualitative techniques such as in-depth interviews and focus group discussions, possible explanations can be sought.

The importance of qualitative follow-up investigations is demonstrated by the experience of the client exit survey and client impact survey conducted by LAPO from 2003–04. While it was difficult for LAPO to draw conclusions on its impact on clients' poverty status based on statistical analyses alone, qualitative follow-up research revealed that it might be incorrect to conclude that LAPO has not had a positive impact on the poverty condition of its clients. The majority of the participants in the in-depth interviews and focus groups revealed that, though they might not be able to give accurate figures on the improvement in their income, they were sure of their improved capacity to contribute to the household income, feeding and the education of their children. Similarly, the in-depth interviews revealed that complaints about loan size might not be limited to the least poor clients. This was because of the wider economic situation in Nigeria, occasioned by the government deregulation policy, leading to a general rise in the prices of goods and services and the associated fall in the value of the Naira, the Nigerian currency.

Lessons learnt from LAPO's use of impact monitoring tools

The design of LAPO's social performance management system shows that the various tools are components of a single system. The participation form is the bedrock of LAPO's impact monitoring tools and is used to generate baseline information for comparative analysis with other tools. The participation form includes the means test and serves as baseline information for a three-year impact survey. While the means test establishes the basis for regular poverty monitoring at every loan cycle, the client/staff learning system uses the poverty score generated initially as a basis for reflection on changes in clients' lives.

As noted above, the application of each of the tools is considered in terms of the nature of information needed and the purpose, as illustrated by Table 3.2. The means test is repeated for a sample of one-tenth of clients to look at trends in clients' poverty status, while for the client/staff learning system, LAPO considers it important to cover all clients in the study and involve individual credit officers in analyzing the impact of the programme on their own clients. The client exit monitoring process contributes information on clients who leave the programme and their reasons for doing so.

The operational benefits of the ongoing integration of the means test into an automated MIS include: 1) having regular ideas of the trends in clients' poverty status; 2) determining when significant positive changes in clients' poverty status are likely to occur; and 3) developing a reliable basis to stimulate further in-depth study of the impact of services on clients. As discussed above, qualitative follow-up research will be undertaken to gain greater understanding of trends in clients' poverty status, and therefore impact of LAPO's microfinance services.

A two- to three-year impact survey, as deemed necessary by LAPO management, will be carried out based on the information gathered from the participation forms. It is felt that this mid-scale impact survey is necessary because LAPO's impact monitoring system can indicate general trends regarding impact, but cannot replace a rigorous impact assessment procedure.

Cost-effectiveness of the SPM

Evidence indicates that LAPO's SPM system does not compromise its overall financial performance and that the system should increase the MFI's ability to

Table 3.2 Use of instruments

Instrument	Purpose	Target respondent
Participation Form (includes means test)	Client targeting and Baseline information	All potential clients
Means test	Regular impact monitoring	10% of existing clients
Client exit monitoring form	Dropout monitoring	All programme leavers
Client/staff learning format	Client/staff impact leaning	All existing clients

attract clients in a potentially competitive environment. The integration of the impact monitoring system with existing operational systems has kept costs, in terms of time and money, to a minimum. The time spent in applying each monitoring tool with clients at different levels only marginally increases the initial time spent in completing the routine operational process. Beyond the developmental costs of the institutionalization process, using the SPM system involves minimal ongoing costs.

Commitment on the part of the LAPO board

There is a strong level of commitment to LAPO's mission at all levels of the organization. The board, management, field staff and clients all have a strong focus on poverty outreach and poverty reduction. The board has a strategic involvement in LAPO's operational decisions and a good understanding of the factors that contribute towards a positive impact on clients, as well as the trade-offs necessary to ensure a financially sustainable organization. The board is particularly keen to receive reliable information about the impact of LAPO's services, and regards the SPM system as being an important step towards this end.

Prior to the design of the SPM system, there was a feeling that LAPO was experiencing some mission drift and that its systems for ensuring depth of outreach were not being used to optimum effective. The SPM system has thus provided an opportunity to strengthen this focus and arrest this mission drift.

Conclusion

LAPO's experience in developing a social performance management system is significant for a number of reasons. First, the organization has developed a minimalist but credible system that uses a few well-chosen indicators for poverty/impact monitoring. Second, LAPO appears to have achieved an effective balance between the need to collect data to monitor overall trends in clients' poverty status and the workload burden on field staff. A one-tenth sample arrangement on all loans approved has led to a system that appears truly workable and valuable in terms of regular poverty monitoring. Finally, LAPO has been clear in separating the functions of different formats for assessment. Instead of using a single monitoring format to achieve a range of aims, different formats are used for different purposes.

The combination of a high level of commitment to a poverty reduction mission with institutionalized informal learning systems means that LAPO is already balancing social and financial priorities in its operations. It has developed its research and analysis skills and has made significant progress in institutionalizing SPM processes throughout the organization. A significant development to ensure the effectiveness of these processes is the creation of a Planning and Research department, which will lead social performance management activities and ensure adequate sharing and discussion of findings, both at the management and general staff levels. Managing social performance in these ways is helping LAPO to avoid further mission drift and to work towards financial sustainability, in addition to achieving its organizational goals.

For LAPO, the value of the SPM system is seen in the improvements it is able to make to its services for clients, as well as being more competitive, increasing its outreach, and operating on a more sustainable basis. The remaining challenge is for senior operations staff to take full advantage of the system to initiate useful analysis and in-depth research to make decisions on service delivery. With this level of cooperation, it will be possible for LAPO to use the information it generates on poverty outreach, impact on clients' poverty status and client exits for improving its services and practices.

CHAPTER FOUR
Cost-effective impact management: the case of the Small Enterprise Foundation (SEF), South Africa

Ted Baumann

Introduction

This paper reviews the experience of the Small Enterprise Foundation (SEF), a non-government microfinance institution targeting poor households in South Africa's poorest rural region. SEF began to use an integrated impact management system in the mid-1990s as part of its Tšhomišano Credit Programme, which targets the poorest households in its area of operations. This impact management system combines in-depth case studies, regular data collection embedded in the loan cycle and constant monitoring of key variables via a dedicated management information system. It has helped the MFI to overcome several potentially serious client-dropout episodes. SEF used the opportunity offered by *Imp-Act* to conduct research and further develop its impact management system.

This chapter describes SEF's impact management system and analyzes its effect on a dropout crisis beginning in mid-2002, which was quickly resolved. It concludes that SEF's pursuit of a proactive impact management system that monitors key variables, enabling corrective action before performance is affected, is highly cost-effective, especially in regarding opportunity costs. It also finds that such an impact management system is particularly important when working with the poorest and most vulnerable, since such households tend to be on the margin of dropout.

The Small Enterprise Foundation

SEF is an 11-year-old non-profit MFI based in the Limpopo province of South Africa, whose mission is to work towards the elimination of poverty and unemployment by providing microfinance services to the poor and the very poor[1] in a sustainable manner. SEF employs a joint liability microcredit methodology modelled on the Grameen Bank. In February 2004 SEF had 20,505 clients, served by 73 field staff, and the total principal outstanding was US$ 2,071,428. In both of these respects SEF is just under the average for African low-income microlenders.[2] Almost all SEF's clients are women, most of whom operate small enterprises from their homes. SEF has achieved remarkable performance in terms of loan losses: from its inception to date, write-offs have amounted to less than 0.01 per cent of disbursements. Portfolio at risk over 30 days has been consistently less than 1 per cent.

SEF's small loans and short repayment schedules were expected to encourage poorer women to join, but the MFI soon realized that it needed a targeting mechanism. Accordingly SEF developed two programmes: the non-targeted Microcredit Programme (MCP), with 10,529 clients, and the poverty-targeted Tšhomišano Credit Programme (TCP), with 9,976 members. SEF's impact management[3] work is concerned with the TCP. Both programmes operate in the same geographical area, but each village within that area is only targeted by one or other of the two programmes.

In per capita terms, South Africa is an upper- to middle-income country, but the distribution of wealth remains among the most unequal in the world. SEF operates in one of the poorest regions, Limpopo province, where much of the population is economically marginalized and dependent on transfer payments from urban relatives or state grants for cash income. Limpopo's Human Development Index is equivalent to that of neighbouring Zimbabwe (121st in the world). Of Limpopo's population 64 per cent live below the most commonly used South African poverty line and 40 per cent of households survive on less than half this income.

SEF is unique amongst South African MFIs in its obsession to reach the very poor. Whereas many MFIs allow themselves to drift 'upmarket' towards clients who can afford larger loans, thereby generating more income per client, SEF has consistently held the 'client variable' as a constant, even changing other variables to enable it to do so. This is because SEF is not interested in microcredit for its own sake, but as a means to eliminate poverty in its target area. Because of this fundamental goal, impact management plays a unique and critical role at SEF. Its impact management system is integral to its success as an MFI, both socially and financially.

Impact management at SEF

Philosophy

SEF's impact management methodology was developed from 1997–99. The goal was to develop an iterative and incremental process that would accumulate information over time, maximize client and staff participation and feedback, and improve SEF's impact on its clients by improving its performance as an MFI.

SEF has a distinct philosophy of institutional impact management based on two fundamental aspects. First, impact management is a holistic, institutional process and is about more than just assessing client well-being. Second, impact is not something to measure occasionally but to manage constantly. This approach is rooted in SEF's perception that impact assessment is often divorced from day-to-day practicalities. SEF's own impact assessment system, initiated during 1997, is an ongoing effort to understand and monitor impact in order to *improve* it, rather than a one-off analytical event to *prove* it. Given this priority, but also bearing in mind resource constraints, SEF's impact management methodology is less comprehensive but also less costly than academic impact assessments.

Key components

SEF's impact management methodology involves the interrelated components of studies, data collection, monitoring and a management information system (MIS).

Impact-oriented studies

SEF uses detailed studies in its impact management work for two reasons. First, detailed studies were initially needed to identify the operational changes necessary to implement an effective ongoing impact management system. It was neither possible nor sensible simply to select an impact management system 'off the shelf' because a detailed understanding of local conditions, clients' habits and needs was required, as well as knowledge of the impact of SEF's existing model. Second, periodic detailed studies are indispensable to maintain the impact management system and to assess the likely impact of changes in the broader microcredit model, such as interest rates and loan terms.

SEF started its impact management work by conducting impact assessment studies in selected TCP villages. Based on careful methodological considerations,[4] these studies sought to develop a qualitative understanding of the role of credit and savings in clients' households and businesses. Specific objectives were to identify changes in clients' livelihoods and businesses since joining TCP and to identify key variables that affect their status. Follow-up visits were made to develop a longitudinal sense of these changes and understand the role of the variables identified. The point of these case studies was to guide the development of operational impact management procedures. However, these initial studies also raised issues that led to immediate changes in SEF's methodology. For example, high transport costs were identified as a problem for some clients. This led to a fuller study of the problem and a change in disbursement procedures to address it.

In all cases, SEF's Development Department – sometimes augmented by consultants – designed the studies, implemented them, analyzed the results and reported back to staff and management through papers and workshops. SEF's Operations staff also contributed to the process, especially design and interpretation of results. Sample sizes and other methodological issues were addressed through discussions with field staff and others who were able to give useful insights. All of SEF's studies were aimed at the MFI's model and needs, rather than to satisfy external stakeholders such as funders.

SEF's use of in-depth studies to monitor and adjust its operations is an integral part of its impact management activity. It is inconceivable that the MFI would have developed its ongoing impact management tools without them. The key finding of almost all these studies is that impact and performance problems are always management problems. Having a model, products and organizational structure that is good on paper, in another setting or even in an MFI's own past, is no guarantee of success either for clients or for the MFI as a whole because circumstances change constantly. The main lesson is that operating an MFI dedicated to addressing the needs of the very poor through microfinance services is an iterative process that requires constant management adjustment, which in turn requires the feedback loop(s) advocated by the *Imp-Act* programme.[5]

Early in its activities, SEF identified client exit as a critical indicator of both impact and operational performance. Exits correlate closely to arrears and portfolio at risk, and are expensive to reverse. Understanding the reasons for exit has thus been a central feature of SEF's work for some years, with studies of the phenomenon being conducted periodically. SEF started its Tshomišano Credit Programme as a pilot in 1996 but before long the exit rate was 38 per cent. SEF then conducted an initial exit study, which resulted in a reduced pressure for programme growth whilst the MFI focused on getting its methodology right. A variety of changes led to a fall in the exit rate to below 12 per cent.

With TCP functioning well, SEF then decided to turn it into a full programme. TCP expanded rapidly and many new field staff were hired and subject to growth targets. Before long, the impact management emphasis started to slip and exits again rose. SEF experienced unprecedented rates of exit during 2001–02. To deal with this, SEF conducted a second in-depth dropout study in 2002. The goals were to understand the reasons for exit from the perspective of clients and to reflect upon the support and services provided by TCP. Critically, separate interviews were conducted with both clients and staff in order to gauge their different understandings and motivations.

The main conclusions of this study were that most dropouts are caused by poor application of the MFI's core methodology. Interestingly, there was no indication of any causal relationship between dropouts and HIV/AIDS or the recent introduction of a national lottery, which had been assumed to drain the income of very poor households. Instead, the main force driving the upsurge in dropouts was found to be an incentive system for fieldworkers that 'over-prioritized' portfolio growth at the expense of quality of service and application of SEF's policies and procedures. This push for portfolio growth was a consequence of donor pressure on SEF to achieve break-even. This was quickly corrected during 2003 through a wide-ranging overhaul of SEF's structure, focusing on field management and a revised incentive system. This in turn set the stage for SEF's remarkable growth in the last 18 months, resulting in its looming attainment of break-even. The success of the exit study led to its extension to monthly exit monitoring, using the same format, by operational staff (as discussed below).

Data collection
Based on the in-depth studies, both initial and subsequent, SEF chose a set of ongoing impact management tools. In general these tools cover all TCP clients, although in respect of client interviews some aspects are relaxed after a number of successful loan cycles. This comprehensive approach to impact management reflects the fact that SEF's impact management methods are an integral part of its microfinance model, not an occasional add-on. There is no point in 'sampling' for impact management if one of its most important benefits lies in the process of impact management itself, as well as in its impact upon clients and fieldworkers.

SEF's qualitative impact management tools are implemented by fieldworkers and overseen by branch and zonal managers, who also consolidate the information collected. Information is further consolidated and analyzed by head office staff. Quantitative tools are implemented by head office staff on the basis of data collected by field staff. SEF's impact management tools are clearly the key constituents of its feedback loop. However, there is more than one feedback loop involved with the same information. For example, information collected during fieldworker visits with clients is immediately fed back to the client at the same meeting. The same information is transmitted upwards to branch managers, along with aggregate information about vulnerable groups and centres, and discussed at branch meetings, creating a feedback loop at that level. It is then fed upwards to senior management at head office. This information is periodically used at staff workshops and board meetings.

SEF's impact management system uses participatory methods (primarily a questionnaire) to monitor key variables at the individual, household and business levels. This leads to a longitudinal view of changes in clients' livelihoods during, although not always as a result of, participation in SEF's programme. Quantitative impact management involves analysis of variables from this level of impact assessment.

There are no control groups in SEF's system, but the generation of baseline information through the monitoring system enables comparisons of clients at different stages of their participation. The in-depth case studies discussed above build up a qualitative understanding of the reasons and processes underlying these changes. By basing the monitoring system on this understanding, it becomes possible to infer causal relationships between SEF's impact and its programme.

SEF's client-level impact management system involves a set of interactions between all TCP clients and fieldworkers at individual, group and centre level. The key elements are centred on the three processes of loan application, centre performance monitoring and loan utilization monitoring. All three processes provide an opportunity for fieldworkers to interact with clients in a way that allows the former to capture information about impact.

The basic tool used is a questionnaire that includes objective variables such as savings, attendance and business value, and subjective indicators such as perceptions of improvement in well-being in terms of food consumption and housing status. Fieldworkers collect this information once in each loan cycle, preferably towards the end, but not at the same time as loan reapplication, to avoid moral hazard in clients' responses. Some of the information is based on records of centre meetings. This information is aggregated and submitted to branch managers, who in turn pass it on to head office. There, it is inputted into an MIS that can be used to generate reports for all levels of the MFI. These reports are provided mainly to the board and senior management, although some field staff have requested that they also receive the reports.

Augmenting this data collection is business evaluation, a process deeply embedded in SEF's methodology. During each loan cycle, fieldworkers visit each client to record the raw value of their business, including stock/materials, accounts receivable and cash on hand. Changes to the overall business value play a crucial role in determining eligibility for an increased loan in the next cycle. This gives the fieldworker an opportunity to see whether or not the client's business is growing and how, and provides a way to investigate the circumstances that affect changes in business value. The primary value of this kind of client-level information is not so much the information itself, although this is important, but the process of collecting it and the resulting relationships and understanding created between fieldworkers and clients.

Dropout and vulnerability monitoring

Dropout monitoring is a simple matter of recording the percentage of clients who do not take out another loan at the end of each loan cycle. This quantitative information is aggregated at branch and head-office levels and used to monitor systemic performance and to guide decisions on whether to conduct further in-depth studies on the reasons for client exit. The information is used at all levels of the MFI.

At face value, exit monitoring does not appear as a facet of impact management. It is a *post facto* measure that by itself says nothing about causality. Through experience and in-depth studies, however, SEF has determined conclusively that most dropouts are closely related to the impact of its microcredit activity on the client's business and household. Because of this knowledge, monitoring marginal changes in dropout rates is a powerful tool that allows the MFI to take corrective measures to prevent wholesale exit from the programme.

SEF is able to distinguish between clients who drop out and clients who graduate out of the poverty-oriented Tšhomišano Credit Programme for two reasons. First, the regular interaction between TCP clients and fieldworkers, integral to the impact management system, means that fieldworkers know very well which clients are dropping out and which are 'flying out'. Second, TCP clients who move beyond the need for TCP group loans more often than not move into SEF's Microcredit Programme for the less poor.

SEF also employs a tool to identify centres that are particularly vulnerable. It is based on three indicators whose 'trigger values' vary depending on the size of the centre, namely, attendance, savings and arrears. Transgressing any one of the three makes a centre vulnerable in SEF's eyes, leading to remedial action by field management. A focus on attendance and savings has always been part of SEF's Grameen-influenced methodology. The introduction of the vulnerable centres approach as a monitoring tool, however, was intended to help branch managers identify vulnerable members in centres and to help zonal managers plan visits to those centres.

It is important to stress here the relationship between vulnerability monitoring and other impact management tools. Statistical vulnerability monitoring by itself would not be enough because SEF needs to know why certain trends imply certain causes. It is necessary first to achieve an in-depth understanding of impact via studies and client interaction in order to use a simple proxy such as vulnerable groups and centres, or even dropout rates. Because of its in-depth impact assessment work, SEF understands that a client's problems will first be expressed through poor attendance and savings, then later through arrears and then finally by dropout. This demonstrates the relationship between impact as social performance and financial performance.

Management information system

SEF's MIS seeks to identify whom SEF is reaching, how the overall system is developing, including trends, and important changes in client status. With a combination of operational and impact-oriented data in the same system, SEF is able to look at relationships and trends on a range of variables, generating standardized reports that can be exported for more detailed analysis. Key to this is the inclusion of three sets of variables: 1) operational (branch, fieldworker, loan size, loan type, loan amount); 2) client profile (age, number of children, business type, start-up, initial poverty score[6]); and 3) client changes (impact management indicators). This combination allows SEF to look for patterns, such as who is dropping out, and use a combination of variables to develop a hypothesis as to why, potentially resulting in a detailed investigation and remedial measures.

Lessons

SEF's actual impact

There are two important points relating to SEF's impact on its clients. First, observing that impact is positive because most SEF clients do not leave the programme does not mean accepting the common and facile argument that impact management is unnecessary because if impact is negative, rational clients will exit. As many have observed, clients stuck in a debt trap will not necessarily leave a microcredit programme, even if impact is negative for them. SEF's impact management methodology allows the MFI to state with confidence that this is not the case for its clients. More importantly, however, the whole point of SEF's impact management approach is to ensure that impact improves, which implies the need for ongoing monitoring and assessment. Without active impact management, there is no way to ensure that impact continues to improve, whether the measure is objective or subjective.

Second, SEF has undertaken in-depth research on actual impact, using conventional measures such as food security and housing. Because of this, the MFI is certain that its impact is positive for clients who stay, and progressively so. The point is simply that SEF does not continually conduct such research because it is neither economically rational nor necessary.

SEF-style impact management is not about measuring absolute poverty, and it is not possible to say in a scientific sense that SEF's impact is such-and-such. That is not the point of SEF's impact management approach. Impact management at SEF serves rather to help clients and fieldworkers assess clients' relative progress, or decline, as participants in a microfinance programme.

Relationship among elements of impact management

The key issue is the relationship between the impact management tools SEF employs. SEF uses a combination of in-depth research, client-level participatory impact assessment and quantitative analysis of operational variables to detect problems before they become systemic and harmful to the MFI and its clients. Most importantly, once SEF had demonstrated conclusively through in-depth studies that dropouts were caused mainly by the negative impact of microcredit on clients, the logical thing was to develop tools to identify negative impact before the client dropped out.

A set of participatory tools and vulnerability measures at client, group and centre levels was devised. The combination of these tools means SEF's impact management methodology is thus divided into: 1) leading indicators of client well-being that manifest early, before systemic problems do; 2) intermediate indicators such as client, group and centre vulnerability; and 3) trailing indicators, such as exits, that manifest themselves once 'the damage is done'.

The key issues arising from SEF's proactive impact management tools are: 1) the process of gathering the information is the most important aspect of the tools; 2) detailed information about impact on clients is more useful to fieldworkers than management, allowing them to intervene before individual client problems become systemic; and 3) the quality of the interaction between fieldworker and client is critical, and management must supervise fieldworkers in this respect, particularly at high productivity levels.

Indeed, the centrality of fieldworkers to the detailed impact management tools is an important conclusion from SEF's experience. This is both a strength and a weakness, however, corresponding to the dual role of both fieldworkers and microfinance. On the one hand, fieldworkers are development workers, trying to help very poor households get out of poverty. On the other, they are employees of a commercial operation with heavy workloads. Detailed impact management tools are strong or weak to the extent that fieldworkers lean, and/or are guided by management, towards one role or the other. In SEF's case, for example, application of its detailed impact management tools suffered during the period when the MFI focused on attaining break-even. Once again, this illustrates the importance of management's role in monitoring the impact management system.

Institutionalizing client-assessment processes and internal learning

SEF clearly illustrates the unique importance of systemic and systematized impact management to an MFI wanting to reach the very poor. It has devoted a great deal of effort to developing and implementing an internal learning feedback loop, involving a combination of client-level assessment processes and systemic indicators, both qualitative and quantitative. Notably, SEF will not make a loan to a client unless impact management information has first been collected and processed.

There are two reasons why institutionalizing impact management is so important to SEF. First, it is important to the board and management to have a positive impact on very poor people, since this is their mandate. Second, SEF has learnt that if it does not pay close attention to how its clients are faring, it will suffer diminished financial performance as a microlending MFI. This is because of the strong correlation between client-level indicators and the systemic indicators that influence financial performance, including client retention, attendance, savings and similar measures.

The key point is that providing microcredit for very poor people is a difficult task, much more so than lending to the less poor. Because clients are so vulnerable, learning cannot stop once an apparently functional microcredit system is in place. The MFI must constantly keep monitoring, assessing and adjusting its system. This learning must be institutionalized, not only to ensure positive impact on clients, but also to ensure MFI survival in a difficult operating environment (particularly true in the case of South Africa).

Well-being versus sustainability

The information collected by SEF fieldworkers serves as an indicator of a client's progress in the MFI's programme, rather than of their well-being. In an operational sense, assessing clients' progress through questionnaires and interviews is important to clients and fieldworkers, but probably not as important as management's monitoring of systemic measures like exit rates and vulnerable centres. The two are consubstantial, however. The specific information generated by the process of measuring client progress – for example, satisfaction with food, housing or savings – may not be as important as the systemic insight that conducting the process provides to fieldworkers and branch managers, but one requires the other. SEF management and fieldworkers consistently reported that the greatest benefit of impact management was to alert field staff to problems at client and group levels before they became problems at centre or branch level. This allowed them to initiate measures to correct the problem at an early enough stage so that neither the client nor the MFI suffered a negative impact.

Operational impact management and academic impact assessment

SEF's impact management tools show that the MFI is having a positive impact on its clients. Again, this impact is not measured in absolute terms, but in terms of relative progress during the course of participation in SEF's programme. By itself this is probably not very satisfying to academic researchers and the donor community, since they both seek objective, scientific measures of poverty performance. Indeed, SEF's client-level impact management tools do not provide the sort of objective, scientific information that could be used to assess the 'net worth' to clients of participation in SEF's microcredit programme.[7]

There are two reasons for this. First, many of the most important indicators collected are subjective, such as satisfaction with food and housing. Second, some objective indicators – such as household income and expense, educational status and non-MFI savings contributions – do not produce very solid data because of moral hazard and the vagaries of client memory. By contrast, indicators such as attendance at centre meetings, compulsory savings and business value can be measured precisely but do not provide detailed insight into impact at the level of the client's household.

SEF's experience shows that objective measures of well-being are not particularly important to the day-to-day needs of an MFI, either for clients or staff. SEF's subjective and relative approach, however, is essential to its success in reaching very poor people and sustaining a positive impact on their well-being. Thus, SEF's impact management activities should be seen as a practical effort to improve its performance as a poverty-reducing organization, not a scientific effort to prove this to someone else. The one does not preclude the other, although it is unreasonable to expect an MFI to conduct scientific impact research on its own account.

This raises another issue relating to practicality vs. 'nice-to-know'. SEF's impact management activities and tools have been developed largely by a dedicated Development Department. In the case of detailed impact measurement tools, however, these must be implemented by operations staff, primarily fieldworkers and branch managers. Managing operations staff's perceptions of the benefits of impact management activity on their own livelihoods is an essential job for MFI management. For just as MFIs have little incentive to conduct the kind of scientific impact management preferred by academics and donors, so field staff often feel distant from the concerns that drive SEF-style impact management activity. In the fieldworkers' case, however, there is clear long-term self-interest in impact management, but when self-interest is long-term it is often not obvious. It is up to MFI management to constantly reinforce this.

Finally, SEF's impact management activities are clearly credible, easily replicable and highly useful. The cost-effectiveness of SEF's impact management system was considered in a separate study for *Imp-Act* (Baumann, 2004), which concluded that it was overwhelmingly positive when compared to a counterfactual in which peak dropout rates were allowed to continue unabated. Here it is important to repeat that the cost of impact management needs to be understood primarily in terms of opportunity cost. This is inherently difficult to do scientifically because it is hard to develop a credible counterfactual against which to test MFI performance with and without impact management. In SEF's case, however, there is a strong argument that the organization's ability to turn itself around, and to grow dramatically in a sustainable manner in a short period, owes much to impact management and the awareness this has generated with regard to field-level impact.

Proactive impact management

Impact management at SEF contributes to the operational performance of the MFI by providing a feedback mechanism that enables fieldworkers and management at all levels to identify vulnerabilities and potential problems before they occur. This is significantly different to finance-based monitoring and performance assessment. Financial monitoring is only able to identify client-level problems indirectly after the fact. Impact management, by contrast, allows SEF to anticipate such problems and take pre-emptive action. This makes it an essential aspect of SEF's business model.

SEF's adoption of two proactive impact management tools – vulnerable centres and client-level impact management – in addition to dropout monitoring, has played a critical role in allowing the MFI to scale up the Tšhomišano Credit Programme over the last few years. It seems clear that the direct and opportunity costs of a *post facto* performance monitoring system would have made it difficult, if not impossible, for SEF to scale up the TCP, or at least to do so in a sustainable manner.

Proactive impact management allows an MFI to anticipate problems and take pre-emptive action in order to maintain positive impact on clients' lives. As with any business, impact management is also a marketing tool that in SEF's case allows it to respond to the way clients are affected by its services with appropriate changes to those services. Impact management also allows an MFI to quickly gauge the impact of changes to its model and/or products, and to make adjustments as needed.

Impact management and microcredit for the very poor

The previous point is particularly true of MFIs targeting the very poor. In a nutshell, impact management is essential for an MFI to survive in the 'very poor market' because such clients are so vulnerable to begin with. In this respect, it is useful to think of impact management in relation to credit scoring. Credit scoring is intended to keep risky clients out of a microcredit system in order to reduce the risks and costs of default. Impact management, by contrast, is designed to keep risky clients in, which is cheaper than mobilizing new clients. In this respect SEF's impact management activities are a logical extension of its participatory wealth ranking (PWR) activities. PWR successfully identifies the poorest and most vulnerable members of a community. But such households do not cease to be vulnerable immediately they enter the TCP. Particularly for the first few loan cycles, it is essential to monitor changes in clients' well-being to ensure that they do not fall out of the system.

For example, at one point the TCP had a 38 per cent exit rate but this has fallen to about 18 per cent over the last three years. Interestingly, in the Burgersfort TCP branch, where an intensive HIV/AIDS awareness programme took place – similar in many ways to client-level impact management in the intensity of attention paid to individual clients – dropouts were reduced to 10 per cent. This suggests that client-level impact management in particular has the potential to contribute significantly to one of the most important performance variables of a developmental MFI. Changes to the management structure and performance monitoring system were also important, but impact management seems to have improved *ex ante* knowledge of clients' trajectories and thereby helped reduce dropouts.

Contradictions of impact management and microcredit

SEF's case highlights the inherent tension between the financial and social imperatives of a developmental MFI. SEF has gone through a major shake-up over the last three years, driven by performance problems and pressure to achieve financial break-even. The MFI did not discount its social development and poverty alleviation mission, but management admit that the specific tools intended to maintain such a focus were allowed to slide. Indeed, during the final review visit it became clear that the balance between social and financial activities in the Tšhomišano Credit Programme seems to have changed. Many of the field-level practices geared to social development objectives – business skills discussions at centre meetings, business valuations and client-level impact management – were not always being practised as intended. Moreover, senior and middle management acknowledged that this was because they were not 'monitoring the monitoring system' sufficiently. While fieldworkers tended to speak in terms of lack of time to undertake impact management properly, and the resulting effect on the quality of client-level data, management recognized that this was at least partly due to their failure, under pressure to break even, to monitor the impact management system more closely and streamline it as needed.

The push for break-even has undermined the client-level part of SEF's impact management system somewhat, and almost certainly reduced its effectiveness. Jettisoning the impact management system, however, is not an option because of its central role as an early warning system, which is essential to success when working with the very poor. It would be better to try to streamline it. Indeed, because of the role impact management seems to have played in allowing SEF to reach break-even, one could argue that allowing it to deteriorate is dangerous.

Impact management and the business of an MFI

Impact management is critical to keep SEF on-mission as an organization, and this alone is an important business rationale for impact management as an activity within the MFI. If nothing else, it serves as a constant reminder to all levels of staff and management that SEF is a developmental MFI and not a commercial microlender. This is particularly important since fieldworkers are subject to incentive systems based mainly on microlending performance, and therefore tend to prioritize actions that affect those indicators.

But impact management is much more than a developmental rallying tool for SEF, it is an essential part of the MFI's business operations. It allows SEF to know its market and to respond to the way clients are affected by its services with appropriate changes to those services where needed. Of course marketing activity of this type is a central part of the operations of all successful businesses. Many businesses, however, are content simply to study their market in order to increase the number of customers. For financial services institutions, as for any business that provides an ongoing service, it is also essential to continue to monitor its market, including existing clients, in order to retain its customers. Unless they are caught in a debt trap – something that impact management should discern – most clients who are not benefiting from a financial institution's services will cease to use them. When clients leave a programme the resources that were initially employed to make them clients and to educate them about the products on offer will have been effectively wasted, with additional resources also needed to recruit replacement clients.

This focus on client retention and impact management is doubly important in SEF's case, as it would be for any MFI committed to serving the very poor. Again, it is useful to contrast a focus on the very poor with generic microenterprise microcredit. In SEF's case the goal is to get very poor households to join the programme and stay in it. Although some clients will not do well, in all cases except those purely related to personal circumstances, the MFI has the opportunity to avoid negative impact entirely if it pays sufficient attention to its clients' needs. To do so, however, it is crucial for MFI management to pay attention to how the impact management system is being applied and to adjust it to respond to changing circumstances.

Impact management and management systems

Given the emphasis on the process of impact management rather than the information obtained *per se*, it is useful to look at impact management in terms of the time spent with clients, which most SEF staff regard as worthwhile; and the time spent on administering the information gathered, which they do not. SEF fieldworkers and branch managers legitimately complain that the additional paperwork associated with impact management is burdensome. Some argue that they already spend a lot of time with clients and that the impact management aspect is redundant because of this.

When under pressure, fieldworkers naturally have an incentive to disregard impact management because their immediate incentives and constraints are not directly related to client impact. They do have an indirect interest in impact management, however, to the extent that it provides an early warning system that ultimately saves them time and lost income. Such cases of contradictory motivation, which are of course endemic to all organizations and processes, always require management to construct systems that balance the different incentives and motivations of field staff in such a way that short-term interests do not result in long-term problems. Impact management is no different and SEF almost certainly needs to build up this side of its impact management system.

Costs of impact management

SEF's experience shows that, although impact management costs money, it is a case of either spending money to anticipate problems or spending money to fix them afterwards. In this respect, impact management should be understood in terms of opportunity cost. Preliminary indications are that impact management is overwhelmingly cost-effective when considered in these terms.[8]

Conclusion

The conclusions that can be drawn from SEF's experience of impact management are as follows. First, the impact management system is integral to SEF's overall functioning as an MFI. It is neither an 'add-on' nor an occasional activity designed to prove impact, but rather an organizational orientation towards continually improving its impact on very poor clients.

Second, none of SEF's impact management indicators measure absolute poverty levels, but rather they measure relative progress – both subjective and objective – during participation in SEF's programme. Third, the indicators are designed to anticipate and therefore avoid negative impact, rather than prove positive impact. Fourth, negative impact is interpreted both in terms of impact on the client and on the MFI as a microcredit organization.

Fifth, SEF focuses on client retention because it knows that clients leave the programme because of negative impact and that losing clients also undermines systemic microcredit performance. Sixth, to achieve both its social and financial goals, SEF must manage impact continuously rather than measure it occasionally. Impact management at SEF is about more than just ensuring client well-being; it is also about ensuring that the MFI can serve very poor clients in a sustainable manner.

Finally, SEF's process of impact management acts as an early warning system, identifying systemic problems before they translate into repayment problems and client dropouts, both of which are critical to financial performance. By focusing on impact, SEF has become a successful, self-sufficient MFI in an unusually hostile operating environment, one of the worst in the microcredit world. For SEF, developing the process of impact management flowed logically from the MFI's belief that, like a doctor, an MFI should 'first do no harm'. SEF has always been concerned to ensure that at the very least it does not make its clients worse off. This led naturally to a focus on understanding the nature of microfinance impact, how it occurs and how it can be managed to optimize the microfinance experience for both client and the MFI. SEF's non-economic, non-market motivation to alleviate poverty is what has prompted it to find a way to survive in a market environment, and impact management has been an essential component of this.

In this respect SEF's experience supports the general thesis that MFIs can cost-effectively collect information from their clients to improve social and financial performance. Indeed, SEF's experience suggests that if an MFI wants to survive at all in the 'very poor market', it must ensure that it is improving the lives and livelihoods of its clients in order to keep them as clients. This is because the poorer the clients, the more vulnerable they are. Clients living on a knife-edge are much more likely to fall off than those with more of a buffer around them. This means that SEF needs to pay close attention to the effects of its microcredit interventions to keep clients from falling off and losing access to the support and services provided by SEF.

CHAPTER FIVE
Methodological and organizational lessons from impact assessment studies: the case of SHARE, India

Marie Jo A. Cortijo and Naila Kabeer

Introduction

This paper brings together some of the findings reported by assessments of the work of SHARE (Society for Helping Awaken Rural Poor through Education) in Andhra Pradesh, India, which were carried out under the *Imp-Act* programme. The studies comprised an initial assessment study conducted in 2001, which included social and economic impacts, as well as exploring aspects of client satisfaction; an assessment of poverty outreach conducted in 2004; and a study in 2004, which focused on wider impacts of microfinance, such as participation in community activities, political awareness and empowerment.

The studies were commissioned by SHARE as a means to obtain evidence of their poverty outreach and the impacts of their approach on the poverty levels of clients, both social and economic. They were conducted by external consultants, but SHARE staff were involved in information collection. This paper asks what lessons might be drawn from the implementation and results of these studies in terms of both impact assessment methodology and organizational strategy.

Regional context

Andhra Pradesh (AP) is neither among the most developed states of India nor among its least developed. According to official estimates, 11 per cent of its population lived below the poverty line in 1999–2000 compared to 27 per cent at the all-India level (Government of India, 2002a). Its human development ranking was 23 out of 32 states and union territories in 1991(Government of India, 2002b). It is, however, one of the country's more dynamic states. Throughout much of the 1990s, the political leadership in power combined commitment to economic liberalization with an active welfare populism. As a result, various government programmes for the poor, including all-India schemes like the Public Distribution System and the Development of Women and Children in Rural Areas (DWCRA), have been pursued with much greater vigour in AP than in many other parts of India.

Of particular relevance for this paper is DWCRA, which offers microfinance services to a similar section of the population as SHARE – mainly poor, rural women. First introduced as a pilot project in 1982–83, DWCRA was subsequently expanded on a nationwide basis. It promotes the organization of women into self-help groups on the basis of savings which are deposited in a bank account for lending on to members. Additional loans are provided through the district-level government agency. Its link with the government facilitates access by DWCRA to various government programmes intended for the poor. As a result of the active promotion of DWCRA groups by the state in AP, it accounts for around 40 per cent of the country's DWCRA groups. Along with the government promotion of microfinance services, there are a number of well-known non-governmental MFIs operating in AP, including Dhan Foundation, BASIX and SHARE.

A brief note on the history of SHARE

SHARE began by providing vocational skills to poor people but relaunched itself in 1991 as an experimental microfinance project modeled along the lines of the Grameen Bank. After a period of institutionalization and expansion, it found its capacity to become self-sufficient and raise funds from the Indian banking sector was constrained by its tax-exempt, non-profit status. In 2000 it registered SHARE Microfin Ltd (SML) as a commercial for-profit entity with the Reserve Bank of India. It also registered a cooperative society, SHARE India MAC Ltd, in order to overcome legal constraints to mobilizing savings within the community.

About 20,000 clients of SHARE have contributed to the equity of the company and it became the first MFI in India to declare dividends of 10 per cent (*The Economic Times*, 2004). SML now has 258 branches spread out in the three main agro-ecological zones in AP – fertile, semi-fertile and arid – as well as in the two neighbouring states of Chattisgarh and Karnataka. By early 2005 it reached 548,775 women, making it one of the largest MFIs in India. SHARE remains the umbrella organization for these different entities and we will refer to them throughout this paper as SHARE.

SHARE's mission and operations

SHARE's mission is the alleviation of poverty among the poorest of the poor, especially women, with an effective and sustainable microfinance programme. This is done by providing credit to individuals so that they can undertake income-generating activities, encouraging thrift through mutually aided co-operative societies, and by providing basic training and motivation in financial as well as non-financial issues.

SHARE offers different types of loans, with general loans making up 87 per cent of its portfolio. It operates using basic Grameen-style principles. Its interest rate is 15 per cent per annum on a flat-rate basis and the loan has to be repaid over 12 months, in 50 equal weekly installments. Its membership is female and organized into 'joint-liability' groups of five members each. Eight groups form a centre. The members are trained on the functioning of the programme and sensitized to the concept of group unity. After that, collateral-free loans are disbursed to clients on a staggered basis with the approval of all the members in the centre. Loans first go to the two poorest women of the group, then to the next two and finally to the elected group leader. This sequence for the disbursement of funds builds peer pressure as loans are only given to the remaining members if the first borrowers are repaying their weekly installments.

Clients meet every week to approve loans, make repayments, express concerns and discuss their projects. The staff closely monitor the business of the clients to ensure that the money is used for business purposes only. SHARE has grown at a very fast rate since its creation but has exhibited an exemplary track record since its inception: 100 per cent repayment rates and no portfolio at risk.

SHARE's astounding repayment results are, without doubt, partly due to its insistence on discipline from both staff and clients. A great deal of effort is invested in training staff to respect the rules of the organization. For instance, they are not allowed to accept even a glass of water from clients in order to avoid any inappropriate influence (Kumar, 1998). Focus group discussions that were held with some longer-term clients revealed good relationships between clients and programme staff. They appreciated the courtesy of staff members and testified to their lack of corruption (Todd, 2001). Annual meetings and workshops with its clients also allow SHARE to understand their needs better.

SHARE has an extremely low staff dropout rate of 2 per cent. It recruits young people with no prior experience and lower levels of education, relative to other MFIs, into junior positions, later promoting them if appropriate. This reflects its belief that qualifications can be a liability in microfinance programmes (Kumar, 1998). Those with more experience or education are less likely to accept the organization's strict codes of discipline. This also has the advantage of lowering operational costs.

High rates of repayment also reflect SHARE's approach to lending. Careful and regular monitoring of loan portfolios, loan management and returns of loans through an efficient branch-level monitoring and information system enable the organization to avert potential problems. Branch offices have been equipped with computers to reduce paperwork so that field staff can spend more time in the field.

SHARE used to follow the Grameen requirement of compulsory weekly savings that were kept in the group fund and could only be withdrawn when a member left or faced an emergency. This policy was changed in 1999 to the principle of voluntary saving, with members pledging to save a fixed amount every week. However, as Todd (2001) notes, it is illustrative of the discipline that the staff exercise on centres, and the centres on members, that the amount saved is almost always the same and that it continues to be collected every week.

Analyzing outreach: reconciling different approaches to poverty measurement

SHARE is now one of the largest MFIs in India. By January 2005 it had a network of 258 branches in 6,292 villages in 38 districts of four states of India. It defines the target group for its lending programme as rural women whose household's asset value is less than Rs20,000 (US$425), where household per capita income is less than Rs350 (US$8) per month, and who live in poor housing conditions. As noted above, one of the core studies commissioned by SHARE aimed to understand the extent to which these criteria help it to reach poor people. As the findings below indicate, the answer is contingent on how poverty is defined and measured.

Findings on outreach

The official estimate of the poverty line in rural AP, based on the 55th round of the National Sample Survey (NSS) in 1999–2000, was Rs262 (US$6) monthly, giving a rural poverty head count estimate of 11 per cent. Using the same methodology, for the purposes of a study conducted under *Imp-Act* in 2004, Rangacharyulu provided an updated poverty line estimate for 2002 for rural AP as Rs293 (US$7) per capita – lower than SHARE's criteria for targeting poor households. Based on 2002 survey data for newly-enrolled SHARE clients, Rangacharyulu estimated that just 18 per cent of SHARE's rural clients were drawn from households below the poverty line (2004). In other words, the vast majority were drawn from the non-poor population.

These findings would appear to contradict the findings of a previous study in 2000 (Sharma *et al*, 2000; Zeller and Sharma, 2000), using the Poverty Assessment Tool, that was commissioned by the CGAP and the International Food Policy Research Institute, as part of an assessment of the poverty outreach of MFIs globally. The PAT tool compares the poverty of recently enrolled MFI clients with a randomly selected sample of non-clients drawn from the same location. It uses factor analysis to aggregate multiple indicators of poverty into a single index, which assigns each household in the sample with a specific weighted value representing its poverty status relative to all other households in the sample, and then ranks it. The distribution of non-client households is then divided into three terciles (poorest, poor and less poor) and the cut-off values of the index score for the three terciles are used to sort client households into one out of the three categories (Zeller and Sharma, 2000).

The tool was used to assess SHARE's poverty outreach in rural areas and the study found that 58 per cent of SHARE's clients were drawn from the poorest third of the survey population, 38 per cent from the middle poor and only 3.5 per cent from the less poor (Sharma *et al*, 2000). Indeed, SHARE was found to do very well in comparison with other organizations that were studied under the *Imp-Act* programme using this methodology, including PRADAN[1] (see Chapter Seven), as shown in Table 5.1, and also compared to other MFIs in India. Its performance in this respect was even better than SEF-TCP, the programme that the Small Enterprise Foundation in South Africa specifically targets at the poorest of the poor (see Chapter Four).

The PAT measure of outreach suggested that, contrary to estimates based on the absolute 'money metric' measure of poverty employed in the Rangacharyulu study, there was very little leakage to the less poor in the population. Where the findings of the two studies converge is in relation to the very poorest. Rangacharyulu's finding that none of SHARE's poor clients came from the destitute poor – those earning just 25 per cent of the poverty line – echoes the finding by the CGAP study that the poorest of SHARE's clients were not as poor as the poorest households among the non-clients.

Measuring poverty

Further analysis suggests that the apparent discrepancy between these two results is likely to be a function of the methodologies used to estimate poverty in the two studies, with one focusing on absolute poverty on a national level and the other on relative poverty within the region. As noted above, according to official estimates of poverty based on the absolute national measure, only 11 per cent of the rural population in AP were living below the poverty line in 1999–2000. Rangacharyulu's estimates suggested that 18 per cent of SHARE's rural clients were drawn from this group. Most of this 18 per cent were also likely to fall into the poorest tercile of the rural population in Andhra Pradesh and hence are likely to be among the 58 per cent of clients in the poorest tercile identified by the CGAP study. However, the poverty line estimates also suggest that the rest of the 58 per cent in the poorest tercile were drawn from non-poor households in absolute terms. In other words, SHARE was drawing on the poorer sections of the population in the rural areas in which it worked, but the majority of these were above the absolute poverty line.

Table 5.1 Share of clients in each poverty tercile

MFI	Lower tercile (poorest) (%)	Middle tercile (less poor) (%)	Upper tercile (least poor) (%)
LAPO	34.5	35.5	30
PRADAN	31	43	26
PROMUC	37	39	24
PRIZMA	26.2	37.2	36.6
SEF	52	39	9
SHARE	58	38.5	3.5

Source: Zeller and Sharma (2000)

Different measures of poverty provide different kinds of information

A second reason for the apparent discrepancy in findings may relate to problems with official estimates of the poverty line in AP. The methodology used in the official estimates has been strongly criticized for using price indices that over-estimate the rate of inflation over time and misrepresent price differences between states and between urban and rural areas. Using alternative price indices to re-estimate the incidence of poverty based on data from the NSS 2000, Deaton (2001) suggests an upward revision of the poverty line for rural AP from the official estimate of Rs263 (US$6) to Rs309 (US$7) per capita monthly expenditure. This gives a rural poverty head-count index of 28 per cent rather than the official 11 per cent. Since Rangacharyulu based his estimate of the 2002 poverty line on the official methodology, it is likely that his study may have also set the poverty line too low.

If we apply the ratio between the official poverty line and Deaton's estimate to re-estimate Rangacharyulu's estimate, we obtain a poverty line of Rs344 (US$8) monthly per capita consumption expenditure for 2002. Unfortunately, as Rangacharyulu aggregates households in the Rs302–375 (US$7–$9) category, we do not know how many in this category earned less than Rs344 (US$8). What we can say is that between 18 and 39 per cent of SHARE's clients were below the poverty line, a possibly much higher percentage than Rangacharyulu suggests.

This analysis of the discrepancy between the two sets of findings draws attention to the importance of the distinction between absolute and relative poverty. It is, in principle, possible for an organization to reach the poorest households in a particular location without necessarily reaching any households in absolute poverty. It would be far more difficult for SHARE to achieve the fine-tuning necessary to reach significant numbers of poor people below the absolute poverty line in a state where official estimates suggest that only 11 per cent of the rural population fall into this category compared to, for instance, PRADAN, which works in Bihar/Jharkhand, where 40 per cent of the population is below the poverty line.

Consequently, we can say that a significant percentage of SHARE's membership is made up of households that are *relatively* poor in the context of AP and that between 18–39 per cent are *absolutely* poor. This should not detract attention from SHARE's outreach to the most socially excluded groups in Andhra, sections of the population that are most likely to be neglected by formal financial institutions and exploited by informal money lenders. These are the scheduled castes, scheduled tribes and 'other backward castes' who occupy the lowest rungs of the social hierarchy in India. According to national estimates, 22 per cent of the population of AP belongs to the scheduled caste/tribes (mainly the former). According to Cortijo and Kabeer (2004), 59 per cent of SHARE's new members and 75 per cent of mature members are drawn from these categories, while 10 per cent of mature members and 21 per cent of new members are drawn from 'other backward castes'.

Analyzing impacts on poverty

A second set of issues explored by the *Imp-Act* studies related to direct and indirect, and economic and social categories of impact. The main evidence for direct economic impacts comes from Todd (2001). She used a number of different approaches to the question of attribution – drawing causal links between an MFI's intervention and positive impacts on poverty. One was a comparison of households of members who had been with SHARE for at least three years and would be expected to have benefited from access to its services, with households of members who had joined within the last six months – too recently to have benefited. A second was a comparison of the situation of mature members at the time they entered SHARE with their situation at the period of the study. Finally, a combination of quantitative data and data from FGDs and case studies was used to track the 'pathways' through which changes in household situations had occurred and the extent to which these could be attributed to membership of SHARE.

Indicators used to measure poverty

Direct economic impact was measured in the study in terms of changes in a composite poverty index based on four equally weighted indicators, listed below, that were selected on the basis of discussions with SHARE staff:

- Sources of income: staff were able to construct a 'ladder' of typical rural occupations based on the magnitude and regularity of income earned.
- Productive assets: this was one of the indicators used by SHARE to identify its clients and hence there was information on this indicator at the time that clients became members.
- Quality of housing: this was the other indicator used by SHARE to identify eligible members and was based on size of the house and flimsiness or durability of materials used.
- Household dependency burden: this was calculated by dividing the total number of household members by the number of earning members. While it was expected that membership of SHARE would have an impact on the first three variables, the dependency ratio was included as an independent influence on household poverty.

Based on the value of this composite index, households were divided into three poverty groups: the very poor, the moderately poor and the non-poor. Figure 5.1 presents the findings from comparison of mature and new clients. It shows that less than 4 per cent of new clients were non-poor according to the composite index. The majority were very poor (57 per cent) while the rest were moderately poor (39 per cent). Of the mature clients, more than a third were non-poor and 58 per cent were moderately poor. Very few were in the very poor category. This is consistent with the hypothesis that SHARE has

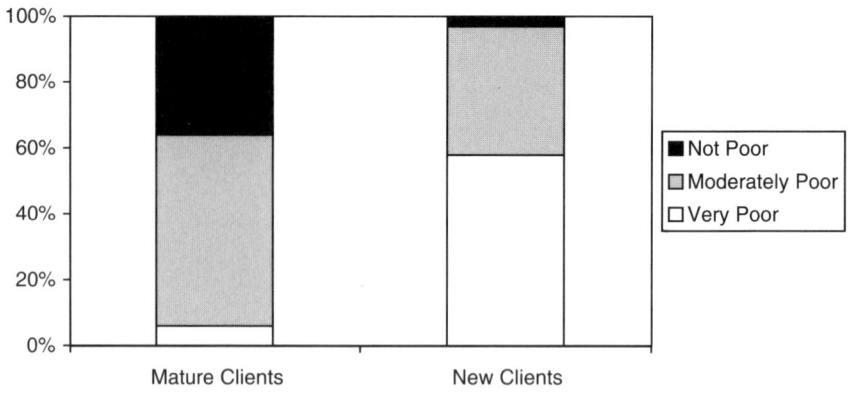

Figure 5.1 Poverty status of new and mature clients
Source: Todd (2001)

had considerable impact on the livelihoods of its clients over time. Such a conclusion is further supported by comparing the situation of mature clients at the time they entered SHARE's programme to their current situation.

The housing index, a list of assets owned and occupations followed by husband and wife were all recorded for clients at the time of entry. Thus, it was possible to compare situation at entry with situation at the time of the survey. The analysis suggested that three out of four of SHARE's mature clients had experienced significant reduction in their poverty level over the four years preceding Todd's survey, and half of them were no longer poor. Nearly four out of ten had moved from being very poor to moderately poor, while exactly the same proportion had come right out of poverty. These results held for all the branches under study.

Pathways out of poverty

A further source of corroboration came from an analysis of case studies and focus group discussions to explore the 'pathways out of poverty' reported by SHARE clients. It found that while new clients were mainly involved in lower-end occupations, where wages are low, paid daily and the work irregular, a large proportion of those who have benefited from credit for more than three years have moved into small business activities, including animal husbandry. However, women's husbands mostly remained daily labourers. In general, loans were used to increase the number of income earners in the household, primarily by creating self-employment opportunities for women, and to diversify sources of income.

Mature clients were more likely to report productive assets – usually livestock – than new ones. A few had invested their profits in purchasing or leasing land, which their husbands were able to cultivate. The big change reported by clients was the more reliable flow of cash. They were no longer dependent on seasonal occupations and could therefore afford to make new investments without putting their livelihoods at risk. The most common pattern observed in loan use was to first invest in the purchase of a buffalo. Once the income began to flow regularly, contributing both to loan repayments and household consumption, clients looked towards other more profitable investments, including husbands' businesses.

Confounding effects

While the various findings reported by Todd establish a strong case for SHARE's impact on the poverty of its clients, a number of qualifying points are in order. One relates to the inclusion of the 'dependency burden' as one of the components of the poverty index. The assumption is that an increase in the number of earners in the household will be associated with a decline in its poverty. This may indeed be the case, and Todd provides evidence that mature households with two or more earners were more likely to report a reduction of poverty than those with only one. However, analysis by Cortijo and Kabeer (2004) draws attention to who exactly these earners are. They found that while mature SHARE clients were more likely to send their sons to school than new clients, mature clients were less likely to send their daughters to school than new clients and more likely to send them to work. Clearly the changes in dependency burden recorded by Todd would have to be assessed very differently if children, rather than adults, continued to shoulder the dependency burden.

A second qualification relates to Todd's finding, with regard to mature borrowers, that 'there is no statistically significant relationship between the total number of loans, the total amount borrowed or the amount of the last loan taken from SML and the poverty status of its clients. Of the clients who have borrowed in total less than Rs14,000 (US$321) from SML, 80 per cent had experienced a significant reduction in their poverty and 34 per cent had come right out of poverty; while among those who had borrowed in total Rs15,000,000 (US$344,549) or more, only 67 per cent had experienced a significant reduction in their poverty, but 36 per cent were no longer poor' (2001).

Given the minimalist nature of SHARE's approach and its focus on provision of microcredit, this absence of a relationship is puzzling. Todd's own explanation is that it is *how* the loan is used that matters, rather than the amount. Those who used it to increase the number of earners/sources of income/assets (particularly milk buffaloes) were most likely to progress out of poverty, regardless of number of loans and amounts borrowed. However, we would suggest that the absence of a relationship between amounts borrowed from SHARE and movements out of poverty could also reflect the fact that SHARE members, both mature and new, had access to other sources of financial services. These were likely to have a confounding effect if they were not factored into the analysis of impact. In particular, membership of DWCRA appears to be most relevant. Indeed, Cortijo and Kabeer (2004) found that 45 per cent of mature members and 34 per cent of new members in their survey of SHARE members were also members of DWCRA; other forms of membership were negligible.

The relevance of DWCRA was also noted in passing by Todd (2001). She pointed to the importance of savings in explaining why mature SHARE members were able to ride out various economic setbacks, such as family crises and natural disasters, which at least half of the members had experienced in recent years. Describing SHARE members as 'prodigious savers', she noted that 98 per cent had 'voluntary' savings with SHARE India MAC Ltd and 84 per cent of these had increased their savings balance in the past year. The average amount of savings for this sample was Rs2,000 (US$42). However, as we noted, the policy climate does not promote saving with non-governmental financial institutions. This may explain her finding that not only were SHARE clients also saving outside of SHARE, but they were saving almost twice as much outside (an average of Rs3,500,000 (US$80,395)).The majority were saving with DWCRA, and indeed many had been saving with DWCRA before they joined SHARE. Several attributed their savings habit to their participation in DWCRA. According to Todd, 'As a government programme, it has a high confidence rating among rural women and it is accessible even in remote rural areas' (2001).

Controlling for dual membership: an analysis of wider impacts

Such evidence suggests that impact assessments of SHARE clients need to factor in their membership of DWCRA in order to avoid the possibility of false attribution of positive or negative impacts to SHARE. This was done in the study by Cortijo and Kabeer (2004), which was designed to explore the wider social impacts of SHARE. Having discovered the high percentage of SHARE members who were also DWCRA members, they used regression analysis to separate out possible effects of years of membership of a SHARE group and whether or not clients were also members of DWCRA.

The study found that the number of years' membership of SHARE had stronger effects on economic relationships (with suppliers and customers) than membership of DWCRA. However, membership of DWCRA was associated with stronger social and political effects. It was also associated with improved relations within the community, improved access to government services, greater likelihood of meeting with elected officials and government service providers, attending political forums and voting in local and district elections. When group membership was confined to SHARE, some but not all of these effects were evident.

The rapid impacts of SHARE on poverty levels of clients reported by Todd may thus also be partly attributable to participation in the DWCRA. It is very likely that clients' prior experience in a government development programme, which had promoted their willingness and capacity to save, as well as the ease of access it provided to other government programmes, played a role in explaining the apparent rapidity of SHARE's impact.

The price of a 'minimalist' approach

As Todd points out, SHARE has, from the outset, been a minimalist programme, designed to lend money to poor people and achieve 100 per cent repayment rates. It is this determined focus that has enabled it to reach 548,775 clients. Through financial intermediation, SHARE has enhanced the business skills of its clients and improved their entrepreneurial ability and confidence. Since social activism was never part of its agenda, it is not entirely unexpected that it does not report major impacts in terms of women's own sense of self-empowerment and agency, or their participation in the wider community. However, the preoccupation with repayments may have had other implications that bear directly on SHARE's avowed goals of poverty reduction.

Todd (2001) makes the point that the very restricted profile of investments reported by clients was dampening the potential poverty impacts that SHARE could have had. The FGDs with mature clients threw up frequent complaints that loan sizes were too small and loans took too long to process. For example, investments in non-traditional activities requiring some degree of technology – transport, tractors, water pumps – were found to be constrained by the size of the loans offered to clients. Such caution with loan size and disbursement may reflect a conscious decision on the part of SHARE to ensure that its clients are able to repay on time, but it could also be hampering the capacity of its clients to take advantage of more productive investment opportunities. In response to these findings, SHARE has increased the size of its loans.

This same strong focus on maintaining excellent financial indicators may be at the source of the high rate of exit (17 per cent) recorded by Todd. Her survey of ex-clients found that their main reason for leaving was not the absence of impact but their dissatisfaction with its lending methodology. They found weekly repayments difficult to maintain when their business was going through a bad time and many found the need to guarantee each other's loans onerous.

Conclusion

Like any other MFI, SHARE faces the difficult task of balancing financial performance, poverty outreach and impact. By all indicators, it has undeniably achieved great success in terms of its financial performance, asset quality, efficiency and productivity. This is confirmed by excellent ratings by internationally recognized agencies, namely M-CRIL and CRISIL.[2] Its poverty outreach as measured by the CGAP PAT tool is also outstanding. However, *Imp-Act*'s studies show that SHARE is less impressive in terms of its wider social impacts, although this may be a deliberate 'trade-off' on the part of SHARE's decision-makers, as a means to ensure that SHARE remains financially efficient.

Taken together, the findings from the *Imp-Act* studies yield a number of lessons both for impact assessment methodology and for organizational strategy. Methodologically, they remind us that how poverty is measured can have an important influence on what organizational outreach is estimated to be. In particular, the findings highlight the need to bear in mind the distinction between absolute and relative poverty in assessing impact. As the poverty outreach results show, SHARE's clients are poorer than other households in the areas in which they are located, but not necessarily as poor as the poor in other parts of India.

The findings also highlight the need to take account of other possible influences that might contribute to the observed impact. In this case, SHARE was drawing a significant percentage of its clients from those who were already members of DWCRA groups and had been for some time. It is clear that many of the wider impacts revealed by the study in 2004 could be attributed to membership of DWCRA rather than SHARE. At the same time, the fact that SHARE membership was more strongly associated with business relationships means many of the economic impacts observed by Todd for its mature members may indeed have reflected number of years of membership of SHARE.

With regard to the organization, the studies make a number of points. As Todd notes, SHARE is today one of the largest microfinance providers in India and is highly cost-effective. It costs only the equivalent of nine cents to lend one dollar and for the last three years it has been financially self-sufficient. However, its record repayment rates may come at a price. Its cautious approach to lending, intended to maximize the likelihood of repayment, may be curtailing its poverty impacts.

SHARE works with a locally adapted version of the Grameen approach to microfinance that was developed to address poverty in rural Bangladesh, where the poor are more numerous and poorer than the poor in AP. As a result, there appears to be some mismatch between the needs of SHARE's constituency and the design of its services. SHARE is likely to be dealing with customers who are better off than its methodology assumes. The studies conducted indicate that its clients want larger loans than it is prepared to offer, despite the fact that there appears to be potential for using such loans to achieve more technology-intensive, and hence more productive, livelihoods in the context in which it operates. At the same time, this cautiousness on SHARE's part in limiting the size of its loans is likely to be a key factor in achieving the remarkable financial performance described in this paper. It may be a conscious choice in the strategy adopted by the management of the organization.

A second organizational issue arising from these studies is the relationship between strategy and outcome. SHARE epitomizes the minimalist approach to microfinance, with the focus primarily on the provision of financial services. Although Todd finds some evidence that through financial intermediation SHARE has enhanced its clients' business skills 'and improved their entrepreneurial ability and confidence', focus group discussions revealed that quite a few of the interviewed clients would have liked some education component and training in income-generation activities to be given at the start of the group formation process. They felt this would have helped them to develop their skills to use their loans more productively.

SHARE's minimalist approach has also meant that social activism is not part of its objectives. As both impact studies found, despite changes in clients' livelihoods, little progress had been made in other spheres of their lives. Clients who were not members of DWCRA in addition to SHARE had little interest in change at the community level and remained dependent on their husbands and community leaders for decisions to be taken. The study of wider social impacts by Cortijo and Kabeer (2004) found some changes in social behaviour, such as family planning and immunization of children, but also reported high rates of child labour, particularly among female children. It also found some improvements in the clients' business relationships over time, but much weaker evidence of change in the wider community or political domain. However, where SHARE members were also members of DWCRA, these wider impacts were stronger.

SHARE could, of course, expand its mission to include some of these other social impacts, which are clearly important in the lives of the poor, but it might, in the process, compromise its financial sustainability. An alternative approach would be to link up with other organizations that are better equipped to achieve these impacts—something which is already happening through the simultaneous participation of its members in DWCRA groups.

CHAPTER SIX

The challenge of sustainability in India's poorest state: the case of the Centre for Youth and Social Development (CYSD)

Anup Dash and Naila Kabeer

Introduction

There has been a growing emphasis on the financial sustainability of microfinance institutions within the development industry. Sustainability refers to the ability of MFIs to cover their operating costs. This occurs initially by expanding their outreach, achieving near-100 per cent repayment rates and providing minimalist microfinance services. However, in time sustainability requires the issuing of larger loans and ultimately, the elimination of any subsidy to the organization and its reliance on formal financial markets to raise funds at commercial rates of interest. MFIs are under pressure to achieve such sustainability in order to reduce their dependence on donor funds. Sustainability is also considered to be an essential ingredient of pro-poor growth.

Reconciling priorities: financial sustainability and poverty alleviation

The alternative to financially sustainable organizations has been described as 'the classic welfare-oriented, low-interest charging, credit-granting NGO that remains dependent on external funding and never quite takes off' (DevFinance virtual discussion, 2004, cited in Greeley, 2005). However, this is a gross misrepresentation of a complex reality. Many MFIs, including some of those who participated in the *Imp-Act* programme, have found that the drive for financial sustainability is at odds with their mission to reduce poverty. Indeed, the contexts in which they work have led them to emphasize the sustainability of poverty reduction over the sustainability of the organization. People in these places are severely deprived, making the recovery of operational costs through loan repayment difficult, if not impossible to achieve. At the same time, the insecurity of their lives and livelihoods suggests that microfinance service provision may have an important role to play.

In this chapter we report on CYSD (Centre for Youth and Social Development), an organization that works in Orissa, the poorest state in India, with some of the poorest and most socially excluded sections of its population.

The first part of the chapter examines the strategies that CYSD has evolved to address this challenge, and describes the notion of sustainability that underpins its philosophy and informs its efforts.

The chapter goes on to report details of a large-scale impact assessment study conducted by CYSD under *Imp-Act*. The rationale for the study was to take impact assessment out of the hands of donors, and to provide a long-term assessment strategy which would be relevant to CYSD's specific aims and approach, and could be applied at regular intervals.

The challenge of working in India's poorest state

The challenge posed by working in India's poorest state can be summarized by some key statistics provided by the *Statistical Outline of India 2003–2004* (TATA, 2004). Around 48–49 per cent of the population in Orissa lived below the poverty line in 1993–94 and this remained unchanged in 1999–2000. In contrast, it has declined in most other states of India from a national average of 36 to 26 per cent over this period. In 2000, per capita income in Orissa was Rs8,547 (US$196), nearly half of the national per capita income of Rs16,707 (US$383). Basic service levels are also poor; only 73 per cent of Orissa's hamlets had electricity in 1999 compared to an all-India average of 86 per cent.

In 2001, 85 per cent of Orissa's its population lived in rural areas (compared to around 70 per cent of the national population) and around 60 per cent are dependent on agriculture for a living. Nevertheless, agricultural productivity is low, yielding 10 quintals of rice (the major crop) per hectare compared to all-India estimates of 19 quintals. Overall per capita food grains production is 134.8 kg against the national average of 188.8 kg, and only 28 per cent of the gross cropped area is irrigated compared to a national average of 39.2 per cent. Similarly, fertilizer consumption per hectare of cropped area is 36.9 kg compared to 87.6 kg at the national level. In the state's small industrial sector, production is also below average with per capita value added standing at Rs645 (US$14) in Orissa compared to Rs1,417 (US$32) at a national level.

The social context of poverty in Orissa

Economic disadvantage is exacerbated in Orissa by widespread social exclusion. Dalits and adivasis, classified for administrative purposes as 'scheduled castes' and 'scheduled tribes' by the Indian constitution, are recognized as historically disadvantaged groups and special provisions have been made in the economic, political and social arenas to address this. While the percentage of dalits in Orissa's population approximates the national average of around 16 per cent, adivasis make up 22 per cent of its population compared to the national average of 8 per cent.

As elsewhere in India, the incidence of poverty among adivasi and dalit groups is higher than that of 'other groups' in Orissa: 72 per cent, 55 per cent and 33 per cent respectively. Tribal groups are concentrated in the poorer southern and western parts of Orissa where poverty rates are higher than in the more prosperous coastal region: 86 per cent compared to 29 per cent. However, even in coastal regions poverty is higher among tribal groups: 92 per cent compared to 78 per cent for the rest of the population. Among the tribal population in southern districts 82 per cent are illiterate compared to 27 per cent of the non-tribal population in the rural coastal areas. According to National Family Health Survey-2 (NFHS) statistics (IIPS, 2001) India National Family Health Survey-2, IIPS Mumbai, 88 per cent of the female tribal population, 73 per cent of dalit women, 56 per cent of 'other backward caste' women and 34 per cent of 'other women' are illiterate.

The social structure of Orissa is dominated by an extremely narrow high-caste elite. In general, political awareness in the state is low but among the poor by Kumar (2001) found that the poor take a great interest in the political system, as indicated by high voter turn-outs. In fact, estimates show that voting turn-out in 2004 in Orissa was 66 per cent compared to 62 per cent in richer states like Punjab (*The Hindu*, 20 May 2004) and 56 per cent at the national level. Even in Koraput, a reserved constituency for the scheduled tribes (because of its numerically strong tribal population), voter turn-out was over 64 per cent.

Despite high turn-out in elections, the knowledge of the tribal population with regard to local and national politics is limited. Though many people could name the *sarpanch* (village head), only 22 per cent of the 'very poor' could name the country's prime minister (against 78 per cent of the upper class) and 39 per cent their Member of Legislative Assembly (Kumar, 2001). Exposure to the media is also extremely limited, with only 6 per cent of the very poor reading newspapers and 17 per cent listening to radio. This is confirmed by NFHS data showing that 84 per cent of the tribal population is not regularly exposed to any media (IIPS, 2001).

Publicly funded efforts at poverty eradication have not been very effective. Most of these are run in a highly bureaucratic and target-driven manner, severely undermining their impact. The dominance of upper castes in the state bureaucracy has meant that it is even less responsive to the needs of tribal and low-caste groups than it might otherwise have been.

CYSD: its programme and mission

The Centre for Youth and Social Development (CYSD) is an NGO that has been working in Orissa since 1982. It began with a core programme of social entrepreneurship development training for youth activists, but has since expanded into a range of development activities aimed at reducing poverty in both urban and rural areas, including microfinance promotion. CYSD finances these activities through external sources, including donor funds and community resources, and attempts to diversify its sources in order to reduce over-dependence on any one.

It uses geographical targeting to determine the location of its programmes so it has experience with working in very diverse contexts within the state and also in some of the most remote areas of the country. It is currently working in 373 hamlets and seven slums across nine districts in the state of Orissa, reaching 36,238 households. This chapter is based on the findings of an assessment study that CYSD carried out as part of the *Imp-Act* programme in Koraput in the southern part of Orissa, one of its least accessible areas of operation.

Poverty, insecurity and social exclusion: description of the study location

Koraput is characterized by rugged mountainous terrain of varying elevations. Many of the hamlets that CYSD works in are situated deep inside the protected forest areas and accessible only by fair-weather roads or walking tracks. The nature of the terrain limits the availability of agricultural land suitable for cultivation. Geographical isolation is thus a key feature of CYSD's operational area in Koraput.

The area is also characterized by extreme insecurity of livelihoods. There are great seasonal variations, ranging from very high temperatures in the summer to severe cold in the winter. While it receives more than the state average of annual rainfall, much of this flows away untapped due to the undulating terrain. Severe deforestation has aggravated the problem, washing away the topsoil and further decreasing the fertility of the land.

Hamlets are small, comprising 20–30 households, and are mainly inhabited by tribal communities carrying out subsistence agriculture on tiny plots of land. Lack of irrigation and the use of traditional agricultural practices contribute to low productivity, limiting production to one crop a year. Households are rarely able to produce enough food to sustain themselves throughout the year and must supplement their livelihood efforts with other activities. Seasonal agricultural wage labour, often involving migration, is one commonly utilized option, but pays very little[1] and availability is dependent on timely monsoons.

Tribal communities also rely on non-timber forest resources such as tamarind, *mahul* and *sal* (forest products used for brewing alcohol, extracting edible oil and as ingredients in a variety of other products) for income during the rainy season, when other sources of income are not available. The lack of local 'value-addition' opportunities forces them to sell their raw produce at the nearest weekly markets or *haats*. These are predominantly 'buyer-driven' because middlemen and petty traders are able to take advantage of the need of tribal producers to sell their goods by the end of the day, thus awarding them only the lowest possible prices.

The district has some mineral wealth but it is largely owned by the state and leased out to state-owned or private firms for prospecting. The mines and mineral-based industries are highly mechanized and do not generate much waged employment. There are no working mines in the project village area.

Given the subsistence level of their economy, tribal households are chronically vulnerable. Any seasonal imbalance (such as monsoon failure) or idiosyncratic shock (such as ill-health) destabilizes their fragile position, frequently forcing them into debt or to sell their assets in order to cope. Widespread incidence of alcoholism is another source of vulnerability. While the routine consumption of liquor is a part of tribal culture, addiction – usually by men – has led many households into even greater poverty and indebtedness. The *sahookars*, or local moneylenders, exercise considerable power over tribal communities. Not only do they charge usurious rates of interest – ranging from 50–100 per cent – but they operate through extremely hierarchical social relations that place their tribal borrowers in positions of humiliating dependence.

The deprivations suffered by tribal communities in Koraput are therefore multiple, overlapping and severe, comprising geographical isolation, social exclusion, economic exploitation and political disenfranchisement. The state has had little impact on this deeply entrenched set of deprivations, which has been transmitted across generations. It has had some outreach through its Swarna Jayanti Gram Swarozgar Yojana (Golden Jubilee Rural Self-help) (SGSY) programme[2] and through a residential school for tribal girls, but this is limited to certain pockets and has largely bypassed interior areas. The regional rural banks are the only formal institutions that have had any bearing on the lives of tribal communities, partly as a result of CYSD's efforts. Tribal groups in turn have little faith in the state, regarding its officials as corrupt and uninterested in their problems. There has been some intermediation by other NGOs in parts of Koraput, but not in the operational area of CYSD.

Adopting a self-help group approach

CYSD began work in Koraput in 1996 but, given the complexity of the physical, economic and institutional challenges of the area, it has taken a number of years to develop an appropriate set of interventions. Tackling the livelihood insecurities of tribal communities and their high levels of indebtedness through some form of microfinance provision appeared an appropriate place to begin. But it was clear from the outset that the strict financial discipline and inflexible repayment schedules associated with some models of microfinance provision would deter many from joining the programme and lead others to drop out. CYSD opted instead for the self-help group SHG approach widely adopted in other parts of India, but this too had to be adapted to the needs and constraints of the community.

Problems with loan take-up and repayment

One major problem was that opportunities for the productive use of loans were very limited locally. Moreover, it was customary for tribal groups to use their loans to address whichever need took priority at a particular point, be it food or festival expenses, treatment of illness, or the repayment of another debt. As a result, very few of those who borrowed from SHG funds could pay back within the agreed period. Almost every loan was behind schedule, threatening the culture of repayment on which the model relied. It was apparent that the role of the SHG as a mechanism for encouraging repayment was not working.

Key lessons learnt about the needs of the target group
What is remarkable, however, was that the groups did not collapse despite mounting arrears. Members continued to meet and save regularly and their funds continued to accumulate. After a difficult formative period, therefore, CYSD reorganized its approach in 1998–9 to incorporate some of the lessons it had learnt in the field:

- That poverty reduction among tribal households living in remote semi-subsistence communities would not occur linearly or at the pace assumed by the logic of market-led models of microfinance.
- That the poor preferred to safeguard what little they had rather than risk it in search of higher returns.
- That savings services were of greater importance than credit in an insecure environment. Savings allow the poor to withstand shocks and increase their willingness to take risks.
- That saving as a group was easier than saving as an individual.
- That access to other services, as well as financial, was just as critical, if not more so, for the poor. Additional services could in fact strengthen capacity to benefit from financial services.
- That the sustainability of the CYSD was not the same as the sustainability of the livelihoods of the poor, and the two might even be in conflict. CYSD's mission required that the latter take priority over the former.

CYSD has adopted a combination of activities designed to bring about the sustainable reduction of poverty in its areas of operation in Koraput. These activities encompass the provision of basic services (such as health training and non-formal education), the promotion of livelihoods, the management of natural resources and the building of capacity for local self-governance. The formation of SHGs, which bring 15–20 women together to meet and save on a regular basis, is a critical element in its strategy. CYSD provides these groups with the support they need to manage their own savings, to provide loans to each other, to develop a culture of thrift and loan repayment and to gradually begin to access various government programmes intended for poor people, including regional rural banks that have been mandated to provide financial services to the poor.

CYSD is not a microfinance provider, but a microfinance-promoting institution. As a promoter of microfinance, it forms SHGs, provides them with various support services and builds their capacity. The longer-term objective is to make these SHGs autonomous, until they eventually become community-based MFIs. Once the SHGs reach a level of maturity, they can access loans from banks or other lending institutions, thus securing their long-term sustainability.

To address immediate problems of food insecurity, CYSD promotes grain banks at the village level to be managed by the community. These are intended to act as a buffer stock for the villagers during the dry months of May to July. The bank accepts grain deposits from members and on-lends them for seed and consumption purposes during the agricultural and dry seasons. The grain loan received has to be repaid to the grain bank on harvesting, with interest. CYSD provides one-off support in the form of the grain equivalent to the amount collected by the community members.

Finally, CYSD has been active in building community-level organizations to express the collective voice of tribal groups against oppressive acts by both state and market functionaries, and against the systematic usurpation of their ancestral rights over forest, water and land. These organizations, which include the SHGs, are provided with training and support to become active at the *panchayat* (village council) level and to lobby government to ensure its greater responsiveness to their needs.

Imp-Act assessment of CYSD's programme in Koraput

CYSD's strategy is to address both livelihood and governance issues with its members. Both are equally essential if poor and marginalized groups are to exercise their rights as citizens. Security of livelihoods is necessary to safeguard tribal groups from exploitative and demeaning forms of dependence on others, while acquiring a voice is essential if they are to play a greater role in the decision-making structures that govern their lives. CYSD's impact in both these areas is explored here on the basis of an assessment of the SHG approach in Koraput carried out under the *Imp-Act* programme.

The programme involved a one-off study designed and carried out by a team recruited for the task, but it was intended to provide a process of learning that could be used to develop CYSD's monitoring methodology. The assessment was based on a comparison of 239 'new' members, women who had been SHG members for less than two years, and 317 'mature' members who had been members for three or more years. They were selected from 31 hamlets in four *panchayats* in Koraput district. Geographical targeting meant that mature SHG members were drawn from different hamlets to newer members.

The study found that mature members were found to be generally more disadvantaged than new members: 35 per cent of them came from hamlets where poverty was over 60 per cent, compared to just 7 per cent of new members. None of the sample hamlets had electricity but new members were more likely to be drawn from hamlets connected by all-weather roads (7 out of 13) than the mature members (3 out of 18). Of the mature members 65 per cent were drawn from the scheduled tribe and 4 per cent from scheduled castes, compared to 71 per cent and 8 per cent of new members. While comparison of mature and new members was the primary strategy for attributing impact, it was supplemented with qualitative information on some of the pathways through which changes might have occurred and the extent to which these could plausibly be attributed to CYSD's efforts.

Addressing livelihood security
Improving agricultural productivity
Agriculture was the mainstay of the tribal economy and most households owned some homestead and cultivable land, although holdings were minuscule in size and made up of poorly endowed land. To address this element of household livelihood, CYSD carried out training in a range of agricultural practices aimed at increasing productivity, arresting the ongoing degradation of land and augmenting the fertility of the soil, particularly on high altitude land. It also introduced improved seed varieties and arranged exposure visits to better developed villages.

The impact study found, as might be expected, that mature SHG members had received higher levels of support from the CYSD programmes than new members. More significantly, a considerably higher percentage of mature members had adopted the practices. For instance, 56 per cent of mature members had taken up land bunding, compared to 13 per cent of new members, a process that entails the construction of earth embankments along slope contours so as to arrest the erosion of topsoil during heavy rainfall. Thirty-six per cent of mature members and 12 per cent of new members were also practising bio-manuring through *danicha* (prickly sesban) cultivation, which restores nutrients to the soil; while 85 per cent of mature members and only 38 per cent of new members had adopted the self-preparation of organic fertilizer through compost pit technology.

The horticulture support programme was intended to increase vegetation on high land areas, to enhance the water retention capacity of the soil and to bind the topsoil, as well as acting as natural hedges obstructing the velocity of the run-off water. Among mature members 67 per cent reported commercial vegetable production, compared to 52 per cent of new members, and 36 per cent of mature members and 14 per cent of new members reported multiple cropping. However, a higher percentage of new members had adopted high yield variety seeds. These are all practices that directly reflect the kind of support provided by CYSD and can therefore be attributed to the organization's interventions.

Diversifying livelihoods
While the overwhelming majority of households reported agriculture as their main source of income, they also relied on other sources to supplement this. While there was very little difference in the number of supplementary activities reported by mature and new members, there was a discernible

difference in the spread of occupations. Of new members 89 per cent reported wage labour, 63 per cent reported non-timber forest produce (NTFP), such as *sal* seeds and tamarind, and just 7 per cent reported small business. By contrast, 55 per cent of mature members reported wage labour as a supplementary activity, 73 per cent reported NTFP and 18 per cent reported small business. The small business activities taken up by mature members included a grocery shop in the village and weekly markets, manufacturing and trading of bamboo products and mobile trading of consumables, all of which could be set up with small amounts of capital.

It thus appears that mature members experienced both a greater spread of economic activities and a shift away from wage labour and into various forms of self-employment. Wage labour played a more important role in the livelihoods of new members and was also undertaken for more months of the year.

Diversifying patterns of savings and loans

Membership of self-help groups also appears to have led to changing patterns of borrowing and saving. One change related to a diversification in the pattern of saving. Excluding their savings with SHGs, 66 per cent of mature members reported three or more forms of saving compared to 39 per cent of new members. Just 8 per cent of new members and 1 per cent of mature members were unable to save. For both mature and new members, the preferred form of saving was cash at home, followed by saving in the form of jewellery. Mature members stated that saving through the grain banks was their third most preferred option, while new members preferred saving grain at home. Along with the strong preference for liquidity of savings evident in these responses, what is also evident was the extremely low use (around 2 per cent) by new and mature members of formal financial institutions, such as the post office or the regional rural banks. Clearly the overwhelming majority of members also saved with their SHGs since that was a condition of membership.

There was also evidence of change in sources of loans. Mature members were more likely than new members to report three or more sources of credit: 60 per cent compared to 46 per cent. Moreover, ranking sources of credit by preference revealed that 98 per cent of mature members preferred to approach their SHG for loans. New members expressed a greater diversity of preferences, with 58 per cent preferring moneylenders[3] and only 27 per cent expressing a preference for their SHG. This may reflect both higher levels of trust among mature members and larger accumulation of funds. In addition, mature members were more likely to have begun borrowing from rural banks than new members (13 per cent and 6 per cent respectively) and considerably more likely to report a decline in the use of moneylenders (64 per cent and 41 per cent respectively). Both trends augur well for the effectiveness of the SHG strategy in mainstreaming tribal groups into the formal banking sector as borrowers and away from exploitative forms of credit, although progress is clearly slower in achieving the latter.[4]

The reasons for the insignificant access to formal financial institutions recorded by these findings were identified through focus group discussions as: the lack of adequate amounts of savings to merit opening an account at a post office or a rural bank; the amount of time lost in going to one of these institutions; the intimidating and time-consuming nature of the procedures involved; and the hostility encountered from staff towards members of poor, tribal communities.

Strengthening the asset base

Along with access to savings and credit, the household's asset base also plays a role in reducing insecurity. Here, CYSD appears to have had some impact in building members' non-land asset base. Almost all members, mature and new, owned some land but the size of their holdings was minuscule. Mature members were more likely to own homestead land, while new members were more likely to report ownership of high land. High land is acquired by clearing the slopes of the mountains. It is less fertile and its slope means it suffers topsoil erosion. Thus, it does not translate into a particularly productive asset.

While there was little difference in the percentages of people owning low land or in the size of the holdings, more systematic differences were evident in five other categories of household assets: trees; poultry/livestock; agricultural tools; consumer utensils; and consumer items. Of mature members 60 per cent owned at least one fruit-bearing or cash-earning tree, compared to 40 per cent of new members. At least one kind of livestock, poultry or one *desi* chicken[5] (generally the latter) was owned by 58 per cent of mature members and 42 per cent of new members. At least one commonly used agricultural tool was owned by 57 per cent of mature members and 43 per cent of new members. Similar percentages owned at least one commonly used utensil, while 57 per cent of mature members and 43 per cent of new members owned a small consumer item, such as a radio, torch light or clock. While the overall poverty level of members is evident from the low rates of asset ownership, it was also evident that mature members consistently reported higher rates than new members.

Securing household food needs

Increases in the productivity and diversity of livelihoods and increased sources of borrowing and lending can in themselves represent an improvement in the well-being of members if it releases them from humiliating relations of dependence and exploitation at the hands of moneylenders or landlords. In addition, however, we would expect such changes to translate into increased levels of income and physical well-being. This was borne out by the findings. A significantly higher percentage of mature members reported that their overall household incomes had increased since joining CYSD (59 per cent) compared to new members (20 per cent), while the majority of new members said that their incomes had remained roughly the same.

Greater security of livelihoods was attested to by other revealing findings. Thirty-one per cent of mature members, compared to just 22 per cent of new members, were able to produce enough food to secure their needs for more than eight months of the year. By contrast, 63 per cent of new members were able to assure their own food needs for less than six months compared to 51 per cent of mature members. In other words, while both mature and new members continued to experience food shortages, mature members experienced them for shorter time periods.

One possible reason for this relates to the pattern of agricultural sales reported by member households. While tribal communities primarily engage in subsistence farming, they still have to sell some of their produce or earn non-farm income to meet their other needs. A comparison of the kinds of crops sold by mature and new members revealed that the former were far less likely to sell crops that represented staple foods, which are the basis of household food security. Mature members were able to keep their primary staples for their own needs, since they had other agricultural stock they could sell. Thus, only 16 per cent of mature members sold rice, compared to 29 per cent of new members; 9 per cent sold millet compared to 13 per cent of new members; and 22 per cent sold maize compared to 30 per cent of new members. While higher percentages of mature members sold non-staple crops relative to new members, the difference was only large in the case of vegetables, which are mainly grown on homestead land. That these are likely to be higher value crops is suggested by the fact that mature member households reported higher mean annual incomes from the sale of agricultural produce than new member households.

A second reason for greater food security reported by mature members may relate to the increased options available to them in coping with periods of food shortage. Reports on this showed that 76 per cent of mature members had procured a food grain loan from the grain bank to cope with food shortage, compared to just 3 per cent of new members. For mature members, this was the most widely reported response. In addition, 63 per cent had also procured rice from government ration cards, 44 per cent had purchased food from the market and 21 per cent had obtained interest-free food from neighbours or relatives. Among new members, by contrast, purchasing food from the market was the most widely reported response (83 per cent). In addition, 69 per cent had procured rice with government ration cards[6] and 65 per cent had obtained interest-free food from neighbours and relatives. Twenty-eight per cent of new members and 16 per cent of mature members had taken an interest-bearing loan of food or money.

While the higher percentages of mature members resorting to the grain bank in times of food shortage clearly reflects the fact that such banks were more likely to have been established among them, it is revealing that it was the most widely preferred option, thus suggesting an improvement on previous options. The purchase of food from the open market – the option most widely reported by new members – is also likely to be the costliest option, since food prices are highest in times of food shortage.

Promoting voice and agency

Building relationships of solidarity and trust between group members has been a central plank in CYSD's strategy for building their capacity for collective action, the key to their greater political agency. However, progress has been much slower on this front compared to impacts reported in relation to livelihood security. Focus group discussions within the hamlets revealed that the members generally had little awareness of the political parties or functioning of the government. They associated voting with the symbols of the political parties but could not name the parties. The idea of voting as a fundamental right and a route to political representation had not taken root within the community. Political parties, government functionaries and elected officials had little interest in promoting local participation in the *palli sabha*.[7] Meetings were not held regularly and when they were, advance notice of the venue or date was seldom given, making it difficult for women in particular to attend. Very often husbands or other male family members went to such meetings on behalf of the women.

However, within this overall context of poorly performing governance structures and political marginalization of tribal communities, CYSD had made a small but discernible difference. For instance, while only 28 per cent of all members surveyed had attended a *palli* or *gram sabha* meeting, 34 per cent of mature members reported attendance compared to 19 per cent of new members. As members pointed out in focus group discussions, such attendance was new for tribals, and particularly for women. For example, one of the women noted that 'We never used to participate in meetings at the village or the *panchayat*. The male members of the village would look down upon the females and talk ill about them if they participate in such meetings. They think tribal women are incapable of participating in meetings as they don't know much about the world because of their illiteracy'.

Voting levels were higher for local elections than national ones. Eighty per cent of all surveyed members had voted in local elections for *sarpanch* and *samitee* members, but only 65 per cent had voted in national elections. While percentages voting in national elections were similar for both mature and new members, mature members were systematically more likely to vote at the local level. Ninety per cent of mature members had voted for the *sarpanch* compared to 83 per cent of new members; 89 per cent had voted for *samitee* members compared to 81 per cent of new members; and 81 per cent had for voted the *zilla parishad* member compared to 73 per cent of new members.

In order to ascertain the extent to which members had access to relevant government officials, they were asked which of a number of officials they had had contact with in the previous year. Access was generally low and did not vary according to duration of membership, with the exceptions of government doctors and forest officers. These were probably the categories of government officials most directly relevant to tribal groups. Sixty-one per cent of mature members had visited a government doctor compared to

54 per cent of new members, while 9 per cent of mature members had had contact with a government forest official, compared to just 2 per cent of new members.

Members were also asked about involvement in various campaigns or protests. The two key issues that appeared to have mobilized them were alcoholism and children's schooling. Fifty-five per cent of mature members had participated in campaigns against alcoholism compared to 30 per cent of new members, while 43 per cent of mature members had protested against the production and sale of liquor compared to 37 per cent of new members. Such protests took the form of organized marches and rallies, as well as through SHG representation to government officials demanding a ban on the selling and making of liquor.

Participation in action to demand improved access to education was undertaken by 34 per cent of mature members and 21 per cent of new members. The SHGs had filed written complaints as well as visited the *panchayat* and block office to lobby for the opening of government education centres under the education guarantee scheme. Five hamlets had been successful in their demands. In one case, the village already had a government primary school but the teacher attended irregularly. The villagers tried complaining to the teacher and the *panchayat* officials, but this had had little effect. The SHG then repeatedly wrote to the inspector of schools about the irresponsible attitude of the teacher. After three such complaints, the teacher was finally transferred and a new teacher posted.

The value of CYSD to its members

We have focused thus far on possible impacts associated with CYSD's activities in relation to livelihood security and local governance. In this section we consider which of CYSD's activities the SHG members judged to be of greatest value to them, and which they disliked most, with information gathered through the survey questionnaire. Very few members found anything to dislike about CYSD, though around 2 per cent complained about the small size of loans and length and frequency of meetings. It was clearly the microfinance aspects of the SHGs that members valued most. However, while new members overwhelmingly voted in favour of the SHG's role in providing a safe and convenient place to save (93 per cent), mature members were divided between valuing its savings aspect (62 per cent) and its lending aspect, with 69 per cent valuing access to quick emergency loans and 15 per cent valuing access to loans without collateral. Eighteen per cent of mature members also valued access to new kinds of skills through participating in SHG training efforts, while 17 per cent valued the feeling of unity with their group members. Thus, while it was savings that might have initially attracted women to join the SHG, over time members began to value other aspects as well.

The focus group discussions provided further information on which aspects of the microfinance services the members valued. Members pointed out that the concept of saving or thrift was not a familiar one in tribal communities. The subsistence nature of their economy provided little scope for generating any significant surplus to meet emergency and other needs, hence their reliance on moneylenders. Widespread alcoholism within the community also eroded the capacity to save. The older groups had started with very small savings of Rs2 (US$0.04), but during their meetings they discussed the possibility of increasing this amount and ways to do so. One member commented that 'If we save Rs3 (US$0.06) on every weekly *haat* [market] then we would have enough money for our month-end compulsory saving'.

The absence of any other formal financial institutions that are accessible, hospitable and can handle the small amounts of money that poor tribal communities are able to save makes the SHG the ideal arrangement for this purpose. By giving responsibility for keeping their savings to the group, they were able to keep it secure, since money stored in the house was likely to be appropriated by husbands for liquor consumption. Thus, a culture of collective saving began to take root and has now become the primary motivating factor for women to join the group.

Finally the focus group discussions also highlighted the humiliations associated with borrowing from moneylenders. According to one participant: 'We had to entertain the moneylender with a good meal whenever he visited the village. We were at his mercy for timely loans. He would give the loan at his discretion. For larger loans we had to mortgage what we had—land, jewellery and brass utensils. We would lose valuables if we did not repay the loan within the stipulated time'. Another person commented that 'In accessing loans from the local shopkeeper or moneylender, we had to "bow down" and beg for the loan. Only then would he be willing to oblige us with the loan'.

With the accumulation of SHG savings, members have been able to access loans without compromising their dignity. As one of them said: 'We take loans from our own money, without any collateral, and that too at our doorstep. Once the *sahookar* asked me why I am not taking any loan from him. I said our SHG has enough money now, and we can give you a loan if he wanted. We have become the *sahookar* now'.

Learning from the *Imp-Act* study

CYSD has benefited organizationally from its participation in the *Imp-Act* project as well from its experience of carrying out this assessment. It is attempting to move away from its earlier 'single loop' monitoring system (one-way information flow) that focused on upward accountability and instead put in place a 'double loop' system along the lines of the feed-back loop model developed by the *Imp-Act* research programme. The monitoring division is being restructured to make it more impact-oriented in its efforts.

The *Imp-Act* research also had a positive output in terms of developing a standardized SHG monitoring system and a self-rating tool for the SHGs. The SHGs had been following different accounting systems and the different project offices were monitoring the SHGs in their own format, hence there used to be significant variations in terms of accounts across SHGs and projects. There were also separate registers (for example for group meetings, cash books, member profiles and general ledgers), making monitoring by the SHGs and central management extremely cumbersome. Generation and consolidation of information and the structuring of reports were time consuming and labour intensive. A standardized and simplified system for self-monitoring is now being put into place and SHGs are being trained to use this new tool. Since the SHGs are now the dominant mode of microfinance, with clear government policy and bank support, many other agencies in the state of Orissa have expressed interest in these tools and the organization is now disseminating them to the rest of the microfinance community in Orissa.

Conclusion

Poor people are not a homogeneous group and it is extremely unlikely that their poverty can be addressed through a uniform set of interventions. The view that microfinance services should be driven by the need to become financially sustainable, a view that is rapidly becoming the orthodoxy in the development community, does no justice to the diversity of poor people's needs and constraints. The goal of financial sustainability may not compromise the poverty reduction mission of an MFI in dynamic economic contexts, where the possibility of growing out of poverty through gradually expanding enterprises is a feasible one. Yet even here, differences between the poor in terms of the degree of their poverty and their social status may lead to unevenness of impact.

In a context where institutions are weak and pressurized into seeking financial sustainability, and where uncertainty is high, the possibility of poor people finding profitable opportunities that will allow them to repay loans at sufficiently high rates of interest seems very unlikely. To force them to do so as a way to increase the institution's portfolio would be to take advantage of the fact that they have so few choices. Yet even very poor people need financial services, to deal with emergencies, to invest in equipment and to meet social needs. What CYSD has sought to do – along with a number of other organizations in India – is to provide such services in a way that promotes a different kind of sustainability. This is the sustainability of its poverty reduction efforts, by building the capacity of the poor to both generate their own microfinancial resources as well as to access mainstream programmes that are mandated to address their needs.

CHAPTER SEVEN

Institutionalizing internal learning systems: experiences from Professional Assistance for Development Action (PRADAN), India

D. Narendranath

Introduction

This chapter summarizes the efforts of PRADAN (Professional Assistance for Development Action) to institutionalize the Internal Learning System (ILS), a system aimed primarily at helping the microfinance group members to reflect and learn about various aspects of their lives and livelihoods, but also for PRADAN to measure and report social performance. PRADAN's choice of the ILS and its mode of application were strongly influenced by the organization's fundamental participatory values that ensure involvement of staff and clients at all stages, from goal setting through to planning and implementation.

PRADAN employs educated individuals who work directly at the grass-roots level and enjoy a great deal of autonomy in the larger organizational framework. The organization neither prescribes nor monitors their day-to-day engagement at the community level. Thus, given that PRADAN's aim is to introduce the ILS into its routine structure, it has been extremely important to ensure that staff support the new system. This chapter describes the process involved in designing and modifying the ILS to make it appropriate to the needs of PRADAN staff and clients, and the challenge of ensuring acceptance of the system throughout the organization.

Background

PRADAN's main focus: building the capabilities of the poor

PRADAN is an NGO working in some of the very poorest regions in India with a focus on promoting the livelihoods for the rural poor. In PRADAN's view, livelihoods are not just a matter of increasing family incomes but rather of building the capabilities of poor people to access and creatively use livelihood resources and entitlements. Therefore, for PRADAN, building capabilities or 'enabling' is an important principle that guides actions in the field. Even though PRADAN's interventions are in the economic arena, the ultimate goal is to enable poor communities to lead a life of dignity. For this reason interventions have been designed and organized in a manner that contribute to the broader well-being of the families involved and they are not restricted to providing access to services.

Microfinance for PRADAN is an important component in a multi-pronged strategy to promote livelihoods. The energy of PRADAN is directed towards creating organizations, systems, processes and an environment that contribute to generating sustainable livelihoods for the poor clients. According to PRADAN, the major missing link in livelihoods for the poor is support for building their basic capabilities, such as the ability to create a vision for themselves, to be able to assess their own resources comprehensively and to plan to optimize these resources for establishing livelihoods.

PRADAN works as an enabler and facilitator, rather than as a service provider. Organizations of poor people are created and enabled to establish sustainable linkages with external resource institutions, such as banks and government departments. As a result, the impact of PRADAN's work is to be assessed not just on the basis of increased access to financial services, but also on the quality of livelihoods, enhancement of clients' livelihood capabilities and the sustainability of the linkages they have established with external resource institutions.

The funding for PRADAN to undertake developmental activities comes from various national and international donors. Most of the funding is project based, though some is institutional in nature. Since PRADAN finds that the kind of work it does – that of building basic human capabilities – is not one that can be 'revenue-driven', it is dependent on grants and service charges to meet its costs. Now that PRADAN has grown to be a very large organization with a staff of about 250 professionals, spread over seven provinces, the volume of funds required annually has grown significantly, leading the organization to lobby the government for economic assistance, which is a challenge in itself.

Working at grass-roots level through self-help groups

It is also a core belief in PRADAN that highly educated and sensitive individuals have to work directly at the grass-roots level to assist poor people in improving their lives and to bring about wide-ranging social and economic impacts. Presently more than 200 professional staff are engaged in a wide variety of livelihood projects with about 80,000 poor families organized into approximately 5,500 self-help groups involved in microfinance through small savings and credit.

Promotion of women's SHGs is an important step in PRADAN's approach to enabling communities. The PRADAN staff who facilitate group formation also provide training and other inputs as required to strengthen institutional values, norms and systems. Once the SHG has become mature and self-reliant, PRADAN helps them to link up with commercial banks to access mainstream finances.

Focus on women: efficiency and equity

The rationale for focusing on women is based on efficiency and equity. In terms of efficiency, it has been PRADAN's experience, as echoed elsewhere, that women are much better money managers and much more conscientious about repayments. Timely repayment and hence lack of defaults is extremely crucial to PRADAN's long-term strategy of graduating into the livelihood promotion arena, leaving the SHGs to deal with the banks to access financial services directly. If this relationship between the SHGs and the banks is to continue sustainably in the future, in the absence of PRADAN's support, then the SHGs have to display extreme financial maturity and discipline. Thus, a major component of PRADAN's training of the SHGs is to deal with issues such as savings regularity, preparing individual loan plans, peer assessment, vetting and repayment norms. Experience in PRADAN has shown that it is far easier to train women's groups in these aspects than men's groups.

It has also been the general experience of PRADAN that women are more disciplined as a social group. They are more regularly available in the village so that it is possible to initiate institution-building processes that require steady and long-term commitment. Men are unable to provide such uninterrupted commitment because they tend to be more mobile. The groups formed around women also tend to be less prone to conflicts. In addition, when money comes into the hands of women they tend to spend it more equitably across the family members than men do. These trends have been observed in many places but are corroborated by the experience of PRADAN's field staff.

On equity grounds the targeting of women is an affirmative action, favouring them as particularly disadvantaged among an already disadvantaged group. They usually own no assets, are not part of any important decision-making processes either in the family or outside and hold quite a poor view of their capacity to achieve. They are often isolated in their homes, which limits their ability to access information and resources and to participate in political activities. Since it is difficult to reach them, welfare and development programmes by government and even NGOs often exclude them.

PRADAN's approach is that women are as capable as men of being actors in the development process, but given their situation special efforts need to be made to reach out to and include them. The SHGs provide a platform to systematically reach out to the women of a community and organize them. They help involve them and incorporate their views in the planning and implementation of microfinance and livelihood programmes. This gives them increased access to their families' economic resources and as the SHGs mature, the women also start establishing linkages with a number of external institutions, which in turn helps to widen their horizons. Using the strength of the collective they are able to have an influence in a wider arena. The most important changes happen at a personal and group level when the women start to view themselves as respectable individuals and feel that they can be instrumental in bringing about changes in their own, as well as others', lives.

PRADAN's outreach to the poor

PRADAN has a mix of geographic targeting to identify pockets of poverty and areas deserving of intervention. It has chosen to work in the poorest seven states in India in areas of intense poverty. The CGAP poverty assessment that was conducted in PRADAN project areas found that the SHG programme reached all but the bottom 3 per cent of poor people in these areas, which themselves were the most underdeveloped in the country. This becomes more significant when one considers that more than 80 per cent of the population in PRADAN's target areas live on less than US$1 a day.

PRADAN's approach to livelihoods promotion and microfinance is derived from the fact that when clients are so poor, they need much more than financial services to set up sustainable livelihoods. First, it is crucial that the basic human capabilities of the women are enhanced, such as the ability to build a livelihoods vision, to see opportunities in difficult situations and to take moderate calculated risks. Once these issues are addressed, the new livelihood enhancement opportunities that are created, such as access to financial services, infrastructure, technology and market linkages, become more meaningful.

Approach to impact assessment

The opportunity presented by *Imp-Act* fed into a number of concerns that PRADAN had in 2001. The lack of a system to provide regular information on impact was already an issue. So it was decided that, with the assistance of *Imp-Act*, the organization would design and institutionalize systems and processes for collecting such information in a manner that would be enabling as well as empowering for its clients. Client learning was an important requisite given the nature of PRADAN's interventions and its empowerment focus.

Objectives of PRADAN's Imp-Act work

The objectives originally set for PRADAN's *Imp-Act* work were: to understand the impact hitherto of PRADAN's work on the poor; to validate internal assumptions about poverty impact that formed the basis of the approaches and strategies followed in PRADAN projects; to understand our ability to reach out to the poorest sections in the community; to improve effectiveness of staff in intervening at the community level; to improve understanding of the ways in which we could help the community set up systems for themselves; and to provide useful information for policy advocacy. Thus, a mix of proving, improving and learning activities and goals formed the basis of PRADAN's agenda under *Imp-Act*.

PRADAN's Imp-Act project activities

Three project activities were chosen by PRADAN:

Poverty assessment of clients using the CGAP tool
Under *Imp-Act* PRADAN was part of a thematic group on issues of extreme poverty and a major poverty assessment was launched as part of its investigation into these issues. The study found that PRADAN's projects were not reaching the bottom 3 per cent of the poor. This data reconfirmed the view of field staff that some of the destitute poor, such as nomadic tribes, handicapped people and very elderly people, were being excluded from the microfinance intervention. The findings of the CGAP study led to new challenges for PRADAN in terms of external proving, internal proving, validation and policy advocacy roles.

Quantitative impact survey of the SHG programme in a mature PRADAN location
An extensive quantitative impact survey was conducted with a sample of 500 families, including members and non-members, and addressed a wide variety of social and economic indicators. Given that members' starting points were extremely low, the study showed a lot of progress for the members on both economic and social fronts. However, on the theme of women's empowerment, the study yielded the significant finding that microfinance alone does not lead to empowerment because other inputs are also required.

Design and implementation of the internal learning system
The internal learning system has been the main focus of PRADAN's work under *Imp-Act*. This tool, created by Dr Helzi Noponen, has a primary role for client learning but also has strengths in making impact assessment and the monitoring of social performance and wider impacts more routine. It comprises a set of pictorial workbooks called the 'learning diaries' to be used by the SHG members and by the PRADAN staff acting as SHG promoters. These pictorial books are designed around a wide set of indicators relevant to the particular level. The member-level books have indicators around well-being, finance and livelihoods, empowerment and participation. The group-level book has indicators around SHG performance, status of the norms and systems in the group and a few area-level indicators on the status of amenities and services. The staff workbook has indicators such as the performance of SHGs under one staff member, the reasons for good and bad performance, possible plans to improve the condition of the SHGs and some area-level indicators.

The member-level workbooks are to be used by the SHG member, wherein she is supposed to look at each picture, reflect on how that indicator applies to her and place a mark, such as a tick, next to the picture that corresponds to her current status. She subsequently revisits that picture periodically to assess the changes that have occurred. There are modules in the book that help the member to plan future action to improve her situation with regard to that indicator. Similarly, the SHG books have indicators that enable the groups to collectively reflect on the past and to plan ahead. The staff workbook provides the same opportunity to the PRADAN staff member working with the SHG.

An existing basic model for ILS was adapted, tested and modified in a series of interactive processes at client as well as staff levels. The design process included selection of the appropriate indicators for each level, distilling them into pictures and organizing them into the workbook in a logical manner. The design of the system underwent a number of changes as a result of these interactive processes and by the end of the *Imp-Act* programme it was fully prepared. It was then launched in two locations and the results were encouraging, with clients finding the system very useful in contributing to their learning. Yet PRADAN management are aware of the need to elicit full commitment from staff if the ILS is to be fully institutionalized into organizational practices. The next section deals with the process of institutionalizing the ILS in PRADAN.

Institutionalization of the internal learning system

Building ownership among staff

PRADAN is primarily a livelihoods-promotion organization. In such a scenario, the staff are exceedingly focused on the issues related to implementing livelihood projects and sometimes there is a tendency to focus just on the income enhancement of clients' families. The finer concerns of building capabilities, bringing about impacts on the broader well-being of the women involved and setting up sustainable systems can be sidelined. Given these factors, it is not surprising that there was initial resistance to the idea of introducing systems and processes that required a broader focus, the initial implementation of which might affect targets for income generation in the short term.

In response to this scepticism, a number of reflective events and discussions were held internally, during which the organizational mission was reaffirmed and staff were encouraged to reflect on the meaning of improved livelihoods and well-being for the families and the communities with whom PRADAN works. In addition, the commitment of staff to these new ideas was sought through their inclusion in design processes from the outset, even though this was time consuming. It was felt that building ownership among staff was a priority because they were the people who were ultimately going to be using the ILS tool, primarily to produce useful information and learning for themselves as well as the organization.

ILS – the design process

The ILS had an existing generic design and had been previously implemented in a few Indian organizations (both NGOs and MFIs). However, the requirements of PRADAN were different owing to a poorer target community, more professional staff, the overarching theme of livelihoods and a learning rather than impact assessment approach.

A number of discussions and brainstorming sessions were carried out with staff and with the local community. The external consultant, Dr Helzi Noponen, and the ILS unit in PRADAN, led this consultation process. In initial discussions with staff the overall framework of the ILS was worked out. It was decided that the ILS would be set up at client level, SHG level and staff level. There would be further consolidation modules for the regional and head-office levels. However, the higher order levels would refer to information collated in the computerized management information system.

Another important consensus that was reached was that the ILS would have livelihoods as a key theme because the day-to-day action of the PRADAN staff revolved around this. Thus, a substantial portion of the workbooks were to be devoted to issues such as analysis of household income and expenditure, ownership of and access to resources, and planning modules for optimal use of resources. In fact this was a major departure for the ILS, as it had previously mostly dealt with impact indicators. The staff themselves suggested that the ILS should not only be looking at impact but also be helping them to guide clients and achieve greater impact. The ILS would not just be a reflective tool but a tool for 'reflective action'.

Extensive consultations were also conducted with staff and clients with regard to the various sections and indicators to be covered in the ILS books. It was an iterative process in which a large number of indicators were listed in the initial interactions and modules were developed around them (see Box 7.1).

Once the design of the first draft was complete, a three-day ILS training workshop was carried out involving about 20 staff members from seven of the 25 locations in which PRADAN works. The SHG members' modules were launched in this workshop and each module was discussed in detail. The participants provided a lot of feedback on the design to make it more comprehensive and also adopted targets to field test the modules. The field testing offered a reality check on the level of detail required while collecting data, on which indicators were most suitable and contributed to maximum learning, and how best to introduce the pictorial modules.

Modules and indicators in the ILS workbooks

The overall structure of the ILS and the modules and indicators that were included is as follows.

Box 7.1

A typical design meeting with the SHG members starts with the consultant showing them a picture of a woman with a sad face. Once the members identify the picture, an open-ended question is asked as to why members think the woman is sad. This leads to a flurry of statements by the women, primarily based on their own experiences. Even those who do not respond immediately get fully engrossed in the exercise. Then another picture is shown of the same woman but with a neutral face, and the question is asked as to what changes might have happened in the woman's life. After giving some time for responses, the next picture of a happy woman is shown and the question repeated. This is indeed a deeply reflective process for the women, who use their personal experiences as reference points. The responses they give for the sad or happy states in the life of this woman are their own stories. For instance, in one village, one of the major reasons given for the sad face was the pressure to have sons. In another village, they mentioned sorcery: branding women as witches. Indicators of women's empowerment were distilled from such discussions.

The member workbook

The member workbook is designed as a rural development curriculum, in which individual sections fit into a logical whole. In the well-being module, a woman reflects on her current standard of living in terms such as living conditions, assets, poverty status and health. In the finance module, she examines how her living standards are affected by her household's pattern of income and expenditure, and its resulting savings and debt situations. In order to improve her finances and living standards, she is next encouraged to analyse her livelihood situation.

The livelihoods module guides an SHG member and her family in critically assessing their livelihood system in order to maximize the use of their total 'availabilities' in forest, land, livestock and labour resources, as well as making more strategic use of their credit opportunities. In the empowerment module, the woman also examines her treatment and status in the home and wider community, either as a liberating or an inhibiting influence on her reproductive and productive roles. Finally, in the programme participation module, the woman reflects on the respective roles that she, her SHG and the PRADAN promoter play in helping her achieve her goals.

The group-level workbook

The group-level workbook deals with the various parameters of interest to the group as a whole. The SHG members fill in this book together in a democratic way. The modules are concerned about whether the group is functioning well together, whether it is following the various norms, systems and disciplines, and whether it is adhering to the values of the group. The group is also expected to assess its capacity as a financial intermediary and a vehicle to influence external agencies such as government departments.

The promoter workbook
The promoter workbook is designed to assist PRADAN promoters to track how well their SHGs are performing in terms of various aspects of group functioning.

The field test

The next step was to field test the workbooks, trying out the modules directly with clients to understand their response to the system, to the individual modules and even individual pictures. It was also important to gauge the time and energy that would have to be put in by the staff for operationalizing the system. It was decided to do the first launch in seven locations after the initial consultation workshop. Unfortunately, the launch happened during the agricultural season, when the SHG members as well as promoters were extremely busy with other activities and could not provide the time required to do the test. Most testing was hurried, leading to a sense of not being able to complete the set of tasks. Yet there were a few cases where the people concerned were personally interested in the process, spent enough time on it and had a positive experience.

In the subsequent feedback workshop there were a lot of comments on the design and content of the ILS books. The staff also shared in detail their experiences of running the process in the SHGs, including problems with recording data both in the ILS books and the data entry template. Some of the staff also talked about the enthusiasm the women exhibited when filling in the workbooks and the rich discussions that followed.

The first drafts of the ILS books were very ambitious in the details they sought to record. This led to the inclusion of quite complex data entry formats, which the staff found very difficult to administer. It also led many of the staff involved to feel that the ILS was an overly comprehensive system that would not work. The staff were looking for a system that would work with minimal external intervention, and the first drafts did not meet that objective. This was further complicated by the dissonance expressed by some staff members who had not had a positive experience when conducting the field tests.

ILS design – revision and launch

With the considerable feedback received from staff, the ILS workbooks were redesigned. A number of factors that the ILS unit had itself identified as shortcomings were also addressed. This time it was decided by the ILS unit that the launch would not happen in a large number of locations but only in one or two where the staff continued to be positive. A second decision was that the ILS would be launched in its totality and not in parts. Third, a lot of attention would be paid to the process aspects of the system and not just the hardware, such as the picture books. It was felt that in the first launch, maybe due to the lack of understanding at the time, inadequate attention was paid to educating the staff on the processes that go along with the pictorial workbooks. Thus, some of the staff used the pictures as data collection devices, and some as reflective tools. Fourth, it was also decided that the ILS unit would monitor practice very closely in the field through regular field visits and troubleshooting, and also collecting progress reports and concurrent feedback.

One of the issues that had been raised by staff in the earlier phase was that the time pressure on them was very great. There was routine work that had to be done in the SHGs and the ILS came as an add-on, rather than a system that was helping to reduce time spent on other tasks. A time analysis of field staff's routine work revealed that a substantial amount of time, about 40 per cent, was spent correcting accounting errors made by SHGs, a task that was supposed to be done by the village accountant. Due to the level of illiteracy in the villages, it was extremely difficult to find reasonably literate people to be trained as accountants, and the ones who were found were not adequately equipped. This resulted in accounting errors that could not be ignored by the professionals because accounts are the backbone of the groups.

Due to these problems it was decided to computerize the SHG accounts and MIS, and install a system called the Computer Munshi[1] (CM). Even though this system was not initiated as part of the ILS development, the ILS benefited substantially from the process. A large amount of time was freed up that could then be diverted to more productive work with the SHGs.

The first phase launch of the revised version of the ILS was done in two locations where the SHG computerization was complete and the CM system was in place. Rather than carrying out centralized training, this time the strategy adopted was to send a central team to the location and conduct a three-day workshop, complete with on-field demonstration, to the whole team that was operating in a location. A team normally consists of 10–12 staff members and without locally-based training, some members would have been unable to attend a central event.

By August 2004 the ILS had been launched in six field locations and interest in its use was gathering momentum. The process was much more gradual than in the initial stages, because there was no time-target pressure and because the emphasis was on building ownership of the system, rather than implementing it. The staff wished to use the extra time freed up as a result of computerization for strengthening the groups.

A guiding concern of the ILS design unit is that the system should not become a set of formats added on to the already heavy workload of the field staff. There is an emphasis on ensuring it is institutionalized, meshing seamlessly with the day-to-day operations of the staff, so that neither staff nor clients feel any additional pressure from its use. Thus, one aspect of the ILS that is constantly highlighted is that the system does not reduce time commitments in the field and neither does it increase them; instead it helps make the time spent more fruitful and rewarding.

Use of the ILS

Response at the community level

ILS workbooks have received very exciting responses at the community level. The ILS got off to an enthusiastic start in the PRADAN projects in the states of Chatisgarh, Jharkhand and West Bengal. As reported by the teams, through the medium of the pictorial workbooks, they are able to ensure active participation of all the SHG members. The workbooks help the members to be more reflective and internalize the inputs provided much more effectively, compared to the earlier mode of verbal interactions. The livelihood modules in the ILS workbooks give the women a broad perspective on making livelihood choices. The other modules, such as those on health and gender empowerment, generate lively discussions in the SHGs, as illustrated in Box 7.2.

> **Box 7.2**
>
> In one of the field test villages the health module received a lot of attention. It generated very involved discussions on the current health and sanitation practices in the village. The effect of such involvement was visible the next week. Many of the SHG members had purchased mosquito nets. It was a malaria-infested area but the women had never before reflected on the cause of malaria or thought about a means to prevent mosquito bits, even given its simplicity!

The modules on SHG norms and systems are an effective training tool for strengthening the groups, as illustrated in Box 7.3.

Advantages of the pictorial workbooks

A noteworthy phenomenon observed from the use of the reflective pictorial methodology is that it gave women the space and opportunity to legitimately speak about a whole range of issues they never spoke about in the normal course of things. In a normal SHG meeting, the facilitator would raise an issue and the women would respond to the topic raised. The discussion would largely be dictated by the depth of understanding of the facilitator. However, using the pictorial mode, the women would become reflective and often lead the discussions. The pictures sparked thought processes that would otherwise not have occurred, for example, in one village in Chatisgarh, the discussion on family income and expenditure turned into a discussion on alcoholism among male members of the family. The SHG rallied around one of their members who felt particularly troubled by this issue and resolved to do something about it.

An important benefit brought about by the ILS is that it is now possible to generate discussions around a wide variety of sensitive issues, notably gender, and more specifically violent behaviour by husbands. Other topics of

> **Box 7.3**
>
> The reactions of the women after they used the group-level workbooks were quite representative of the effect of the system overall. One woman commented that 'This book has everything about our life', while another said 'We will buy the ILS books and run our SHG properly'.
>
> The discussions in one of the cluster meetings[2] in the Chatisgarh project, where 54 representatives from 18 SHGs had assembled, concentrated on the SHG workbook. The cluster leaders assessed their own individual SHGs using the ILS pages. One of the issues they themselves identified was that the SHG leadership was not rotating so other members were not getting the opportunity to take up leadership roles. It was quite remarkable that the SHG leaders themselves identified this issue. The PRADAN staff member was surprised when he discovered that in the next monthly meeting, most of the SHGs had changed their representatives.
>
> In the SHG in Namodadar village in Chatisgarh, one member mentioned quite casually that after doing the income-expenditure tree in the ILS, she and her husband sat together and reviewed the household finances. They discovered that they were spending more than reasonable amounts on purchasing sweet meats and confectionery, which they promptly cut down on.
>
> In one SHG in West Bengal, the facilitator asked the women at the beginning of the meeting if they had dreams, but their response was 'No! We only worry about a hundred things!' Subsequently the ILS module on good living conditions was done and the women got around to reflecting on their quality of life. By the end of the exercise all the women agreed that they understood what 'dreaming' meant – it was the positive side of worrying, where instead of getting lost in problems, they set rational goals and adopt practical ways of achieving those goals. One of the women actually presented her plans to the group for converting her thatched house to a concrete house: she would invest her SHG loan to dig a well on her little piece of land and take up vegetable cultivation. She would keep reinvesting her profits and over a period of three years she would save up enough to put a concrete roof on her house.

discussion include women's reproductive health and family planning, which the male staff member may previously have found difficult to raise.

In another village in Jharkhand, the group-level workbook led to a different phenomenon. In one group there were a few members who were poorer than the rest and were not being treated well by the group. During the ILS session they talked about SHG values such as equality of opportunity and equal access to resources. This gave the very poor members a voice to talk about the unequal treatment they were receiving in the SHG. They thus decided to move out of the existing SHG and form another one specifically for women as poor as themselves. Somehow they had not thought about doing this in all of the two years they had been part of the first group. Staff members unanimously observed that the level of discussions in the SHG is more intense, whatever the topic, due to the use of the ILS. The level of ownership of the women of any issue or any decision is also much greater than was the case previously.

Response from staff

More staff members in the second round found the ILS modules both useful and exciting. The ILS was not just a system for routine data collection; the use of pictures gave it enormous versatility that made it equally useful as both a learning and training tool. The ILS was also excellent as a group facilitation tool. Facilitation skills varied from person to person but the ILS helped standardize this process considerably. Once the pictorials are introduced, the women are often inspired to talk and rich discussions are generated. Often women followed up the discussions with discernible action. This was unlike the earlier times where ownership of key issues was with the PRADAN staff and it was necessary to conduct follow-up to ensure some action was generated.

The ILS was also an equally effective tool for data collection. The women would often think quite seriously before putting a mark against any one indicator. The sampling and data collection system has now to be put in place, once the initial issues related to finalizing the design and staff acceptance have been resolved. Computer software that will be managed by the decentralized Computer Munshis is in process, and this will simplify the data collection system.

There have also been other important lessons about the system that have emerged from the field. The ILS helps the SHG members reflect on their lives and take appropriate decisions but it is a process-intensive tool. It does take a lot of facilitation time in SHG meetings but it also helps the professional use that time more effectively in providing structured inputs to members based on a comprehensive curriculum designed around the lives and livelihoods of those members. Those who have been using ILS regularly state that over a period of time their facilitation skills develop, so that it demands less and less of their time.

An immediate effect of the experience of using the pictorial methodology is that the staff members are branching out and devising their own pictorial modules to address specific needs. Two such examples already in practice are the modules prepared for streamlining paddy cultivation in the West Bengal project and for improving dairy farming practices in the Rajasthan project. Drawing on these experiences, the plan is now to design ILS workbooks around individual livelihood activities. They would not only include improved practices but would also provide space for each woman to take a critical look at the activity in the context of her resources, monitor the activity across a season, make concurrent changes and, at the end of it, track the income generated from the activity and monitor the use of that income.

Plan for institutionalization

At the time of writing the plan was to extend the ILS to all PRADAN teams and SHGs. Appropriate methodologies, such as cluster forums and use of SHG leaders, would be used in addition to the PRADAN professional directly facilitating use of the workbooks, thus reaching out to the large number of SHGs already in existence. The basic idea was to make the ILS part of the ongoing procedure of working with the community and not design it as a separate monitoring system for which additional efforts will be required. Thus, PRADAN was designing a standard operating procedure for SHG promotion that would have the ILS as an integral component.

One of the issues PRADAN faced was that there was already a backlog of 5,000 SHGs with about 76,000 members. Most of these groups had matured and did not require or receive day-to-day monitoring assistance from PRADAN staff. Staff time was largely used to develop and implement various livelihoods programmes so more time could be devoted to intense activities with new SHGs. Since the ILS requires a significant amount of time to be spent at the group level, the full set of books was only to be implemented with new members. The group-level books were to be introduced gradually in all new and existing SHGs. All staff members were to use the staff book that was being computerized. For impact monitoring, the full set of books were to be implemented with a panel of clients selected in a sampling process. This data was to be collected once a year.

ILS as a social performance measurement system

ILS is concerned with measuring social rather than financial performance. It is best suited to measuring indicators related to the well-being of the client's family and impacts on livelihood, gender equality, social and political empowerment as well as wider impacts in the community. The difference between the ILS and other social performance measurement systems is that the ILS looks at these issues from the perspective of clients. In this way the system responds to PRADAN's view of itself not only as a provider of financial services but as an organization that will contribute to the empowerment of its clients.

The complexity of the system and emphasis on inclusion of staff and clients means that, as with most SPM systems, significant costs are inevitably involved in institutionalizing the ILS. In PRADAN's case, it is clear that the costs of the ILS will not be passed on to the clients, at least not in the medium term. This is principally because the impacts of using ILS are subtle and the results are not tangible, thus uninitiated clients are unable to see the potential benefits of using it. Therefore PRADAN is not yet at the stage where a dialogue about charging clients for the ILS can be initiated. At the time of writing PRADAN was mobilizing subsidy funds to provide the first set of books to the clients and SHGs. Nevertheless, in the long run it is envisaged that the clients will be interested in buying the books for themselves because they will see the value they add to their lives as well as to the quality of their groups.

Conclusion

The ILS is a comprehensive social performance assessment system, designed as a participatory learning tool. The process of modifying and running the system, developing the indicators and assigning levels of assessment depends upon the priorities of the organization. However, once this initial period of development is completed, the ILS can make an enormous contribution to the organization's work, providing extremely useful feedback from clients as well as enabling the organization to access valuable impact information.

PRADAN's experience has shown that ultimately it is the conviction and support of the organization as a whole that makes the system a success. There has to be the basic belief that social performance will contribute to the achievement of a broader impact on clients than an assessment of financial performance only. Thus, as this chapter has shown, it has been important for PRADAN to build ownership of the system among staff because they are the primary users. This has been achieved by involving staff from the outset and eliciting their responses to the concept, design and implementation of the system. These factors have contributed to the acquisition of a necessary level of staff 'buy-in' to the ILS process.

CHAPTER EIGHT

Measuring and managing change in Bosnia-Herzegovina: Prizma's steps to deepen outreach and improve impact

Sean Kline

Introduction

There is growing evidence and recognition that serving poor people requires intentional outreach to the poor. However, translating intent into action requires strong management commitment, deliberate management of the process and the effective use of information systems – electronic or manual methods of systematically collecting, analyzing and acting on information in a timely manner. This chapter outlines some steps that Prizma has taken to strengthen its social performance by enhancing staff understanding of poverty, shaping its organizational culture around its pro-poor mission, designing appropriate incentives to align staff behaviour with this mission, and developing systems to assess the poverty status of clients and changes in this status over time.

Bosnia-Herzegovina

With one corner touching the Adriatic, the country of Bosnia-Herzegovina in Southeastern Europe was the smallest and poorest state of the former Yugoslavia. Out of a pre-war population of 4.4 million, the war in the early to mid-1990s left 250,000 people dead or missing, and over 50 per cent of the population displaced. Significant displacement and the destruction of housing and production facilities led to a dramatic reduction in living standards and an equally dramatic increase in poverty (Bosogno and Chong, 2002). The devastation that war brought meant that Bosnia-Herzegovina's loss of GDP exceeded that of any other transition country, even those that had also suffered war during their transition (ibid.). Despite an estimated 23 per cent loss of the population as a result of death and migration, per capita GDP dropped from US$2,000 in 1990 to an estimated US$500 in 1995 (World Bank, 1999).

In this country of 3.5 million people, there are an estimated 42 registered financial service organizations (Dunn and Tvrtkovic, 2003), which has transformed in Bosnia-Herzegovina into the most competitive microfinance environment in the region, and one of the more competitive environments in the world. Prizma faces at least five competitors in any community in which it operates.

Prizma's background and mission

Founded in 1997 by an international NGO and registered as a local institution in 2001, Prizma's vision is to provide people with choices to improve their lives. Its mission is to improve the well-being of large numbers of poor women and their families by providing long-term access to quality financial services. It has pursued this mission by providing enterprise, shelter repair and emergency loans employing solidarity group and individual methodologies. Since its inception Prizma has recognized social performance and financial sustainability as fundamental imperatives. Managing the tension between the two has pushed the institution to clarify the essential indicators of its effectiveness as a social enterprise.

Participating in the *Imp-Act* programme has provided Prizma with the opportunity to pursue three objectives critical to its social, financial and institutional performance: 1) measuring and deepening outreach in an environment of poverty and growing inequality; 2) improving service quality and institutional performance in an environment of growing competition; and 3) measuring and improving social impact.

Pursuit of these objectives under *Imp-Act* has led the institution to appreciate and better understand the need to explicitly manage the inherent tension between its primary developmental imperative to contribute to positive change in the lives of those it serves and its institutional imperative to survive. The steps Prizma has taken to strengthen social performance, to increase internal and external accountability for depth of outreach and impact, and to position itself strategically to remain competitive, have been based fundamentally on board and management analysis of the context and needs of poor people in Bosnia-Herzegovina, as well as an increasing body of research that demonstrates the potential, diversity and flexibility of microfinance service providers to achieve social impact while strengthening their institutional viability.

A number of important findings have informed Prizma's work. First, microfinance can help reduce extreme poverty more than moderate poverty (Khandker, 2003) and second, microfinance organizations do not necessarily face a trade-off between sustainability and outreach (Barrès, 2002). Third, institutions can become self-sufficient and reach a poor clientele with productivity and efficiency gains based on solid credit methodology, streamlined operations, an effective management information system and skilled staff (Nègre and Maguire, 2002). Fourth, microfinance can be effective for a broad range of clients, including the very poor who make up the bottom half of those living under a country's poverty line. Fifth, excellent financial performance does not preclude strong outreach to poor households and sixth, reaching the poor is not at odds with maintaining such performance standards and professional business practices. Finally, organizations that seek to address poverty and vulnerability as an explicit goal and make it a part of their organizational culture are far more effective at reaching poor households than those that prioritize financial performance (Morduch and Haley, 2002).

Understanding context for social performance

Understanding poverty

There is still much to learn about the extent, nature and severity of poverty and vulnerability in Bosnia-Herzegovina. Employing qualitative and quantitative research methods and drawing on available external research, Prizma has sought to better understand who is poor in this post-war and transitional setting, and to what extent the institution is reaching these people. In addition, Prizma has sought to identify and mitigate biases that lead to exclusion of the poor.

Prizma has 'mined' rich existing information in its MIS to understand seasonality, risk and other salient features of poorer segments of its clientele. The institution has worked with staff of the Microfinance Centre for Central and Eastern Europe and the New Independent States (MFC) to adapt participatory rural appraisal tools, used for many years in the developing world and recently adapted to microfinance by *MicroSave*,[1] to the culturally specific context of Bosnia-Herzegovina. Employing these adapted tools, Prizma has sought to understand the multidimensional nature, complexity and dynamism of poverty, the daily challenges and vulnerability people face, client, non-client and staff perceptions of the poor, and the landscape for financial services more generally.

With financial support from the Consultative Group to Assist the Poor and the Ford Foundation-funded *Imp-Act* programme, Prizma also contracted an independent research firm in 2002 to carry out a poverty assessment to determine the poverty level of clients relative to non-clients, and a national omnibus survey, which incorporated the questions from the poverty assessment to assess poverty more generally across the country. In addition to contributing to Prizma's understanding of the character of poverty, this research highlighted areas of the country where poverty is most prevalent and, thus, ways in which Prizma can strengthen its targeting and outreach.

Among other findings, Prizma's research indicated that 64 per cent of new clients are among the poorest and moderately poor relative to non-clients in the same communities. It was found that poverty is particularly prevalent among ethnic minorities, returnees and refugees, women, people in rural areas generally, most communities of the Serb Republic and many communities of the Federation. In addition, the character of poverty in the country is complex, encompassing a relatively educated 'new poor' who may have a significant asset base but limited and intermittent income, as well as a more 'traditional' poor who have few assets, little or no education, and limited and intermittent income. The research also highlighted that some regions of the country have a greater concentration of poor people and there are dramatic differences in poverty among regions and within each region due to the ethnic and rural character of poverty. Shelter, an asset that has proven a critical indicator of poverty in the developing world, was found to be only modestly correlated with poverty among the 'new poor' (Kline, 2003).

Understanding exclusion

Drawing on Simanowitz' analysis of exclusion (2001), Prizma identified areas and means by which poor people have been left behind through informal and formal exclusion. Understanding exclusion has been central to Prizma's organizational learning, leading it to re-evaluate aspects of its operations and re-engineer its performance management system, including incentives, to deepen and broaden outreach.

Informal exclusion by the institution

One the most significant ways in which poor people are left behind is through informal exclusion by the institution as a result of branding, promotion, sales approach, informal operating policies, product attributes, location of service delivery and staff biases, all of which communicate to poor people that the institution and its services are not for them. Though work is ongoing, Prizma has identified and taken steps to address informal exclusion at a number of levels.

Through ongoing focus group and drop-out research plus regular feedback from field staff, management have sought to better understand clients and non-clients' perceptions of Prizma, to ensure that poor people find affinity with its image, public projection and staff approach. Understanding poor people's perceptions has also been critical to Prizma's efforts to monitor and clarify its strategic position and identify market opportunities in an increasingly competitive environment. In fact one of the clearest opportunities for Prizma has been the fact that most of its peers have begun moving upmarket. Thus, for both developmental and competitive reasons, Prizma has continued its move to serve a larger number of poorer people, particularly in rural areas.

Through regular market research Prizma has also identified ways in which its products, policies and procedures have contributed to informal exclusion of poor people. Branch managers have undertaken focus group research with non-management staff to understand and develop strategies to mitigate staff bias towards poorer people. Prizma is also piloting new means of delivering service to poor people in rural areas, leveraging organizational infrastructure and capacity and community networks and trust. Given that many solidarity groups are formed along income and ethnic lines, and this excludes poor and very poor people who are less influential in forming or joining groups of less or non-poor members in small communities, Prizma is facilitating group formation by poorer members. It has also taken steps to simplify paperwork, minimize eligibility requirements and shift tasks requiring literacy from applicants to trained field staff.

Finally, Prizma reassessed its approach to arrears – one of the most important areas of informal exclusion among lending organizations – based on the knowledge that poor and vulnerable people often face family and business crises, intermittent pension, salary, or remittance payments, or otherwise struggle to maintain smooth income flows that allow them to provide for their and their family's basic needs. Though branch managers have full autonomy to approve renewal applications from clients who have previously been in arrears for understandable and compelling reasons unrelated to willingness to repay, field staff bias and Prizma's previous loan officer incentive programme led officers to screen out and exclude larger numbers of clients with repayment difficulties. As a result many poorer applicants' cases never made it to the credit committee.

Recognizing that minimizing arrears is fundamental to the institution's long-term viability, Prizma has maintained strong portfolio quality since its inception.[2] However, with experience it has also recognized that portfolio quality, like financial self-sufficiency, is a means to an end and something that can be maintained through a combination of incentives, disincentives and arrears management approaches.

In addition, management has never rewarded loan officers for the size of their portfolio, recognizing that this incentive usually encourages loan officers to seek out less and non-poor clients capable of borrowing larger loans. It may also encourage them to push existing clients to borrow progressively larger loans as quickly as possible and exclude from their portfolio clients incapable of absorbing progressively more debt over time.

Under *Imp-Act*, management analysed historical trend data from the institution's MIS and reflected on the nature of credit risk in Bosnia-Herzegovina before abandoning repayment rate altogether as a measure of short-term portfolio quality. In addition, management shifted loan officers' monthly bonus weighting for portfolio-at-risk (PAR) from more than 1 day to more than 30 days past due. Given that repayment for all products is monthly, this step effectively freed branch managers and loan officers from the pressure to maintain zero PAR for arrears of 1–30 days.

At the same time, branch managers have emphasized stronger outreach to poor people, analysis of poor clients' circumstances when any payment becomes one day overdue and sensitive differentiation between clients' *ability* and *willingness* to repay. This combination of new and existing steps and policies has helped diminish a long-standing tendency for loan officers to practice zero tolerance for arrears by screening out and informally excluding clients who did not contribute to perfect portfolio quality calculated at one day overdue, thereby undermining the officers' monthly incentive pay and professional standing in the branch.

Prizma's portfolio quality has remained very strong but field staff now have somewhat greater flexibility to understand and negotiate repayment with those clients who occasionally suffer a family crisis or other setback. Preliminary evidence also suggests that greater flexibility towards arrears in the first 30 days of arrears is helping reduce voluntary and non-voluntary dropout. Though flexibility towards arrears may seem heresy in some corners of the industry, it is one of a number of areas in which Prizma has identified opportunities to strengthen social and institutional performance by increasing efficiency, reducing dropout generally, and better retaining those most often left behind.

Formal exclusion by the institution

Prizma has also identified formal attributes of the institution and its services that have led to exclusion of poorer people. Recognizing that some product attributes – such as a high minimum loan size or stringent collateral requirements – discourage poorer applicants, Prizma has refined product terms better to match poor people's needs and capacities. Prizma has also researched, pilot-tested, costed and launched new products to meet a wider array of needs of poorer segments of its broad low-income clientele, including non-enterprise needs such as small sums that help clients smooth income flows. Unfortunately, the restrictive legal framework in Bosnia-Herzegovina has thus far precluded non-credit service provision by microfinance institutions and, despite significant research that points to the important non-enterprise needs poor people have, the largest microfinance interventions in Bosnia-Herzegovina since 1997, most notably the Local Initiatives Project of the World Bank, have discouraged non-enterprise lending.

The institution has affirmed ongoing support for start-up enterprises, including those that require modest inputs and limited risk. Branch offices approve the large majority of all applications for start-up enterprises and collateral is rarely a 'deal breaker', provided a client can demonstrate some knowledge of the risks and needs of the enterprise. While significant evidence indicates that most start-up enterprises fail, the experience in Bosnia-Herzegovina may seem counter-intuitive because many start-up businesses are actually re-start businesses that operated prior to the war. It is also worth noting that significant remittance income from relatives abroad has buoyed many families' ability to manage business and personal risk. Finally, though Prizma remains a lending-only organization by law, ongoing research is helping it to position itself to address poor people's critical non-credit needs when the legal environment allows it to engage in broader activities.

Self-exclusion by clients

Self-exclusion is another area in which Prizma has taken steps to understand and mitigate bias. Analysis of historical arrears data from its MIS and branch practices confirms the degree to which group loan sizes grow over time as a result of disbursement pressures and explicit or implicit step lending. Though many poor and low-income clients can and do absorb larger loans over time as their capacity grows or seasonality leads to periods of higher demand, emphasis on automatic increases over time, particularly within groups, can lead to poorer clients' self-exclusion. To understand this informal bias Prizma has undertaken focus group research with poorer clients and non-clients and, among other measures, introduced a new quick-access individual product with a modest collateral requirement, to address poorer clients' smaller, short-term needs. Prizma has re-emphasized lending based primarily on clients' identified need rather than on automatic increases.

Client exit

Prizma has taken steps to understand and address client exit, a phenomenon that is costly to Prizma's bottom line and its effort to achieve sustained social impact over time.[3] In order to understand who is leaving voluntarily and why, Prizma tracks dropout in general and in particular among poorer clients. It follows up on trends highlighted through dropout monitoring using exit interviews and focus group discussions with clients who drop out in order to explore causes of exit in greater depth.[4] Drawing on important learning from the Small Enterprise Foundation and other organizations active under *Imp-Act* or otherwise breaking new ground in poverty outreach, Prizma now includes dropout in its loan officer and annual team incentives, matched with strategies to help loan officers and other front-line staff better retain clients. Prizma management has also begun monitoring cross-selling among products and involuntary dropout, which offer opportunities to improve client retention.

In addition, Prizma has re-evaluated the causes and costs of forcing people out as a means to maintain very high portfolio quality. For example, in 2002 Prizma began using activity-based costing (ABC) to calculate product and other costs of its operations. This yielded the cost of underwriting each loan product at the first and follow-on cycles and the time spent pursuing serious arrears.

A policy of zero tolerance was a prudent step to minimize credit risk as an inexperienced organization in a fast-changing post-war environment in 1997. However, with more experience, increasing competition and the desire to support clients' longer-term needs and wants, Prizma now recognizes the financial, competitive and social costs of forcing people out and the need to encourage greater service flexibility and alternative strategies to manage risk. For example, in 2004 it began developing a scoring system to not only predict each client's likelihood of going into arrears, but also their likelihood of dropping out or being poor. This initiative is intended to allow the institution to better manage risk, improve efficiency and deepen outreach.

Measuring social performance
'Scoring' poverty and measuring change

Internal and external research and other organizational learning has moved Prizma along a continuum of three critical objectives: 1) determining the relative and absolute poverty level of its clients; 2) strengthening targeting of and service to poor and very poor clients; and 3) measuring change in the lives of these people over time. Working closely with the Microfinance Centre and members of the Microfinance for the Very Poor working group under *Imp-Act*, Prizma developed a scoring approach intended to serve two critical purposes. First, to enable the institution to report on the poverty level of every client in absolute terms in relation to the national poverty line. Second, to enable it to measure change in clients' poverty status over time in order to inform internal and external stakeholders of how such changes are occurring. While this system was not intended, on its own, to capture the complex, dynamic, multidimensional and context-specific nature of poverty in Bosnia-Herzegovina, it was intended to enable Prizma to understand and demonstrate more clearly and on a regular and cost-effective basis the extent to which it is reaching the people it wants (and claims) to reach and fulfilling its social mission.

Characteristics of the scorecard
The scorecard is a composite measure of household poverty based on some of the strongest and most robust non-income indicator proxies for poverty in Bosnia-Herzegovina. It was triangulated using the 2002 Living Standards Measurement Survey (LSMS),[5] United Nations Development Program (UNDP) data, a Consultative Group to Assist the Poor poverty assessment and findings from staff and client focus group research.

The scorecard consists of two sets of indicators. The first set of three indicators – education level, residence and household size – reflect poverty risk categories. The subsequent four indicators measure change in household poverty status and in addition to contributing to the poverty risk profile of each new or renewal applicant's household, these four enable Prizma to measure change in poverty status over time. Prizma's scorecard is simple, with seven indicators and 0/1 weights. Using statistically optimal weights gives more weight to those indicators with greater predictive power, but only a little because one indicator – how often the client eats meat – is dominant. Very simple one-indicator scorecards overstate the likelihood that any one given Prizma client is poor. In particular, loan size does not identify poor clients more accurately than the poverty scorecard (Schreiner *et al*, 2005). Constructing and applying Prizma's poverty scorecard involved:

- Measuring the absolute, expenditure-based poverty status of households in a national random sample.

- Selecting non-expenditure indicators that were not only simple and inexpensive to collect but also correlated with absolute, expenditure-based poverty status.
- Constructing a scorecard by assigning weights to the non-expenditure indicators to reflect their correlation with expenditure-based poverty status.
- Adding up the weighted non-expenditure indicators to produce poverty scores for the surveyed households.
- Collecting from Prizma's clients the non-expenditure indicators used in the scorecard and using them to produce poverty scores.
- Defining the poverty likelihood of a Prizma client with a given poverty score as the observed poverty rate among surveyed households with the same score.
- Defining Prizma's overall poverty rate as its clients' likelihood of being poor, on average.
- Checking that poverty scores for Prizma clients made sense for different branches, products and geographic areas.

Prizma worked with the Microfinance Centre for Central and Eastern Europe and the New Independent States to select non-expenditure indicators (Matul and Kline, 2003) that: correlated strongly with poverty status, both in the past and future; appeared in the national survey, enabling linkage to an absolute poverty line; kept data-collection costs low – already collected as part of the loan evaluation or easy to start to collect and not too sensitive for loan officers to acquire; elicited truthful reports that an internal auditor could verify; and took different values across clients. Figure 8.1 provides a graphic representation of the scorecard indicator domains, questions and ranges.

Measuring relative and absolute poverty

The scorecard provides a relative measure for Prizma to assess its depth of outreach in each area of operation (Schreiner, 2001). For example, a household that has a composite score of two can clearly be said to be poorer than a household that has a score of four.[6] Just as the data sources identified above can be used to identify indicators and determine appropriate ranges for each, so then LSMS, other national data sets or data generated from a short survey focused on key areas of interest can be used to define cut-off points for categories of absolute poverty status.

Absolute poverty status was derived from the 2001 LSMS for Bosnia-Herzegovina that recorded expenditure and a wide range of other data for a national random sample (Schreiner *et al*, 2005). A household was poor if annual per capita consumption (adjusted for the local cost of living) was less than KM2,200 (US$1,158) (World Bank, 2002). At purchasing power parity, this poverty line is estimated to be US$14 per person per day. The overall poverty rate in Bosnia-Herzegovina was 19.3 per cent.

Poverty Scorecard

Poor and Very Poor 0-2 ¥ Vulnerable Non-Poor 3-4 ¥ Non-Poor 5+

		Indicator		0	1	2
Poverty Risk		Education	What is the education level of female household head/spouse/partner?	≥ Primary	> Primary	
		Residence	Where is residence?	Rural/Peri ≥ 10,000	Urban > 10,000	
		Household Size	What is household size?	≥ 5	< 5	
	Change	Household Assets	Does household possess a stereo CD player?	No	Yes	
		Transport Assets	Does household possess a transport vehicle?	No	Yes	
		Meat Consumption	On average, how often does household consume meat each week?	Rarely 0-2 times/week	Sometimes 3-5 times/week	Often 6+ times/week
		Sweets Consumption	On average, how often does household consume sweets with main meal each week?	Rarely 0-2 times/week	Sometimes 3-5 times/week	Often 6+ times/week
			Poverty Status Score (0-9)			

Figure 8.1 Poverty scorecard

Using the scorecard

Enabling staff to generate reports on client household poverty status by branch, product, dropout, gender, portfolio quality and an array of other variables already captured in the MIS, represents a milestone in Prizma's efforts to enhance social performance. In addition to enabling it to better meet its developmental objectives, this system is enabling Prizma to meet critical institutional objectives, including:

- *Positioning the institution in a competitive market.* Understanding its clients better has helped to position Prizma strategically to compete in an increasingly competitive market for financial services.
- *Segmenting the market.* Poverty variables strengthen Prizma's efforts to segment its clientele and improve its services. Segmenting its clientele by poverty status allows Prizma to develop more effective promotion strategies and delivery channels to attract, serve and retain the clients its mission says it must serve.
- *Developing products and services.* Understanding its clients better allows Prizma to understand how they can use and benefit from existing services.

The institution can then adapt these services to the developmental needs of poorer clients, as well as to segments critical to institutional objectives.
- *Improving efficiency.* A powerful use of the scorecard includes integrating poverty scoring data into Prizma's existing activity-based costing system.[7] This enables the institution to better understand its cost structure generally and the specific cost of products targeted to poorer segments of its clientele. It can then use such information to identify means to provide more efficient services to poorer clients and focus greater attention on those drivers most important to improving efficiency.[8]
- *Managing credit risk.* In addition to finalizing a system to score poverty and drop-out, Prizma is preparing to employ credit scoring based on arrears data since 1997 and credit bureau data. It is anticipated that measures to assess poverty status will be crucial to assessing credit risk among different segments of its poor clientele. However, rather than seeking to use credit scoring to exclude poorer people, Prizma seeks to enhance its understanding of credit risk to further deepen its outreach.[9]
- *Managing human resources.* First, demonstrating that depth of outreach is not only fundamental to the institution's mission but also critical to operational performance, strengthens staff commitment to the system. Second, depth of outreach and change in client status are incorporated into the incentive system intended to motivate staff and affirm the primacy of social performance.
- *Monitoring client dropout.* The system enables Prizma to track dropout by poverty status, enabling it to better understand the appropriateness of its service to different clients who leave and, in turn, what can be done to retain and help these clients.

Preliminary results

Prizma's overall poverty rate is its clients' average poverty likelihood. Loan officers collected the required scorecard indicators for 5,177 first-time borrowers from December 2003 to September 2004 (Schreiner *et al*, 2005). Given the resulting scores, the poverty likelihood of each client was defined as the poverty likelihood of households in the national survey with that same score. Prizma's average poverty rate is quite close to the national poverty rate of 19.3 per cent. This would seem to represent significant depth of outreach given the steps taken to reach poorer people, but has sparked important internal discussions about the relative performance of each branch and product.

This important new information raised several questions, including: is this poverty outreach high or low? At this early stage it is not clear that there is a simple answer. For example, the distribution of creditworthy borrowers in Bosnia-Herzegovina might not be uniform over the distribution of poverty. At the same time, Prizma's poverty outreach may be high compared with the (unknown) poverty outreach of other MFIs in Bosnia-Herzegovina or compared with the (unknown) poverty outreach that is sustainable in an environment in which MFIs are still only allowed to engage in lending. In any case, Prizma has an explicit mission to serve the poor and measuring poverty outreach helps the board to monitor the fulfilment of the mission as it pushes managers to look for ways to improve. By measuring poverty, however, Prizma risks 'looking bad' *vis-à-vis* competitors who lack such measurements and can thus claim to have greater poverty outreach because there is no evidence to the contrary (Pritchett, 2002).

While external stakeholders may focus on Prizma's overall poverty rate, managers are interested in poverty rates by loan product and by branch. Disaggregating poverty rates can help pinpoint products and branches with greater or lesser poverty outreach, possibly suggesting ways to deepen outreach. For example, as shown in Figure 8.2, the poverty rate at Prizma's Sarajevo branch using the original scorecard is 23.9 per cent, which is above the national average and significantly above the weak 4.7 per cent rate for Banja Luka.

Overall, poverty outreach varies more by branch than by loan product, perhaps highlighting the importance of branch placement and branch managers' outreach within their service areas. Also, newer and smaller, slower-growth branches – those that had fewer 'new' clients between December 2003 and September 2004 – had lower concentrations of poverty, perhaps because older and larger, faster-growing branches face more pressure or are more able (due to their experience) to go beyond less-poor clients. Finally, the current law only allows MFIs in Bosnia-Herzegovina to lend but the opportunity to offer savings, money transfer and insurance services promises to enable Prizma to improve poverty outreach by addressing a wider array of needs of its poor clientele. In any case, the most powerful and immediate change that poverty

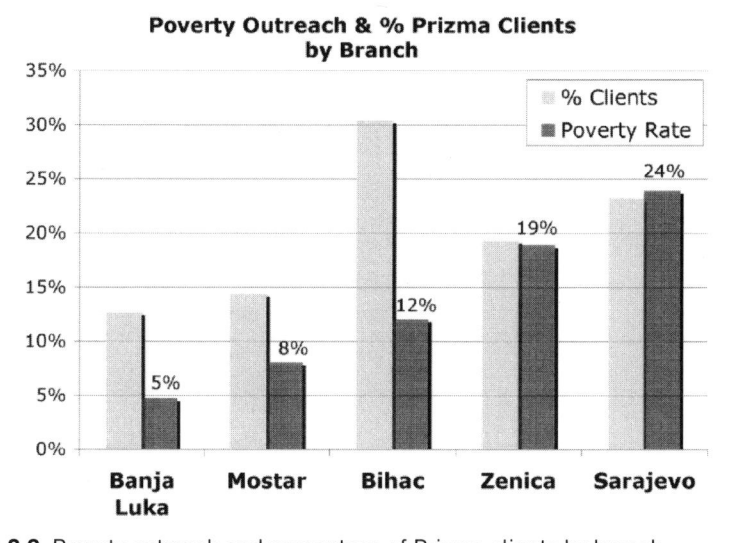

Figure 8.2 Poverty outreach and percentage of Prizma clients by branch

assessment is bringing to Prizma is explicit dialogue and greater understanding about the level and nature of poverty outreach it can achieve as a result of intentional action.

Managing social performance

'Anchoring' activities to mission

Above all, Prizma's inquiry under *Imp-Act* was about translating the intent to serve and have a positive impact on the lives of many poor families into action. As a foundation for this process and to demonstrate to internal stakeholders (staff, managers and board members) that it was, in fact, heading in the right direction, the institution used its mission statement as the anchor for all activities. This is illustrated in Figure 8.3.

Leadership

Leadership has proven critical to Prizma's progress on its social performance agenda as senior and middle managers have strengthened the institution's pro-poor orientation and reaffirmed the pro-poor mandate embedded in its mission. First, management have considered formal documentation in light of what it has learned about bias and poverty outreach. It has added to or revised where there were opportunities to reframe operations – methodology, policies and procedures – in terms of targeting, attracting, serving and retaining poor clients. Second, while senior management has led the social performance agenda, they have also sought to develop and nurture middle and non-management leadership on this agenda across the institution, recognizing that any effort to deepen outreach, improve service quality and strengthen impact must be broadly supported and implemented by field staff engaged with poor people in communities across the country.

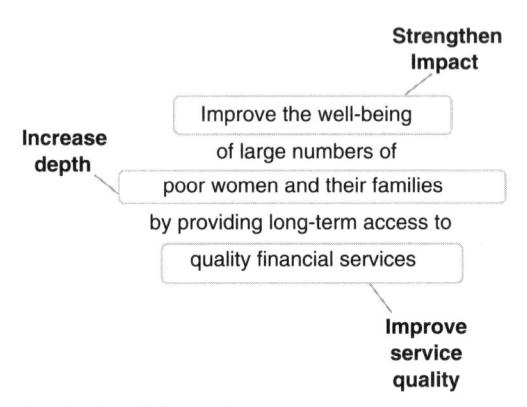

Figure 8.3 Prizma's mission statement

Culture

Organizational culture is fundamental to Prizma's historic and future social and institutional performance, and senior management have taken important steps to communicate and reshape culture across the institution to balance developmental and institutional objectives. First, management have revised and strengthened the recruitment and induction process to ensure mission, vision and organizational values are central to every applicant and employee's introduction to, and training within, the institution.

Second, management affirms mission and values on an ongoing basis via the organization's intranet, memos, annual retreat and regular office visits. Third, it has been clear from Prizma's inception that communicating branch, product and organization-wide performance results to staff on a regular basis yields accountability for results and strong consequent performance. Thus, headquarters provides social, financial and portfolio performance reports to staff on a monthly basis via the intranet and regular branch-level meetings. The next section highlights ways in which Prizma has integrated appraisals with performance reporting in six core performance areas to tightly align incentives and performance with the institution's fundamental social and institutional objectives.

Incentives

Perhaps one of the most important areas where Prizma has taken steps to enhance and institutionalize social performance has been in re-engineering its performance management system – appraisal, reward and communication – to better align employee interests and rewards with greater depth of outreach, improved service quality and the financial health of the institution. On one level, loan officers are rewarded monthly for performance on a few select indicators,[10] including those in four of Prizma's six core performance areas: depth, breadth, dropout, administrative efficiency, productivity and write-off.[11] This monthly incentive focuses on short-term social and institutional performance. On a second level, each member of a branch team receives a percentage of the institution's annual surplus as a flat profit share based on their team's aggregate score across the six core performance areas.[12] Rather than a reward for short-term results, this incentive affirms strong team performance towards the institution's social and institutional objectives on an annual basis.

Affirming the fundamental role of headquarters to facilitate branch and, in turn, client success, each member of the headquarters' team is rewarded based on the performance of the branch network overall; if those in the field succeed, headquarters is rewarded.[13] Figure 8.4 summarizes eligibility at each level of the institution and the six core performance areas on which the bonus is based. Among other benefits, this system has contained personnel costs by tying them more closely to the financial health of the institution. It has increased the regularity, consistency and relevancy of formal performance appraisal (now every trimester) and clarified what good performance is for every position at every level of the institution. It has also balanced reward for individual and team performance, balanced short and medium-term performance, and helped maintain focus on sustaining social performance.

Conclusion

This paper has outlined the primary ways in which Prizma has set out to enhance and sustain social performance by building capacity for and undertaking ongoing research, leveraging leadership, shaping organizational culture, crafting appropriate incentives and developing systems to assess poverty status and monitor impact. Through this process Prizma has learned or affirmed a number of important lessons.

First, people's poverty status does not determine if they are able to access microfinance services; this is determined by institutional design – leadership,

Annual Team Incentive

Performance Area	Weighting	Calculation	Scale	Notes
Depth (%)	TBD Annually	# of new poor[1] clients during the year / Total new clients during the year	60% 40% 25%	Based on sampling, baseline determined in 2003
Breadth (%)	TBD Annually	(# of active clients at the end of the year) - (number of active clients at the end of last year) / # of active clients at the end of last year	50% 40% 30%	Audited statements Weighted by product
Drop out (%)	TBD Annually	# of clients who took a follow on loan within 90 days of paying off their previous loan / # of clients who could have taken a follow on loan within 90 days of paying off their previous loan	30% 40% 45%	Calculated in loan tracking system
Productivity (#)	TBD Annually	# of active clients at the end of the year / Total number of paid employees at the end of the fiscal year	350 250 150	Audited statements
Administrative Efficiency (%)	TBD Annually	Personnel + office supplies + depreciation + rent utilities + transportation + other administrative expenses / Average total gross outstanding portfolio for the fiscal year	15% 20% 25%	Calculated from audited statements
Write-off (%)	TBD Annually	Total loan amount written off for the year / Average total gross portfolio outstanding for the fiscal year	< 1.25%	Audited statements, based on 180 day policy
	100% of Bonus			

Figure 8.4 Annual team incentive sheet

structure, culture, incentives and systems. Second, organizations committed to effective and sustained poverty outreach and positive impact must maintain absolute focus and clarity of purpose. Third, organizations committed to serving large numbers of poor and very poor people must be ruthless about efficiency and transparent about performance. Fourth, a sustained service that leads to positive impact requires understanding and differentiating between poor people's developmental *needs* and market *wants*. This understanding, in turn, will allow organizations to sustain social performance by effectively balancing developmental and institutional objectives.

CHAPTER NINE

Achieving the double bottom line: a case study of Sinapi Aba Trust's (SAT) client impact monitoring system, Ghana

Lydia Opoku

Introduction

For a long time the microfinance industry has focused mostly on providing standardized products and has not paid much attention to its clients' needs, leaving them with few choices. However, along with a large increase in the number of microfinance institutions, there has been a paradigm shift in recent years to attempt to meet the diverse needs of clients. Studies have shown that the most successful MFIs are those that listen to and know their clients and the market as a whole. Getting information on how clients are transforming their lives and how MFI interventions are helping the poor raise their standard of living is essential, as is obtaining information to develop strategies to satisfy clients' needs and thus retain more clients. All these are geared towards helping MFIs move towards a 'double bottom line' of reaching and helping to transform the lives of poor people in ways that are financially sustainable.

For MFIs to achieve their social performance goals, it is critical for them to be client sensitive, with a primary focus on learning about clients' needs and responding to them by offering appropriate products and services. Different MFIs use different formal and informal approaches to track clients' progress. This paper provides a case study of the experience of Sinapi Aba Trust (SAT) in designing, testing and implementing a Client Impact Monitoring System (CIMS).

Background

Sinapi Aba Trust is an implementing partner of Opportunity International (OI) network, providing financial and business advisory services to over 45,000 economically active clients in Ghana for the past 10 years. It is in the process of converting into a regulated savings and loans company. In collaboration with OI and the *Imp-Act* programme, SAT has been developing and implementing a Client Impact Monitoring System over the last three years. The CIMS survey is used to track changes in clients' lives to assist management in making informed decisions. The information gathered enables SAT to learn lessons on how its products and services are affecting clients, either positively or negatively, and also to map out strategies for further improvement in the quality of SAT's service delivery and efficiency.

Rationale for designing CIMS

SAT's focus on developing the CIMS was driven in part by the organization's mission. This is based on its commitment to serve the poor by focusing its energy and efforts on clients so they can have the dignity to provide for themselves, their families and communities. It is imperative for SAT to measure its progress in achieving these goals to capture benefits and counter or prevent possible problems. In this way, the institution can ensure that it will continue with its mission to help poor people as efficiently as possible. This need to measure the mission of holistically transforming the lives of clients to escape from poverty was the starting point for the CIMS.

SAT is among the leading MFIs in Ghana and, until recently, had not experienced fierce competition. Nevertheless, following recent developments where even some commercial banks are targeting the traditional clientele of MFIs, there is the need to prepare for this eventuality. Market research information about the needs and wants of clients is necessary to respond effectively and stay ahead of the competition, hence the need for the CIMS.

In addition to SAT's imperative to fulfil its mission, there is also an increasing need to prove impact to donors and funders to validate their financial interventions in terms of achieved developmental value, and also to contribute to the Millennium Development Goals (MDGs). All of these factors played a role in the design of the CIMS. Not only do donors now want more measurement of developmental goals, but also USAID is to make it a requirement that all MFIs measure the poverty level of their clients.

CIMS design process

Adaptation of the AIMS-SEEP tools

With financial support from the Ford Foundation/*Imp-Act* programme and OI, phase I of SAT's *Imp-Act* project was geared towards building an understanding of its clients. SAT began by reviewing its impact assessment and market research (MR) studies to better understand its impact areas, the methodology and indicators used, and how the organization utilized this information. The review found that conclusions from the three-year longitudinal studies were generally positive in the economic, social and spiritual domains, while SAT's contribution in the political domain was not clear. The MR studies also prompted SAT to review some of its products and services. One downside of the existing studies was that they were conducted by external consultants with little involvement of staff. It was therefore concluded that SAT needed to build its internal capacity to bring IA in-house, hence the establishment of the Research, Transformation and Impact Assessment Unit.

Based on the findings of the review, a focus group discussion was conducted with management and staff to define SAT's impact priorities from staff perspectives. The FGD tried to establish what the impact of SAT's programme should be and which indicators should be used to measure changes in impact, taking into account indicators SAT already has information on from the loan application form/management information system.

A number of indicators were identified in this discussion. However, staff realized that the existing data gave little information on social empowerment and religious/community involvement. A gender research study was therefore conducted in November 2001 to define empowerment from both a staff and client perspective. A total of 24 loan officers representing all 16 branches of SAT participated in the FGD and topics discussed included: indicators for successful transformation for SAT clients; definitions and indicators of empowerment in the Ghanaian context; and how SAT's programmes contribute to the transformation and empowerment of clients.

In-depth client interviews were designed to understand how, and under what circumstances, participation in SAT's programme leads to significant transformation, but also to identify areas and types of transformation that typically occur in SAT group loans. Particular attention was paid to changes in relationships, skills and capabilities, while the in-depth interviews with clients' spouses gave a richer picture of transformation in clients' lives.

The findings from this study were used further to adapt and refine the series of hypotheses and indicators in the AIMS impact assessment tools in order to better capture the social, political and spiritual impacts that are a key part of SAT's mission. These indicators include: business income and assets, business employment, personal cash savings, housing, food consumption, decision-making, self-esteem, healthcare, children's education and welfare, community and religious involvement, training, borrowing patterns and coping strategies. The indicators were pilot-tested in December 2001 for suitability in the Ghanaian and SAT context.

AIMS workshop and implementation

The purpose of the field research was fourfold: 1) to discover the level of poverty of clients upon entry to the programme in order to improve poverty targeting; 2) to understand the types of impact SAT has on its clients; 3) to gauge levels of satisfaction, including what clients like about SAT's products and services and what they dislike; and 4) to examine rates of retention, looking at the numbers existing the programme and why. After receiving a one-week intensive training course, SAT staff and volunteers set out to administer the tools to a total of 1,025 clients, including prospective and former clients, as revealed in Table 9.1.

Table 9.1 Sample by type of client and by tool

Client type	Impact survey	Exit survey	L&S use interview	Empowerment	Client satisfaction
Mature clients	312		56	49	171 (19 groups)
New clients	259				
Former clients		178			
Total	**571**	**178**	**56**	**49**	**171**

Source: SAT (2004)

Highlights of findings and management decision-making from the AIMS tools

Poverty movement

To measure the poverty level of clients at entry, SAT used the means test form – a scorecard of assets and housing conditions. Those who scored up to 15 points qualified as very poor (level 1), 16–25 points as poor (level 2) and above 25 points as not poor (level 3). The data from SAT's management information system revealed that sampled clients scored an average means test of 16 when they entered the programme. At the time of the survey, the average score had increased to 18.7 for the same sampled clients, reflecting the changes that had occurred since they entered the programme and utilized the services offered by SAT. The difference was statistically significant at 95 per cent confidence level. The spread of the survey population among poverty levels is illustrated in Table 9.2.

What is more interesting is the means test point of new clients who were admitted to the programme at the time of the evaluation as eligible clients, but had not yet received a loan. As Table 9.2 shows, non-clients depicted a similar poverty level breakdown to mature clients at the time of the evaluation. Although most fell into the poor category, 17 per cent of the new clients were scored as non-poor according to the means test. Their average means test score was 16.4, which is higher than the average score of 16 of the mature clients at the time they entered the programme.

These findings appear to suggest that SAT might be taking on better-off clients. However, the difference was not statistically significant (p value 0.57).

Table 9.2 Means test point of mature and non-clients

Poverty category	Mature clients (%)	Non-clients (%)
Very poor (up to 15 points)	32	38
Poor (16–25 points)	52	45
Not poor (above 25)	16	17

Source: SAT (2004)

Moreover, in terms of food security, 10 per cent of clients interviewed said there was a time when they did not have enough money to buy food for their household, while for new clients this figure was 20 per cent. This finding suggests that new clients were more food insecure and thus were not likely to have been better off than mature clients.

Impact

SAT anticipates that participation in the programme leads to positive changes in four domains of clients' lives: spiritual, social, political and economic. Changes in these domains were measured through a number of indicators and compared before and after joining the programme. In addition to this comparison, the study employed a cross-sectional design where responses from mature clients and new clients were compared on the assumption that any differences found were attributable to programme participation. Overall, the findings indicated no consistent pattern but instead mixed results in each of the four domains.

For example, improvements were significant in terms of economic progress, especially with regard to clients' household standard of living and clients' businesses, but not so significant in terms of increase in political involvement. There were signs of negative impact, such as having less time to attend to spiritual and political activities. Also, when it came to decision-making in the community and their businesses, clients were taking an active part. However, at the household level, men still had the final say because of the cultural set-up, except in the acquisition of household assets, where the women sometimes had an equal say because they now contributed significantly to the household budget. Furthermore, 94 per cent of the mature clients had added new products to their existing businesses. But despite an increase in business expansion, only 33 per cent of the mature clients employed someone other than themselves in their businesses and only 29.9 per cent mentioned an increase in business employment over the last 24 months.

Client exit and reasons for clients leaving

The study revealed that the first three years were critical in determining whether a client would leave. When respondents were asked to specify the main reasons for leaving, problems with SAT's credit policy and group lending were cited. The most common reasons were respondents' inability or unwillingness to attend all the group meetings, either because they took up too much time or because they conflicted with other commitments. Figure 9.1 illustrates the range of reasons behind client exit.

Client satisfaction

Loan disbursement was one factor in client satisfaction. Despite the fact that some groups had fully repaid, they were told that the loan cheques were not ready. This delay sometimes resulted in group break-up and negative impact

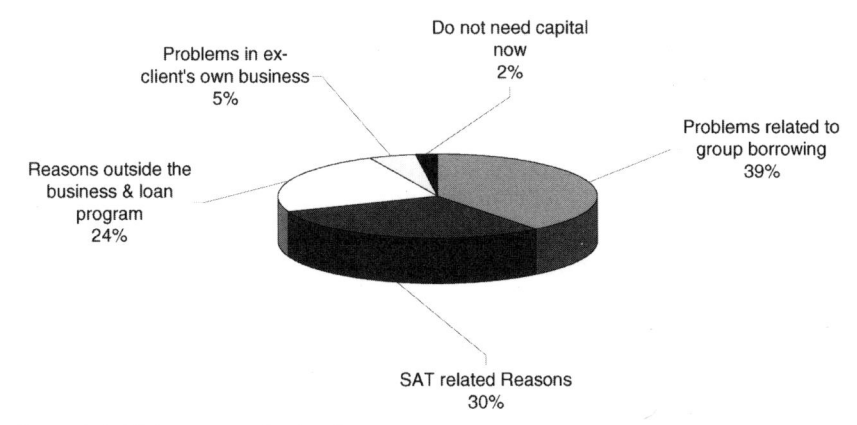

Figure 9.1 Main reasons for leaving

- Do not need capital now 2%
- Problems in ex-client's own business 5%
- Reasons outside the business & loan program 24%
- Problems related to group borrowing 39%
- SAT related Reasons 30%

Source: SAT (2004)

on clients' businesses. SAT identified a number of possible solutions to the disbursement issue, including adapting policy so that groups could become formalized financial institutions in order to accept deposits. Also as another measure to address the issue of delayed disbursement, SAT introduced a pool system to manage funds. Funds were previously treated as a 'branch fund' and only the branch could have access, irrespective of whether other branches were in need of funds or not. Hence, disbursement in some branches would have to be delayed until they were able to mobilize funds. The pool system has helped ease the problem of delayed disbursements.

Clients also offered several recommendations on new products. First, group loan clients do not appear to be accumulating significant business or household assets during the initial two to three years. Yet one of the key strategies for poor people to move out of poverty is to accumulate assets, both household and business. Further research was conducted into this issue and SAT has introduced a new product, an asset loan, together with training to help clients acquire productivity-enhancing assets to expand their business. The findings on client satisfaction, such as smaller loan sizes and repayment schedules, led to the revision of the credit policy.

With respect to poverty targeting, SAT appeared to be reaching clients who were at a similar level to those reached two or more years prior to the impact assessment. However, as noted above, it is important to stress that there were some indications of mission drift to better-off clients. It was therefore recommended that SAT develop a monitoring system to assess more accurately the poverty level of its clients.

Process and lessons learned in developing the CIMS

Components of the CIMS

SAT is seeking operational client monitoring information to make immediate short-term management decisions based on client progress and satisfaction, as well as seeking to monitor client status with impact indicators to understand how clients are benefiting. The innovative approach consists of the following four components, answering four key questions, as illustrated in Figure 9.2.

The design process

Selection of indicators for monitoring
A brainstorming session was held with SAT management, staff and OI consultants to select indicators for the monitoring system to answer the four key questions above. The team agreed that the indicators:

- Should be able to address the four critical domains of SAT and OI's mission in transforming the lives of its clients in social, spiritual, economic and political/empowerment dimensions.

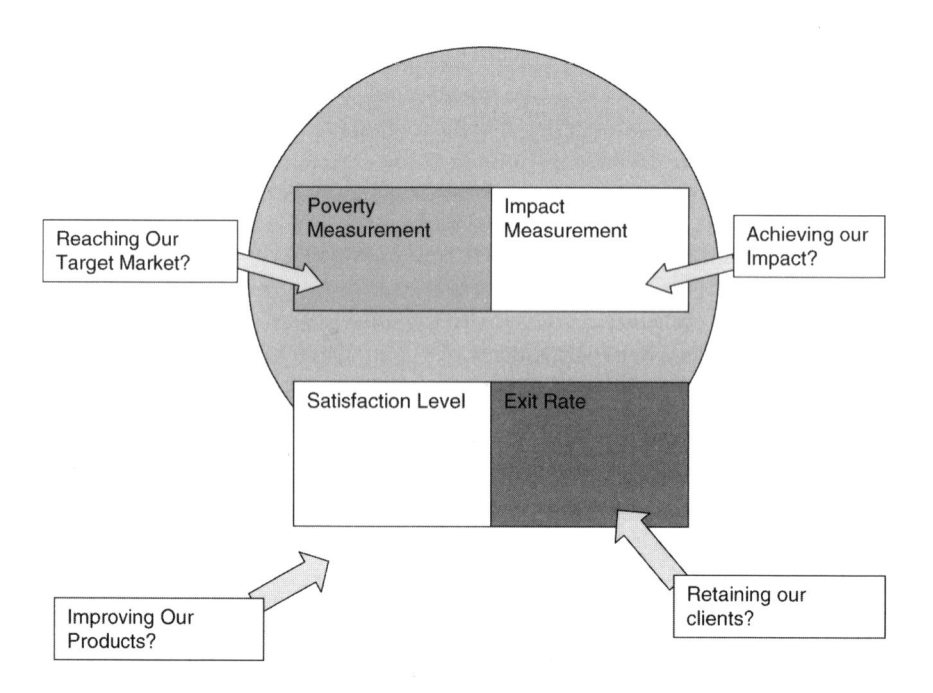

Figure 9.2 Components of the Sinapi Aba client impact monitoring system

- Should be reliable, SMART (simple, measurable, achievable, realistic and timely) and complement each other.
- Should be easily understood by both staff and clients, conclusive in their meaning as well as easy to collect.
- Should generate continuous, numeric data that will change over time.

Mapping out existing loan application form, MIS and information flow
Based on the above criteria, a team of staff and OI consultants met to examine the information that was already being collected from clients, including from the existing loan application form and MIS data. The purpose was to determine the most relevant information and avoid any repetition in data collection in order to save time and money, and to make sure there was not too much data for SAT to handle effectively. The following indicators were selected to be included in the CIMS: business income and employment, personal cash savings, housing, health, children's education, decision-making, community and religious involvement and client satisfaction.

In the initial process it was agreed that the CIMS would be integrated into the normal loan application process to avoid the need to repeat the demographic information on the CIMS form. This was later revised so that the information would be repeated on the CIMS form, but officers were advised to copy it directly from the loan application form. It was also determined that SAT would use the existing loan application process, whereby the supervisor/branch head would be in charge of the first line of quality control and occasionally do field spot checks on an ongoing basis, while the manager would carry out random checking of the form.

Designing the CIMS questions and preparation for field-testing
The CIMS questions were designed based on the outcome of the aforementioned discussion. The group reconvened to look at the design of the questions and a few staff were trained to pilot test the form with some clients to determine the applicability and relevance of the questionnaires, and how easy or difficult the questions were for both field officers and clients.

Pilot-testing phase

SAT spent a lot of time testing its impact monitoring system before rolling it out to all its branches. The pilot testing took place over three phases.

Phase I: Testing the water
Phase I occurred in September 2002 with the objective of assessing the effectiveness and utility of the questions for both loan officers and clients, to find out if they needed to be revised. Forty clients were interviewed and focus groups were held with the loan officers who conducted the interviews to get feedback on which questions needed to be revised or deleted. It was clear from

the discussion that it took some time to get absolute income figures from clients.

Phase II: Wading in (getting staff and clients on board)

After revising the questions used in Phase I, the Kumasi branch was chosen for the CIMS Phase II pilot testing between November 2002 and February 2003 because of its proximity to the head office. Staff received training in basic interviewing techniques and the importance and intent of each question. The loan officers and managers then worked in groups to translate the questions into local dialects. During the brainstorming session it was agreed that, due to the complexity of translating the questions into the Akan local dialects, only technical terminology would be translated. The translations, together with the English version of the CIMS questions, would be sent to the field to ensure that all interviewers were asking the questions in the same way.

Monitoring played a key role at this stage of implementation. The CIMS coordinator supervised some of the data collection by paying regular visits to the field with the field officers. The coordinator also held a series of meetings (focus group discussions or one-on-one) with field officers to address any problems that came up. During this phase, the target was to interview all fresh and renewing clients in the Kumasi branch. However, to make the task more manageable, a decision was made to interview a sample of clients only.

The majority of clients were happy that they were given the chance to provide their opinions to SAT. However, despite the enthusiasm and commitment shown by staff of the Kumasi branch during the preparatory training in September, the initial stage of implementing the CIMS did not go as smoothly as expected. It was soon realized that very few CIMS forms were being filled out, even though officers were making loans. As a response to this, meetings were held with the field officers to encourage their use of the forms, explaining the reasons and benefits of the CIMS. In addition, a decision was made that all loan forms submitted without the completed CIMS forms would not be approved, which would eventually delay disbursement. From that time onwards, the CIMS forms were filled out.

Loan officers began to be convinced when they were able to see the initial results of the CIMS, especially its capacity to highlight aspects of client dissatisfaction, such as delays in disbursement. They knew the clients had been complaining about this and were glad to see that the CIMS had brought this to the attention of management. However, it was realized that, in estimating the cost, time and resources for the pilot test, full consideration was not given as to how this would affect loan officers' workload. Loan officers did not have time to interview all their clients at each loan renewal. There was also concern about the possibility of clients telling their loan officers what they wanted to hear, especially if the form was administered before the loan disbursement. It was therefore agreed that the CIMS form would be introduced soon after the loan disbursement to offset probable bias. Interviewers were also given training in interview techniques to reduce bias.

Phase III: Launching CIMS SAT-wide

Following this pilot stage, CIMS is now being launched in all SAT branches. Although at the time of writing, the data collection and analysis are still in their early stages, the process has yielded some interesting results that point to some of SAT's positive impacts. The data reveals that clients who have been using SAT's services for some time – mature clients – had significantly higher average monthly income than new or intermediate clients. The data also indicates that mature clients are less likely than new clients to miss workdays due to sickness in the family. In terms of non-financial impacts, mature clients are more likely to report improved self-confidence and, compared to country-wide figures, have better access to education, healthcare and household utilities.

Changing organizational culture

Designing the monitoring system and sharing the CIMS findings has resulted in ripples of changes affecting the rest of the organization. Principally it has provided an opportunity for staff, management and the board to understand clients better. While the use of the AIMS-SEEP tools served as the research and diagnostic phase for the development of the CIMS, it was also very valuable from an operational perspective because real changes were made in response to the findings.

For example, based on the finding that clients were complaining about loan sizes, SAT has reviewed its loan sizes and intensified staff training on client cash-flow analysis so that appropriate loan sizes are granted at the right time. Delays in disbursement of loans have also been addressed by streamlining the loan renewal processes, making the administration more efficient. As a result, clients no longer seem to be complaining about this. In addition, listening to clients through impact assessment and the CIMS has led to a new product, the asset loan, combined with intensive training to help promote women's empowerment through business growth as part of the wider strategy to achieve our social development goals. SAT continues to appreciate the value of the monitoring system in improving its ability to meet the needs of its clients. However, further CIMS data will need to be collected to enable in-depth analysis of other areas, such as impact and changes in poverty level.

Attribution

Attributing changes in clients' lives to the provision of credit or savings is not straightforward because a cross-sectional analysis does not adequately address the extent to which other factors might have contributed to any changes. Using new clients as a comparison group can help monitor client profile and identify what changes are happening in clients' lives, but it remains to be seen how useful this is in substantiating claims about impact. This calls for a higher level of complexity and skill, requiring longitudinal analysis. Some of the obstacles in trying to interview the same client repeatedly in a longitudinal system include client fatigue, the necessity of starting with a larger sample size to still have enough clients left after a couple of years and the logistical difficulties of keeping track of the sampled clients. SAT might need additional technical assistance in order to manage this component.

Delayed feedback
Although a great deal of time and effort was spent on designing and testing the monitoring system, less time was spent on developing systems for data analysis, reports and the overall 'feedback loop' of data collection, analysis, reporting and decision-making.[1] These are all steps that should be planned and tested before the wide-scale data collection begins. The success of the CIMS depends on an effective feedback loop and on institutionalizing an efficient mechanism to give feedback to staff at all levels, including loan officers and even clients. In view of this, SAT is planning to embark on an initiative to introduce branch analysis for CIMS operational questions so that branches can analyse and utilize the information.

Additional challenges
Having set up a system that best meets the needs of SAT, there is a further challenge to be addressed: that of comparing CIMS data with national or international data. In collaboration with OI, SAT is part of a study in four countries to compare CIMS poverty level indicators to the World Bank's Living Standards Measurement Survey to see how valid the CIMS indicators are in measuring poverty in Ghana.

As SAT transforms itself into a savings and loans institution, another challenge will be to integrate additional savings questions into the monitoring system, along with a new sampling strategy for savings clients. With the anticipated increase in client population as a result of the conversion, SAT will need to strike a delicate balance between learning even more about its clients at an increasingly higher cost and keeping it simple enough to ensure that learning is not abandoned when the workload mounts up.

It has been learnt from the pilot testing and analysis that some impact indicators are not susceptible to change over a short period of time, such as education, housing ownership, community involvement and decision-making. In such areas, changes should be analyzed over a longer period of time, for example, three to five years.

Key lessons

Cost-effective sampling and pilot testing
In order to facilitate cost-effective implementation of the CIMS to all its branches, SAT has learned to scale down its survey sampling methods.

However, even if adapting a pre-existing tool, an MFI should never try to skip the development and pilot testing phases, though they require an investment of time and money.

Staff involvement and 'buy-in'

SAT has learned that, for the CIMS to be successful, both management and staff need to be fully trained to appreciate the benefits of the system. As much as possible, all attempts should be made to build the monitoring system into existing work patterns. Time needed for interviewing and data capturing should be kept to a minimum so that staff will not see it as an additional burden of work. If staff are forced to collect the data without seeing the need for it, they will either rush the client through or cut corners, thereby invalidating the information given. For these reasons, staff from all levels should be involved at the early stage of development so they see it as part of the core activities of the institution. Regular 'buy-in' meetings should be held, and training given to ensure that staff understand the objective of the data collection and that they feel involved in the entire process.

Minimizing bias versus maximizing efficiency

The early stages of CIMS have indicated that there are 'trade-offs' with regard to using loan officers to collect data from their own clients. If loan officers interview their own clients then staff time is minimized because the process can be integrated into existing activities. Furthermore, they do not need to spend time gathering background information from clients. However, one major drawback is that clients may be less willing to give frank and open responses for fear that it will affect approval of their next loan. The most effective solution has been for staff to be trained to explain the importance of the survey to their clients and to assure them that the information given will not affect the loan approval process. As noted above, the interviews only take place after the client has received a loan for that cycle in order to reduce bias.

Analyzing and using data

SAT emphasizes that the effort put into data collection by staff and clients is wasted unless it provides findings that are timely and useful and can lead to operational changes. A 'feedback loop' is therefore employed[2] to ensure that information is analyzed and used effectively. The feedback process involves reporting back information, not only to management and donors, but also to clients and staff members as a way to show them the benefits of the CIMS.

Conclusion

CIMS is not a replacement for a more rigorous, issue-specific impact assessment but this level of detail and accuracy is not what is needed for SAT's routine work. CIMS is a system that enables the ongoing collection of relevant information so that the organization can keep track of clients' development and make changes to products or operational practices as necessary. CIMS also acts as an early warning system to highlight problems before they become damaging for the organization, as well as flagging up areas of potential research. Above all, SAT is investing in the process and culture of listening to its clients and staff. It is this investment in staff training, capacity building and data collection, along with a commitment to impact monitoring and assessment, which is moving SAT closer to achieving a double bottom line of both tangible poverty reduction and financial sustainability.

CHAPTER TEN
Institutionalizing feedback from clients using credit association meetings: the experience of FOCCAS, Uganda

Regina Nakayenga and Susan Johnson

Introduction

FOCCAS (Foundation for Credit and Community Assistance) Uganda is based in Mbale in the east of the country and serves clients in six districts. It was initiated in 1995 as a programme of a US-based NGO, the Foundation for Credit and Community Assistance. Since 1996 it has been an affiliate of Freedom From Hunger International (FFH), and since 2002 has been operating entirely under local management.[1] Its mission is to provide sustainable financial and educational services that are responsive to the basic needs and wants of poor families in rural Uganda. While the main street of Mbale now contains the branches of many microfinance institutions, FOCCAS has the most significant presence beyond the town, stretching into rural areas. It has some 16,000 clients and, as shown in Table 10.1, has been making steady progress towards financial sustainability.

FOCCAS uses the Credit with Education methodology promoted by FFH and targets women in groups called credit associations (CAs). The product is a 16-week loan paid in equal weekly instalments and is complemented by adult education sessions during the midweeks of the loan cycle. The field agents, who also manage the loans, run the education sessions, which cover issues such as health, family planning, nutrition and business management. FOCCAS is committed to this methodology although it presents challenges for financial sustainability compared to a minimalist approach.[2]

Table 10.1 FOCCAS – key performance indicators

Indicator	March 2001	March 2002	March 2003	March 2004
Clients	10,691	15,740	16,965	16,124
Loan portfolio (US$)	393,417	578,597	712,933	896,247
Operational self-sufficiency (%)	42	62	80	82
Financial self-sufficiency (%)	39	59	79	77
Portofolio at Risk >30 days (%)	2	0	2	5

FOCCAS was setting out to implement what FFH called a 'progress tracking' system when it started its partnership with *Imp-Act*. The central philosophy of this system was based on empowering field officers to respond effectively to clients' needs, and embedding these activities in the programme's regular operations. The purpose of the plan was to evaluate: 1) if FOCCAS was reaching food insecure households; 2) if it was providing good quality Credit with Education; 3) what changes were occurring in the lives of clients and their families; and 4) if clients were satisfied with the Credit with Education model, including any adaptations necessary to help retain good clients.

The first issue was to be assessed using a poverty assessment tool; the second, through a range of tools including spot audits and assessment of the quality of the facilitation of the education sessions; the third was to be assessed through mini-surveys, qualitative client interviews and Participatory Learning and Action (PLA) exercises, focusing on food security, vulnerability and coping strategies, and child health and nutrition. The last issue was to be addressed through focus group discussions on client satisfaction and exit interviews.

FOCCAS started by examining how satisfied its clients were with the services provided. This then led to the institutionalization of meetings to get feedback from clients, which in turn has improved the capacity of the organization to retain clients and respond to what is becoming a dynamic microfinance market-place. In addressing the issue of client satisfaction, much information was raised on the other three areas of concern. However, this has also meant that systems for data collection and analysis to monitor these aspects of social performance have not yet been developed and are still needed to produce a sufficiently comprehensive system of social performance management and assessment. Although some monitoring tools were developed to monitor the quality of services, they are not discussed here. This case study explains how the work on client satisfaction was carried out, how the product was adapted to respond to the findings and how the feedback mechanisms were institutionalized.

Starting out: how satisfied are the clients?

In collaboration with FFH and before joining the *Imp-Act* programme, FOCCAS had already experimented with a number of data collection tools – mostly participatory research techniques and some semi-structured interviews – seeking ways to tailor them to the issues of most interest to FOCCAS. As a result, the first activity that was implemented on a larger scale was a client-satisfaction tool very similar to the AIMS-SEEP tool.[3] The aim was to examine clients' likes and dislikes in relation to a number of features of the product: the loans, savings, education sessions and the management of the credit associations themselves.

The work was led by the training manager who worked with operational staff at all levels to develop and implement the tool. This approach continued throughout the project so that undertaking the work was seen as the responsibility of operational staff. The implementation of the client-satisfaction tool was carried out in late 2000, with each staff member being trained to carry out a focus group discussion in one of her credit associations.

There were four key findings. First, clients appreciated the assistance loans provided but found the initial loan size of USh50,000 (US$25) too small, as were the subsequent incremental increases. Clients commented that they felt 'stuck in P1!', that is, the first grade of primary school. Second, they appreciated the education modules but identified food security and health issues – such as malaria and diarrhoeal diseases – as key concerns about which they wanted to know more. Third, they liked saving but disliked having their savings cut to pay the loans of defaulters. Fourth, clients liked CA procedures that safeguarded their money but disliked management committee members who misused group funds and could not control their groups.

FOCCAS's first and immediate response was to increase loan sizes. However, without mobilizing additional funds for the loan portfolio, the increased loan sizes quickly exhausted the available capital and led to a liquidity crisis. In wanting to respond quickly, the implications for the MFI's own cash flow had not been adequately considered. This is a good example of why it is necessary to follow through the different stages of a feedback loop, which ensures that information gathered on clients and services is reported to management and informs decision-making (McCord, 2002). The organization must carefully consider the impact of any proposed change, most critically for cash flow, profitability and the capacity to implement.

The findings from the client-satisfaction exercise also highlighted the need for new educational modules, especially one on malaria, and the need to undertake further research into the food security issues these clients faced. Since this latter concern fitted closely with the overall objective of whether the programme was reaching food insecure households, it became the focus of the next stage of work.

The use of the client-satisfaction tool proved that it could generate issues of concern to the clients that the organization needed to follow up. However, having identified these concerns, the tool gave only a shallow coverage of the issues and it was then necessary to undertake further research before adjustments to the programme could be considered.

Crisis and coping: understanding and responding

Difficult seasons and coping strategies

The next step was to identify the main crises faced by clients, both their nature and their seasonality, and how families coped with them. To do this a research tool was devised to explore difficult seasons and coping strategies. This again used focus group discussions. FOCCAS wanted to better understand the major difficulties that clients faced, which members of the household were most affected by them, when they tended to happen, how the family coped and what they needed to do in order to overcome these difficulties. The discussion guide is given in Box 10.1.

> **Box 10.1**
>
> Life is generally not easy and we all struggle to survive in our households. However, there are times when you state/admit/confess that you are in 'crisis' (very difficult times). What major difficulties do you encounter/face/meet in your household?
>
> Ask the respondents to rank the listed difficulties according to their magnitude (frequency and number of people affected in the household).
>
> Ask the group to select one major crisis that occurs for all of them and then ask what factors cause this difficulty.
>
> Which people are most affected by this difficulty in your household(s), and how?
>
> Which particular months in a typical year does your household experience this difficulty and why? Probe by asking: in which months a difficulty occurs and note this on the calendar provided; what exactly happens; and ask respondents to select the most difficult months on the calendar and allocate a number of seeds/stones out of 10 to indicate the degree of difficulty, then record this on the calendar.
>
> How have you and your household(s) been coping with this difficulty?
>
> List coping strategies and use pairwise ranking to order them.
>
> What support/strategy would you and your household need to enable you to control or prevent this difficulty from occurring in future?
>
> Record coping strategies for each difficulty ranked (note, solutions do not have to involve FOCCAS).

The tool was used as a one-off exercise with 18 focus groups of five to seven people each (106 clients in total) selected from within CAs, and also selected to cover the range of locations: urban/peri-urban; rural communities with relatively high commercial activity; and rural communities with low commercial activity. The groups were also selected to reflect the length of time they had been in the programme: those who were in their first cycle; those in their third to fifth cycle; and those in their seventh loan cycle or beyond.

Analysis of the data was carried out in a workshop of branch managers and field officers with the specific intention of building understanding and ownership of the findings. The findings were, in fact, broadly consistent between the locations, though with some small differences in terms of the exact months involved. They highlight the importance of knowing the market.

Factors contributing to seasonal difficulties

The months between April and June were found to be particularly difficult for clients. This is due to a number of reasons. First, as it is the rainy season, people suffer from malaria and diarrhoea. Second, at the same time, food is in short supply and therefore diet is poor, but due to it being the planting season, the demand for agricultural labour is at its highest. Third, this period is also that of lowest business demand because available funds are used for farming inputs and consequently demand for other goods drops.

Female household members are most vulnerable

Women are clearly most severely affected by these problems; they prefer to go without food to ensure that their children eat something. The women explained that they were overworked because of the farming activities and therefore more vulnerable to sickness, while at the same time they lacked cash generated from business activities to seek and pay for treatment. In addition, when others in the household are sick it falls to the women to care for them and this caring role can cause great psychological strain. Finally, the situation is particularly difficult for single mothers who have to cope with all of these responsibilities alone.

FOCCAS loans used as a coping strategy

Clients further explained that they use loans from FOCCAS as a coping strategy and struggle to stay in the programme. Field agents noted that repayment and meeting attendance fell off between April and June. There was also a clear pattern of demand for school fees, peaking in February, May and August. Some more worrying features of the coping mechanisms employed also came to light. Strategies to increase the amount borrowed had involved: first, 'ghost' clients – members who were only there to take loans for others; second, multiple borrowing, where clients were members of more than one CA; and third, internal lending, whereby clients wanting larger loans got others to borrow for them and then hand over the funds to top up their loans. These factors had, in turn, resulted in loan delinquency, default and client exit.

Recognizing the need for greater programme flexibility

While rigid policies regarding loan increments from cycle to cycle made it easy for field officers to predict their portfolio growth, FOCCAS now clearly recognized the need for greater flexibility. Extensive discussions among staff and management raised a number of options about the ways in which the product could be improved. These included: allowing smaller/larger loans depending on the season; changing repayment frequency from weekly to fortnightly during the difficult seasons; allowing for grace periods; introducing emergency or medical loans and revising savings policies to encourage savings for these difficult times. However, it was clear that there was still insufficient information on which to base a decision as to how the product should be redesigned and that clients' preferred loan features would need further investigation. In order to take the work forward, a product development committee was tasked with the job of investigating clients' preferences for loan features in more detail and making more specific recommendations.

The next step was, therefore, some further research on how to make the loan product more flexible. This involved the development of a tool to find out what clients' preferred product features were. This time a discussion guide was developed and used with focus groups of clients involved in similar types of business activities so that a better understanding could be developed of how capital requirements related to the seasonality of particular types of business. Twenty-five field agents undertook the research with small groups of five respondents from each of the 27 CAs.

Ensuring well-designed qualitative research techniques

In developing the discussion guide, steps were taken to ensure that those carrying out the work properly understood the meaning of the questions and recorded the types of responses being sought. Particular problems arose due to language and hence the best translation of the questions. In FOCCAS's operational area a number of different languages and dialects are spoken, which made initial attempts to produce a range of translations of questions unfeasible. Instead it was necessary to spend more time training the field agents on the intent behind the questions. A second issue was creating a specific format for recording the responses, because although the questions were designed to be open-ended, the responses needed to be clear and address key issues.

The exercise highlighted the difficulties of involving a large number of staff in research of this kind, rather than using a small number of staff who are more experienced in qualitative research techniques. In the former case, it is necessary to train and structure the research more specifically. This approach has the advantage of engaging staff in developing an understanding of the issues involved, but may take more time than using a small number of more specialist staff.

Implementing changes to the loan product

The findings of the research came at a time when FOCCAS was experiencing pressure to reach operational self-sufficiency and had also undergone a change in key senior managers. As a result, the piloting of proposed changes was slow to take place. In addition, there was resistance from field staff to implement a move to fortnightly repayments – even though many clients had requested it – since they feared that clients would be unable to repay the higher amounts due, thus damaging portfolio quality and reflecting badly on the field staff. However, moving to fortnightly repayments offered the potential benefit of expanding staff productivity because it would enable field staff to handle higher numbers of clients and hence portfolios. This would, therefore, have an immediate impact on the financial bottom line. At the time, discussions of a staff incentive scheme were just beginning. The incentive scheme now being pilot tested incorporates an indicator of client exit intended to ensure that staff are motivated to respond to clients' concerns. Pressure for sustainability eventually added impetus to the need to make these changes. The adjustments made to the loan product are shown in Table 10.2.

Institutionalizing feedback: credit association management meetings

Opening new channels of communication

Management started to realize that information they were receiving direct from the clients was often conflicting with the feedback they were getting from the field agents. As a result, they held meetings with representatives of a number of credit associations to open new channels of communication. These meetings have now evolved into a format FOCCAS calls 'credit association management meetings' (CAMM). These consist of a meeting to which two representatives of each CA in the locality are invited; they are usually members of the management committee. Local leaders are also invited, offering them an opportunity to learn more about the programme, while at the same time securing their support for the CAs.

Initially the meetings involved large numbers of people, perhaps 100, and took all day. After feedback on the format, the meetings have been made more local and now cover around 20 CAs. This reduces the travelling time for clients and means that the business can be conducted much more efficiently, so taking around three hours. The format has evolved into a mechanism

Table 10.2 Summary of changes to loan product

Loan product features	Before	After
Loan sizes	Initial loan of USh50,000 (US$28)	Initial loan between USh50,000–150,000 (US$28–85)
	Fixed increments per cycle	Increment depends on client's performance: repayment history, attendance and business activity
	Could only go up	Client can take lower amount if so wishes
Loan length	16 weeks fixed	8, 12, 16, 20 or 24 weeks
Repayment frequency	Weekly	Weekly for 3 cycles, then fortnightly
Grace period	None	One week
Disbursement mechanism	Administrative delays in office-based system led to women waiting for a long time	Bank disbursement system, which is quicker for clients

through which FOCCAS can invite feedback from the CAs and have the opportunity to discuss its policies and procedures with clients. The current policy is to involve each CA in one of these meetings per year.

Building on the experience of focus group discussions

The means of doing this has been to build on the FGD experience gained in the previous research. The participants are broken up into small groups facilitated by a field agent. This is a key opportunity for the groups to meet and talk to field agents other than the one who normally attends their meetings, and hence to raise issues they might have felt they could not discuss with their usual agent. In essence, the format uses the client-satisfaction tool to find out likes and dislikes about FOCCAS and to explore the problems faced by CAs. The results are taken back to the office for analysis and report back.

In meetings held during 2002, the main problems identified were not new to FOCCAS itself but clients had not articulated them so clearly before. Many of the problems were interlinked: weak CA management involved officials manipulating records and being slow to bank money; ghost borrowers; encouragement of multiple borrowing; embezzlement of group funds; and poor follow-up of defaulters. These issues also reflected on the performance of the field officers who had not adequately supervised the CA management committee. Issues around the poor performance of field officers were also raised and in some cases this enabled management's own concerns to be confirmed, enabling them to take clear action. In 2003 these meetings were particularly used to educate members on the role of the management committee in financial record-keeping and banking procedures, a need which became apparent through the previous round of CAMMs.

Staff now see the CAMM as central to the organization's activities, a means of both receiving feedback from clients and giving them information on policies and procedures. They reported that the CA management meetings 'have become part of us' and that activities based on listening to clients are the 'lifeblood of the organization'.

Improving the loan product, improving overall financial performance

The financial performance of the organization has improved significantly over the last three years (see Table 10.2). The changes made in order to make the product more flexible have strongly contributed to these improvements, especially the move to fortnightly repayments. This has allowed significant portfolio growth and improvements in financial self-sufficiency, although client numbers have remained stable and been achieved with fewer staff. At the same time, giving clients a voice has made them feel that FOCCAS listens and cares about them and hence has improved client loyalty. The exit rate (between cycles) has dropped from 12 per cent in 2000 to 4 per cent in late 2003.

Lessons learned

Changes in products should be supported by organizational changes

The implementation of progress-tracking activities coincided with FOCCAS's transition from an affiliate of FFH to a locally-owned and managed MFI. Coming at this time, the progress-tracking work has played an important role in adapting the Credit with Education product to respond to the context of Eastern Uganda, while at the same time building ownership of the organization among its staff and enabling them to recognize the importance of being responsive to clients.

Although FOCCAS has not yet addressed all of the four issues of concern it initially set out to address, staff were trained with the assistance of FFH and *Imp-Act* and they developed the skills and experience to adapt the basic FGD format to answer the operational questions that the organization needed to answer. Moreover, the involvement of field staff and a cross section of management in the main activities of data collection, consolidation and analysis improved their understanding of the changes once they had been decided upon by management, and were thus more easily communicated when implementation was underway.

Carefully consider how to best utilize field staff

While FGDs fitted well into the operational methodology of the organization with its strong focus on education, and are also a useful tool for collecting data, the strong facilitation skills required to implement them mean that investing in training all staff is quite costly. In this context, use of staff for data collection needs to be very clearly focused with clear questions and well-designed formats for recording the responses. It may be more cost-effective in future to involve only those field officers who have shown themselves most capable in carrying out this kind of work.

Challenges facing FOCCAS

The experience has also highlighted a number of challenges for FOCCAS. First, its overall cycle of listening to clients, then devising, piloting and implementing responses, has been rather slow. This has, in part, been due to organizational constraints that arose from the pressures of transition towards operational sustainability. At the same time, changes in key personnel also affected FOCCAS's capacity to adapt. As competition is now starting to extend further into rural areas, FOCCAS will need to learn how to respond more quickly in order to retain clients.

Second, while FOCCAS learnt from its mistake of increasing loan sizes without adequately considering the consequences, it did not fully appreciate the need to think about the reverse situation. That is, in needing to make a decision led by the needs of the organization, it should have considered adequately the implications for its clients and how they would respond. Hence senior management, responding to organizational needs to improve sustainability, imposed a 2 per cent administration fee but failed to adequately consider how clients would react. For clients, this has undermined some of the progress made through making the loan product more flexible. During a CAMM, the clients told FOCCAS that in implementing this policy it had disregarded them, failing to capitalize upon the advice that they could have provided had they been consulted. It is important to consider how clients should be consulted on changes originating from the MFI's own needs, just as it is important to consider those changes that are known to respond to clients' needs.

Third, communication of policy changes to staff requires investment of time to ensure that they understand them. It is also necessary to consider the changes in light of the circumstances in which field agents operate and ensure they can explain the changes properly to clients. Failing this, field agents interpret policy in the way that makes most sense to them and is most in accordance with their own needs in doing the job. This was particularly found in relation to the communication of the policy around the shift to fortnightly meetings, which field officers had had their reservations about. Methods of explaining the changes themselves need to be tested with field agents and piloted with clients before being rolled out. Furthermore, in the process of communicating these changes to clients, it is helpful to use as many channels of communication as possible. The presence of management in the field to back up what field agents say is particularly important. FOCCAS could also produce simple leaflets for clients that explain the changes.

The need for quantitative as well as qualitative data

FOCCAS has primarily used qualitative methods of assessing client satisfaction, and while these have played an important role, they need to be complemented by quantitative data that monitors client profiles and performance in order to develop an overall system of social performance management. It is these elements of the original plan that have not yet taken place. FOCCAS makes claims about its rural outreach and depth of outreach but does not yet generate data of its own to substantiate those claims. Apart from enabling verification of the extent to which it has achieved its social mission, such data is critical to developing a clear understanding of client behaviour.

Conclusion

The experience of FOCCAS demonstrates that research to investigate client satisfaction can be a good place to start and can use a relatively straightforward approach, building on the MFI's existing methodology and skills in group facilitation. The findings of this work naturally led to new areas that FOCCAS needed to investigate in order to make effective changes to its products and services, and FOCCAS developed its skills in using focus group discussions to explore these. The experience of using this technique then enabled the development of a mechanism of regular consultation with clients that can assist FOCCAS in the future to respond to its client's requirements and to changes in market conditions.

CHAPTER ELEVEN
Microfinance networks and the evaluation of social performance: the case of FINRURAL, Bolivia

Irina Aliaga, Reynaldo Marconi and Paul Mosley

Introduction

FINRURAL (the Association of Financial Institutions for Rural Development) was established in Bolivia in 1993. It is funded by private donations, including research grants, and subscriptions from members. The FINRURAL network consists of non-governmental microfinance organizations whose objective is to improve the living standards of vulnerable groups through microfinance and, in some cases, to provide complementary services. As of December 2004, FINRURAL comprised 14 member MFIs, which are not subject to government regulation but are subject to a system of self-regulation.[1]

Most of the 14 members are sponsored by international NGOs and, in spite of the stresses inflicted by the global economic crises of 2000–02, they continue to maintain good financial discipline. At the end 2003 they had an average arrears rate of 8 per cent. Two members of the FINRURAL club, PROMUJER and CRECER, are 'village banks' lending to women only, and these have a financial performance outshining any other financial institutions in Bolivia, with arrears rates consistently less than 1 per cent.

FINRURAL promotes the development of the microfinance sector and innovation within it, with a particular focus on the rural sector. A number of activities are pursued at the local level, including: the operation of a risk-assessment centre for microfinance institutions; a statistical bulletin and information service; an impact assessment service for the local microfinance community; and a closed-circuit television link between member NGOs. At the international level, apart from its membership of the *Imp-Act* consortium, FINRURAL is a member of the Latin American Rural Finance Forum.

Conceptual framework for impact assessment activities

The framework for the evaluation of the financial and social performance of MFIs is displayed in Figure 11.1. The horizontal axis shows the main sources

MICROFINANCE NETWORKS AND EVALUATION OF SOCIAL PERFORMANCE 139

```
                    ┌──────────────┐
                    │  Microfinance│
                    │supply (provider│
                    │  institution)│
                    └──────┬───────┘
                           │
Monitoring of social goals, targeting etc   Financial performance assessment
                           │                Default prevention
                           │                Risk assessment
  ┌──────────┐             │                              ┌──────────┐
  │  Social  │             │                              │ Financial│
  │performance├─────────────┼──────────────────────────────┤performance│
  └──────────┘             │                              └──────────┘
        Social impact assessment    Monitoring of client satisfaction
           (case-study enquiry)     Studies of client exit and loyalty,
                           │        characteristics of defaulting clients
                           │
                    ┌──────┴───────┐
                    │  Microfinance│
                    │    demand    │
                    │   (clients)  │
                    └──────────────┘
```

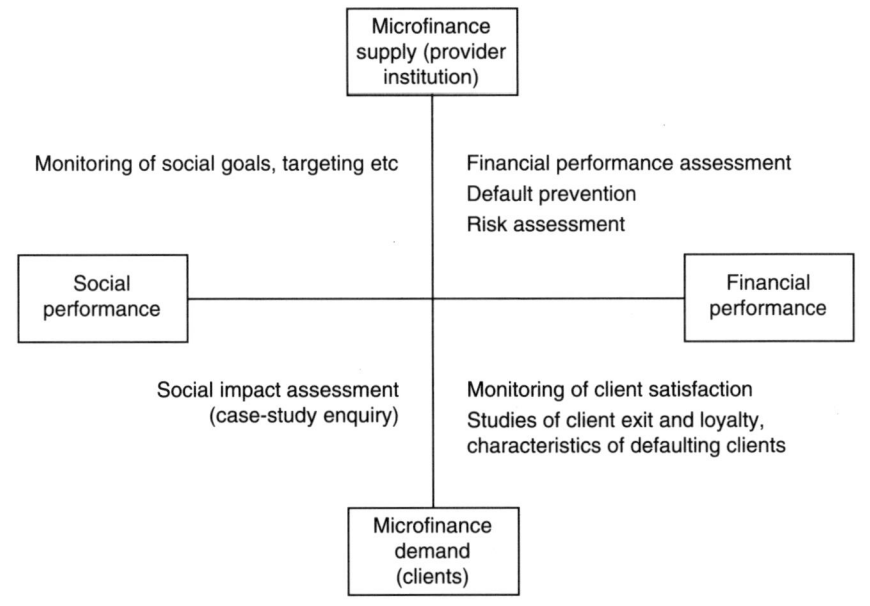

Figure 11.1 Conceptual framework for evaluation of the financial and social performance of MFIs

of information for performance assessment – the MFIs (or supply side) in the upper half of the diagram and their clients (or the demand side) in the lower half. The vertical axis shows the characteristics required for financial assessment in the right-hand section and those required for social assessment in the left-hand section.

As the diagram illustrates, proper evaluation of both the financial and social performance of MFIs requires information from both the supply and the demand side. Financial performance (the right-hand section) can be evaluated on the supply side by means of assessments of standard financial benchmarks (notably profitability) and by means of risk assessments, and on the demand side, by various measures of client satisfaction, including studies of default and of clients who have left the institution. Social performance (the left-hand section) can be investigated on the supply side through assessments of targeting derived from monitoring exercises, and on the demand side, by case studies of social impact on individual clients and communities, which often measure subjective as well as economic impacts.

FINRURAL's strategy for assessing MFI financial and social performance

A fundamental characteristic of FINRURAL's approach to impact assessment is to intervene directly in the area of *social* impact only. In relation to indicators of financial performance, FINRURAL's intervention is indirect, in other words, the intention is to understand a correlation between financial and social performance. Table 11.1 lists the various initiatives that FINRURAL has taken in the impact assessment field.

The rationale for this particular *modus operandi* was to maintain impartiality of assessment, achieve economies of scale and minimize the costs of participation for those MFIs in the FINRURAL consortium who lack the staff time and specialized skills, even more than the financial resources, to initiate such assessments themselves. However, the intention is to devolve the studies of client exit and client loyalty, which are less technically demanding, to the participating MFIs themselves. As mentioned earlier, the function of client credit scoring is already heavily devolved to commercial rating organizations. We now describe the evaluation process in more detail.

The FINRURAL impact assessment service

In its three years of participation in the *Imp-Act* programme, FINRURAL designed, marketed and consolidated its impact assessment service (IAS). The Ford Foundation, through *Imp-Act*, financed the consultancies required to bring the service into being, and also provided methodological and practical support through global meetings, regional meetings of the Latin American members of *Imp-Act*, and the services of the UK technical support team, represented by Professor Paul Mosley, University of Sheffield, who advised on methodology, offered analytical ideas and provided technical accreditation for the initial evaluation reports on each of the participating MFIs.

The aim of the IAS is to provide objective, timely and cost-effective information on the social performance of MFIs at an acceptable level of statistical

Table 11.1 FINRURAL initiatives in the assessment of MFIs' social and financial performance

General impact assessment	1. *The impact evaluation service*, directly operated by FINRURAL, aimed at MFIs and MFI support organizations (donors, investors, second-tier organizations) and assessing: economic impact; measures of social performance; measures of empowerment; and exit from poverty and its determinants
Social performance assessment	2. *Social performance rating*, directly conducted by FINRURAL, applied to MFIs not subject to the regulatory authority. Produces standardized indicators that are published each month by FINRURAL in the bulletin *Autoregulación*
Financial performance assessment	3. *Development of methodologies to assess client loyalty*, client exit and determinants of default
	4. *Development of client rating systems* on an internationally-approved and transparent basis, in association with the commercial rating firms PlanetFinance and MicroRate

reliability. The IAS contains a complementary market research component, which develops methodologies for explaining client loyalty, desertion and default and transfers them to participating MFIs, developed in collaboration with a firm of external consultants as discussed above. Table 11.2 outlines the various components of the IAS.

Table 11.2 Characteristics of FINRURAL's impact assessment service

	Impact evaluation component	*Market research component*
Clients supported	Four NGOs, associates of FINRURAL: CRECER, DIACONIA-FRIF, FADES, PRO MUJER-Bolivia	Seven FINRURAL associates: CRECER, DIACONIA-FRIF, FADES, PROMUJER-Bolivia, ANED, FONDECO, SARTAWI
	Four NGOs, not associates of FINRURAL: ECOFUTURO and FIE, both FFPs and Trinidad and Comarapa cooperatives	FFP EcoFuturo (not a FINRURAL associate)
	MFI support organizations: ICCO (Holland), PROFIN and Ford Foundation *Imp-Act* programme	MFI support organizations: ICCO (Holland), PROFIN and Ford Foundation *Imp-Act* programme
Services provided	Impact assessment service (at both household and aggregate level)	Market research, based on an aggregative analysis of MFIs
		Studies of exit, loyalty and default amongst MFI clients
Modus operandi of the service	FINRURAL designs research methodologies with the assistance of a steering committee of MFI representatives	As for impact evaluation component, except for the last step, in which FINRURAL transfers responsibility for execution of surveys of client exit, loyalty and default to participating MFIs
	Collection of field data is delegated to a specialized market research company	
	FINRURAL enters and analyses the field data, provides reports to users and publishes the results (at an aggregate level), with the permission of MFI clients	
	FINRURAL maintains responsibility for survey administration and for all large-scale surveys (for example, those involved with poverty impact or with spillovers on to non-clients)	*(continued)*

Table 11.2 Characteristics of FINRURAL's impact assessment service——continued

	Impact evaluation component	Market research component
Source of finance	To March 2004: principally Ford Foundation through its *Imp-Act* programme, with some contributions from clients	
	Subsequently: wholly financed by contributions from clients	

The IAS generates information, based on data from the demand side, in a manner designed to combine timeliness, rigour and credibility. As a distinguishing feature from other MFIs within the *Imp-Act* consortium that conduct their own impact evaluation, the entire evaluation process – from design to analysis to dissemination – is here delegated to FINRURAL as intermediary. The studies that present individualized data on particular MFIs are confidential to that organization and are released only if authorized by the organization. By contrast, those studies that present aggregate data on all MFIs contain no information about individual organizations and so are published immediately. The market research studies in Table 11.2 are gradually transferred to the participating MFIs to be executed by them in future years, in contrast to the impact assessment studies, which remain with FINRURAL because of their greater requirements in terms of rigour and specialized skills. The common methodological characteristics shared by both the impact assessment and the market research studies are as follows:

- *Use of a standardized methodology*, which generates results to suit the individual needs of each MFI as well as an aggregated report containing a weighted average for all MFIs.
- *Participatory design*, with leadership supplied by FINRURAL and feedback from a steering committee containing representatives from specific MFIs.
- *Use of both qualitative and quantitative methodologies* for analysis, with the qualitative results in particular used to infer patterns of causation.

The methods developed by FINRURAL for both impact evaluation and market research are standardized and can be replicated with any type of MFI. At the same time, they are straightforward and produce results that are cost-effective (Marconi and Mosley, 2004). In this way, the methodologies used can be adapted and validated for different types of MFIs.

Methodologies used by FINRURAL for impact assessment and market research

The impact assessment methodologies included attribution, involving a cross-section approach with control groups and with the results then cross-checked against clients' perceptions. It also entailed interviews with current

MFI clients (ideally with two or more years' exposure to financial services), in addition to a control group of non-clients having the same characteristics as the MFI clients under evaluation. The impacts assessed were economic, social, empowerment, social capital and social change. Impact was assessed at the levels of the client, the client's household and the client's enterprise. The analytical tools included a questionnaire administered to the treatment group and control group, in-depth interviews and specialized in-depth interviews of those clients who exit or are chronically poor. Social and economic analysis of mechanisms of impact included correlations between instrument and target variables, differences between treatment and control group sample means for target variables and impact modelling. These methodologies were not transferred to participating MFIs.

The market research methodologies were completely separated from the impact assessment process. This involved analyzing three distinct fields of investigation: 1) client loyalty, with interviews directed at experienced clients of the institution (ideally with at least two years' membership); 2) client exit, with interviews directed at ex-clients with a low probability of return (who ideally had left the organization at least one year ago, thereby excluding clients taking a temporary break from financial services); and 3) clients with arrears, with interviews directed at clients with loans more than 90 days in arrears. The analytical tools used were questionnaires and interviews with clients and MFI loan officers. These methodologies were transferred to participating NGOs.

Outputs produced by the FINRURAL impact evaluation service

In terms of the impact evaluation component, FINRURAL used a standardized methodology for the evaluation of impacts at individual and aggregate level. It executed two studies based on the results: first, social impact assessment studies on eight MFIs,[2] with six summaries published on this in 2003; and second, a study of the aggregate impacts of microfinance in Bolivia, published in 2003. Complementary studies were also produced, such as a methodological synthesis of findings (FINRURAL, 2003b) and a study of the cost-effectiveness of the FINRURAL impact assessment service (Marconi and Mosley, 2004). A further study looked at how clients escape poverty, drawing on the case of CRECER and PROMUJER-Bolivia. Some of the results can be found in Marconi and Mosley (2004).

In terms of the market research component, this was centred on issues of customer loyalty, exit and default at individual and aggregate levels. The outputs from these studies included client loyalty studies, client exit studies and studies of default and its causes in eight MFIs. The methodology opts for a separation between measurement of social impact, a task that remains with FINRURAL to be repeated every two years, and research into clients' needs and satisfaction, a task devolved to members of the network, enabling the survey instruments to be redeployed at the will of the MFI.

FINRURAL impact assessment service: timeframe of activities planned and executed

In 2002 the FINRURAL impact assessment service formally began operations with studies of eight local MFIs. The results of these studies were published at the beginning of 2003, together with a composite study, which used the information from all eight studies to draw conclusions about relationships at the aggregate level and about the relative performance of different types of institution. Numerous activities still remain that require further work, not least the handover of the market research studies to collaborating MFIs and the conversion of the impact assessment studies conducted by *Imp-Act* on to a fully self-financing basis, which is planned for 2005. In addition, in the field of social performance assessment, FINRURAL is working with two of its associate organizations, PROMUJER-Bolivia and DIACONIA-FRIF, in a pilot of a new methodology in collaboration with the French NGO CERISE. Table 11.3 shows a timeframe for the main activities undertaken or planned for the future.

Conclusion

FINRURAL's achievements over the last four years in the impact assessment field give reason to believe that this is a model capable of being successfully scaled up and adapted for use in other contexts. There are six key lessons from our experience. First, there are considerable advantages in developing an impact assessment product for a range of institutions all at once. These consist not only of economies of scale but also of the possibility of comparisons, exchanges of ideas between institutions and the derivation of aggregative

Table 11.3 Timeframe of activities planned and executed

Year	Activity
2001	Specialized impact assessment unit created in FINRURAL
	Impact assessment methodology designed
2002	Impact assessment service launched, with eight participants
2003	Eight individual impact assessment studies, plus one study of aggregate impact (FINRURAL, 2003a)
	Summary versions of the studies prepared for publication, with methodological annex (FINRURAL, 2003b)
	Market research methodologies developed (for assessment of client loyalty, exit and default)
2004	Studies of client loyalty, exit and default in eight local MFIs (24 studies altogether)
	Transfer of market research methodology to MFIs who request it (in progress)
2005	Second round of impact assessment studies projected

results on developments in the microfinance sector in response to policy shocks and stimuli.[3] More lessons can be extracted from the studies already done at low marginal cost because the baseline data for 2002 already exists and the only costs of further analysis consist of the labour required to do the additional data processing.

Second, in addition to the cost advantages, there are also advantages of independence in the FINRURAL model, with evaluations conducted by an intermediary rather than the organization itself. As a good proportion of the data collected consists of objective rather than subjective performance ratings such as client assets, any possibility of the results being distorted by the self-interest of the organization's employees is removed.

Third, FINRURAL has derived two advantages from the operation of the IAS – one tangible and the other intangible – that other institutions considering providing a service of this kind could benefit from. The tangible benefits consist of the conversion of the IAS into a source of revenue for the FINRURAL member NGOs, who appreciate the professional expertise and impartiality of the service, and for FINRURAL itself, enabling it to promote the service amongst other MFIs in Bolivia and further afield. The intangible benefits derive from the acknowledgement of the FINRURAL network as a source of credible professional and advisory services. This increased credibility has enabled FINRURAL to act more effectively to promote good practice and policies within the Bolivian microfinance community. There is potential to broaden the role it took on in 2001 when it negotiated between the MFIs, the Superintendency of Banks and representatives of defaulting debtors.

Fourth, the 'network model' of impact evaluation developed by FINRURAL has not only made these services available to participating institutions, but has also helped them integrate and build social capital between them. It has provided a forum for them to share ideas about how to improve their effectiveness, that is, to serve clients better and in particular to help them ride out shocks. In the face of the global recession of 1999–2003, which culminated in a severe political crisis, the financial institutions of Bolivia displayed varying degrees of resilience.[4] The severity of the crisis may be ascribed in part to the sufferings of microfinance clients, which might have been averted if their financial services had been better managed (Marconi and Mosley, 2003). It is hoped that through mutual learning, as well as learning directly from clients, MFIs in Bolivia and elsewhere can achieve greater resilience and thus help make their national economies more resistant to future macroeconomic shocks.

Fifth, the FINRURAL model also provides flexibility to respond to the evaluation needs of particular organizations, especially in relation to the range of performance targets selected for assessment. This avoids the constraints involved in using ready-made evaluation packages, for example, the AIMS tools. These may be more costly than the 'local product' and may not provide opportunities for local organizations to develop their creativity and crisis-response capacity. The skilled manpower required to develop a local product exists, as we have seen, in Bolivia and assuredly in other developing countries as well.

It is not suggested that the FINRURAL model is perfect yet. What has been designed in the course of the *Imp-Act* programme is only a prototype; many errors have had to be corrected and the process of learning that has been initiated needs to continue. Nonetheless, the fact that the model expects to expand its clientele in 2005, even in the absence of external subsidy, is a good omen. The lessons detailed above provide reasons to believe that the model is not only original, but can also provide ideas for improving the poverty-reducing potential of MFIs on a sustainable basis well beyond Bolivia.

CHAPTER TWELVE

The potential of regional networks to stimulate innovation in microfinance: lessons from the Microfinance Centre (MFC) in Eastern Europe

Katarzyna Pawlak

Introduction

The Microfinance Centre (MFC)[1] for Central and Eastern Europe and the New Independent States (CEE and NIS) is a regional network that contributes to the development and spread of microfinance innovations in 26 countries. In a region characterized by newness and fragmentation, the experience of MFC shows that a regional network can successfully play a role in filling the vacuum created by limited access to relevant information. The *Imp-Act* programme has provided MFC and its partners with the opportunity to develop client-monitoring approaches that benefit microfinance clients, individual organizations and the wider regional sector. This chapter describes the learning that has occurred at the network level.[2] Through these processes, MFC has developed the 'innovation scaling-up model' (ISM), which enables it to deliver practical solutions to its partners across the region. MFC's experience provides insights into how regional networks can use low-cost approaches, not only to support regional microfinance as a service provider, but also to use their unique position to stimulate and enhance sector development.

Microfinance in Central and Eastern Europe and the New Independent States

In the early 1990s the concept of microfinance was virtually unknown in CEE and the NIS. In some post-communist countries, only credit and savings cooperatives served low-salaried populations. Furthermore, small loans to invest in microenterprise development were not available to those made redundant. However, when the demand for credit was demonstrated by pilot microcredit projects, the international aid community provided a great deal of support to encourage development of the microfinance sector. Within a short time, microfinance achieved significant outreach and sustainability in the region, with most MFIs being NGOs with missions focused on self-employment and microenterprise development. This growth was not without constraints as there were legislative barriers often not found in the developing world, however, in time other institutions began to recognize the success of microfinance and enter the market. There is now competition from dynamic microfinance banks and downscaling commercial banks. All have seen the potential of extending outreach to financially excluded market segments.[3]

Obstacles to innovation in the region

Since its inception, the nascent microfinance sector in CEE and the NIS has faced a paucity of region-specific practical solutions and knowledge to draw upon. This factor, combined with a difficult regulatory environment, has set the costs of innovation high. The lack of capacity within many MFIs also makes it difficult to undertake innovation. Additionally, the sector's donor-driven origins and slow transition from product to market-led microfinance has resulted in few market incentives to innovate. Lack of market focus and blind replication of microfinance blueprints widely used in other parts of the world have resulted in low client retention, low demand and/or huge levels of client exclusion, especially from lower market segments.

At the same time, the region possesses high quality human capital and has proved its potential to absorb knowledge, to learn quickly from others and implement 'ready-made solutions'. This has been demonstrated by successful efforts in implementing best practices related to the Consultative Group to Assist the Poor sustainability principles, allowing many institutions to achieve operational self-sufficiency in a very short time compared to other regions where microfinance is more established.[4]

Regional diversity, although posing a challenge in terms of innovation, development and delivery costs, can also be considered an advantage in terms of learning potential. In CEE and the NIS, there is a wide variety of MFIs working in different contexts, including post-conflict situations and transitional economies. These organizations are generally recently established, different in size and utilize different lending models, which in itself stimulates industry-wide learning. In a context such as this, promotion and development of innovation and a client-focused learning culture has been a challenge, even though it is critical to the long-term growth of the sector in the region and the expansion of outreach to excluded populations.

MFC's involvement in regional innovation processes in CEE and the NIS

MFC was established in 1997 by regional practitioners and supports the emerging microfinance sector in CEE and the NIS. Its mission is to build a strong and sustainable microfinance sector that delivers high quality solutions to poor families, particularly those of microentrepreneurs. It has a membership base comprising 84 MFIs from 26 countries in the region. It provides both members and non-members with a wide range of services they can use to become more client- and market-led. These services include: information on global and regional industry developments; innovative solutions developed through action-research activities; networking opportunities; and capacity building, through training and on-site technical assistance.

MFC not only serves practitioners but also collaborates with donors, investors and other support organizations, including academics and consultants. It has a unique position, being close to the field by virtue of its practitioner-oriented services, but at the same time has close relationships with global and regional industry stakeholders, as shown in Figure 12.1. These relationships allow MFC to monitor the current state of the industry, identify barriers and opportunities, and initiate innovation efforts, as well as document such efforts to contribute this knowledge to wider industry learning.

Examples of MFC's innovative work in the region

The first steps in the development of regional innovation evolved around adapting existing solutions for diverse contexts. Dynamically growing MFIs in some of the regions, primarily Bosnia and Herzegovina, and other countries

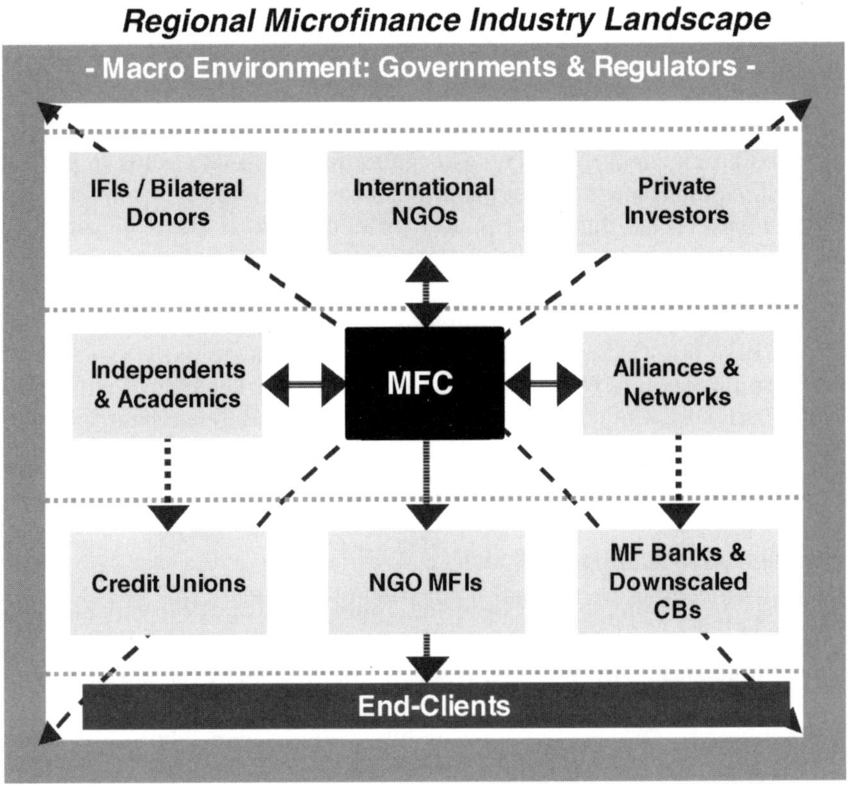

Figure 12.1 Regional microfinance industry landscape
Source: *Imp-Act*/MFC (2005)

in the Balkans, moved towards more market-oriented services. This resulted in their increased interest in market and client-level information. During 1999–2001 MFC, together with a few selected partner MFIs, conducted regional pilot tests of the AIMS-SEEP impact assessment tools as well as *MicroSave*'s market research toolkit.[5] This helped fill the regional gap in practitioner-led, client-friendly instruments that would allow MFIs to better understand their clients, markets, contexts and effectiveness of operations. The result of the project was not only adapted tools ready to use in the transition context, but documentation of lessons learnt, development of MFC's technical assistance (TA) capacity, training modules and TA services on tools, their selection process and building MFIs' internal market research capacity.

Client assessment work indicated practitioners' need for an institutionalized system that would integrate a mix of tools into daily operations. These could provide different types of information over different time periods for different purposes. The resulting system would have the potential to produce timely and relevant information at low cost. Taking the opportunity presented by the *Imp-Act* programme, MFC and seven of its partners engaged in an action-research process to develop efficient, cost-effective systems for assessing and improving impact by practitioners, based on identified goals and information needs and suited to the individual MFI's capacity and operational context.

The action-research format provided a great opportunity to learn and innovate on the one hand, and on the other hand posed a challenge to the young network and its members to clearly formulate its needs and develop a framework to address them. The diversity of partners that elected to participate in the project meant that it was a challenge to develop a coherent regional action-research plan that could be adapted to different contexts. In addition, all were very young institutions with different levels of experience in client assessment. To address this challenge, MFC developed and trained its partners in client assessment approaches and tools to ensure they all had the requisite level of basic knowledge. The training provided the means to clarify partners' needs and develop individual implementation plans. The plans then served as the basis for an emerging regional level research agenda, research implementation plan and a documentation and dissemination strategy, through which the goals and strategies were communicated.

The innovation scaling-up model

Building on lessons learnt from its innovation and capacity-building experiences, MFC has integrated all its activities to form a new innovation scaling-up model. The ISM builds on the MFC operational model, where ongoing data collection on trends within the regional industry informs action-research. This research then results in innovative solutions that are subsequently disseminated through networking, training and consultancy services. After some time, such solutions can be evaluated and the results used to further inform regional good practice and standards.

The ISM reflects the process of the new product development cycle. It consists of four phases: 1) identification of the need for innovation; 2) the laboratory phase; 3) the adaptation phase; and 4) the scaling-up phase. The model works in such a way that the high cost of innovation is offset by breaking down the innovation development process into manageable stages. The network's comprehensive knowledge of the regional industry is used efficiently to allocate resources across different innovation development phases, identifying possibilities for cost savings and/or sharing. During the different phases, and working with well-selected partners, the network develops and analyzes new solutions to identify those that can be standardized and those that require customization on a case-by-case basis. This enables MFC to develop technical advice packages as part of the assistance it offers to a range of MFIs at low cost.

Identification of the need for innovation

The process starts with a comprehensive overview of the sector's current situation and trends. Since development of any new solution takes time and costs money,[6] it is important to consider the needs of, and benefits to, the industry in the longer term. It is also crucial to consider the cost of scaling-up the solution. All this needs to be taken into account to allow informed and controlled innovation development, leading to cost-effective solutions.

The difficulty in identifying latent needs in CEE and the NIS results from the newness of the industry and dynamic change within it. Many MFIs are still gaining experience and have been growing in different directions at different paces. As noted above, the industry is very diverse and consequently certain sub-regions are more or less developed than others. In the past MFC observed that demand for certain solutions demonstrated by more mature regions subsequently also became important in less developed ones. This is why MFC observes innovation in better-developed markets like Bosnia or the Caucasus, so that it can develop solutions of interest to other sub-regions like Central Asia. In some countries, the situation has not changed much for years due to regulatory constraints or other factors. Thus, innovation for those sub-sectors requires a different approach.

MFC, through its sector monitoring and analysis, as well as its ongoing field presence, has permanent access to necessary information. It is therefore in a position to identify burning issues within the industry today and to ensure that innovative solutions, when developed, will be highly relevant.

The testing phase

During testing, an idea is translated into a prototype solution, thereby operationalizing a theoretical framework through testing it in the field. The network chooses partner MFIs and other stakeholders to participate in action-research to develop the prototype using their expertise. Indeed, drawing on existing experience and expertise is one key area of concern. It is important to draw on global microfinance knowledge and similar solutions developed outside the microfinance sector to fully understand the needs and potential constraints to developing and implementing solutions. Networks are well positioned to obtain the required knowledge and information, thanks to established relationships with other stakeholders. They are able to select relevant information from existing resources and deliver it in the most effective format to MFIs engaging in innovation processes. This enables cost savings for MFIs who often do not have the capacity, resources or skills to filter the necessary information.

Another focus is upon selecting good partners for experimentation. The nature of experimentation implies selection of open-minded partners, pioneers in their area who have the interest and capacity to experiment as well as to overcome the consequences of potential failure. Networks are in a good position to select appropriate partners to maximize the benefits to themselves and the industry. Good selection is determined by comprehensive knowledge of local contexts, capacity of MFIs and their needs. A long-term relationship between the network and an MFI allows it to carefully manage the experimentation process and not overburden or negatively influence the institution. This is done through ongoing supervision, capacity building and help in problem solving.

The testing phase is the most risky because experimentation is an iterative process through which one tries to find the best way of translating ideas into practice. Developing practical solutions requires participatory processes involving MFIs at field level in order to monitor factors that influence the experiment's success or failure. The issue of confidentiality is particularly important during this phase, as competitive markets tend to be more innovative and/or more open to innovation. A balance has to be established between ensuring confidentiality of the partners and sharing practical examples of lessons learnt as a way to facilitate innovation by other MFIs.[7]

The adaptation phase

During the adaptation phase, innovative prototype solutions are further adapted to different operational contexts, taking into account the maturity and capacity of different MFIs. The goal is to identify features that can be standardized and to generate a protocol that will allow for cost-effective, customized solutions.

Again it is important to select MFIs that will be different enough from each other and representative enough of sub-regions of the regional sector. This is so that lessons learnt from the adaptation process can be generalized into a set of recommendations that, with customization, will allow every MFI to implement solutions without a problem.

The scaling-up phase

During this phase, the solutions developed are widely implemented across the region. For wide-scale implementation there is a need to strike a balance between customization and standardization in terms of cost-effectiveness. The sequencing activities presented above lead to standardized toolkits and a well-defined protocol for customized technical assistance and field coaching. The solutions that have proved to be successful are delivered on a cost-recovery basis to interested MFIs. The scaling-up phase consists of three parallel and sequential activities, as outlined below.

Market needs segmentation

Addressing the needs of similar groups among a diverse range of MFIs allows for cost saving. The outcomes of capacity building or innovation within one MFI can be of use to others with a similar profile, facing similar challenges and/or working in a similar context. This process adds value and maximizes benefits to individual MFIs.

Development of a balanced mix of services, including both standardized and customized products

Each market segment requires a different approach in terms of delivery of final solutions. Small, unsophisticated MFIs may require knowledge on principles that can be delivered through standardized packages, while more mature MFIs will require greater customization and will be faced with more complex problems. Across the region, MFC delivers ready-to-use solutions through its training and consulting arm. The training courses provide a general overview of the concept, main principles and practical tips for institutionalizing processes, as well as case study examples from regional MFIs. They are delivered in English, Serbo-Croatian, Russian and Polish by a network of 20 regional trainers and consultants. The courses, combined with customized technical assistance, help MFIs to implement solutions and adapt them to the context and capacity of their organizations. For example, having accomplished the successful adaptation of the AIMS-SEEP and MicroSave tools, MFC has been disseminating the client assessment methodology and tools through a series of open enrolment and in-house training courses, as well as on-site coaching and mentoring to assist with implementing the tools. The wide dissemination of adapted toolkits has advanced the limited knowledge on client assessment throughout the region and provided MFIs with the capacity to obtain client-level information and adjust their operations accordingly. Once developed, internal capacity has been used by many MFIs to further improve their operations.

To promote *Imp-Act* programme learning, apart from a series of briefing notes and reports, MFC has developed a Social Performance Assessment Training course.[8] The training serves as a social performance overview and helps managers to develop the system implementation plan and identify areas for more focused technical assistance follow up, where necessary.

Marketing and knowledge management

Since the ready-to-use solutions have been tested and proved successful, they serve as case studies to encourage other MFIs to invest in such solutions. However, marketing efforts need to start early on to prepare the market. Good regional knowledge and assessment of demand within the market enables the network to plan appropriate marketing strategies and to make sure needs are satisfied with timely, high-quality products.

While the training and TA services are the best way to deliver ready-to-use solutions to practitioners, it is important to engage early on in other dissemination and knowledge-sharing activities. This not only prepares the ground for later scaling-up solutions but also stimulates ongoing learning by project participants and the industry as a whole.

To manage regional knowledge and promote innovation MFC undertakes ongoing information-sharing on its activities through its website, publication of working reports and presentations, bimonthly MFC updates, regular project updates and electronic list serves. It conducts regional knowledge documentation and dissemination through the MFC semi-annual newsletter, annual conference and publications. In addition, global knowledge dissemination is undertaken through inviting interested MFIs and other organizations to the regional annual conference, publishing articles from outside the region through the MFC Newsletter, website and list serves, and translating key books and publications into Russian for dissemination across Russian-speaking countries.

Conclusion

The regional industries, with their specific characteristics, diversified contexts and operating bases of MFIs and/or other stakeholders, represent challenging environments for innovation and scaling-up. The diversity limits possibilities for pooling needs, necessitating customization that is particularly difficult in nascent and fragmented markets. This poses a challenge regarding the initial investment costs for developing new solutions. Hence, outside support is often needed to cover them.

To enable regional networks to successfully develop and promote innovation, a focus on ideas is needed that will lead to industry development. The regional network, thanks to its comprehensive regional knowledge, close links with various industry players and broad overview, easily identifies the most pressing needs for dynamic industry growth, as well as demand-driven solutions.

Also necessary is the sequencing of activities to develop and scale-up innovation and facilitate low-cost implementation across the region. The network, due to its unique position, has been able to develop innovative solution concepts through a participatory process with well-selected pioneering MFIs and other stakeholders. Action-research activities are valuable to test new concepts in real situations in the field, thereby minimizing potential failure. The network identifies approaches for adaptation of the solutions to different contexts, taking into account variables determining their viability, and thus further reducing the risk of failure in the region-wide scaling-up. Finding the right balance between standardization and customization of new solutions, and packaging the product to respond to various segments' needs, further increases the cost-effectiveness of the scaling-up phase.

Optimal allocation of regional resources within each of the sequenced phases is also a prerequisite for innovation. The network is well positioned to select relevant partners for different stages of the innovation development, thus increasing the likelihood of the success of each phase. It identifies a representative group of institutions for testing, making further generalization of results feasible.

Innovation also requires that there is provision of an ongoing knowledge-management platform for broader, deeper and faster learning. Through a sound understanding of the characteristics and operating context of each partner MFI, a network is well positioned to adjust its technical assistance to the required scope and scale in order to foster vertical learning. A network can decide what inputs are needed and how available resources can best be used and protected from risks. This is particularly important in the most common situation, where there are considerable resource constraints. Vertical learning is also beneficial to the network, as it can immediately apply lessons learnt in other vertical relationships, thus possibly resulting in cost savings.

Providing vehicles for information and a knowledge-sharing platform, a network can stimulate horizontal learning by allowing peers to exchange lessons learnt, to inspire new concepts and solutions, and to motivate each other. Having good linkages to different stakeholders and information on their activities both in the region and beyond, a regional network can keep everybody in the loop with regards to recent innovations and developments in the microfinance industry. Peer learning also has an important function as a quality check.

An additional requirement is the provision of ready-to-use, tested solutions that are attractive to MFIs, ensuring sustainability and low-cost scaling-up. Participatory and process-oriented action research, used both in the development and adaptation phases, strengthens the internal capacity of the MFIs and the network itself. While MFIs continue to use the solutions and work to improve them, they also serve as an example for other industry players. This demonstration effect allows the packaging of ready-to-use solutions as marketable products, and the network is ready to scale them up. Institutionalized skills at the network level, once developed, do not leave when the consultant does but remain available to any MFI in the present and future. Serving as a repository of technical skills and solutions development protocols, and being well grounded in the regional context, the network is always ready to provide necessary assistance whenever demand is manifest. This helps to overcome the challenge of the uneven level and pace of industry development.

To achieve innovation, cost-effective dissemination is also essential. A regional network can maximize the impact of new solutions and knowledge dissemination through coordinating various stakeholders' activities. It can promote the work, both within and beyond the regional industry, through its own network of partners. In turn, partner MFIs may disseminate the findings in local markets among their peers and local industry stakeholders. Such specialization helps to adjust the outputs to different audiences' needs and adds leverage to existing contacts and partnerships.

Lastly, facilitation of industry growth and the production of high quality solutions that benefit the client are essential if new ideas are to emerge. A main advantage of regional networks is their sincere interest in fostering regional development. Being distanced from vested interests at national-level politics, which can corrupt the network leadership seeking to capture advantage, the regional network can stay impartial and focus on maximizing benefits to the whole regional sector, not just certain groups of particular interest.

The example of MFC shows that strong regional networks with a focus on technical services have a comparative advantage in promoting and developing innovation, benefiting the whole regional sector in cost-effective ways. To achieve innovation and learning without the support of a strong network can be especially problematic in such challenging settings as those described in this case.

CHAPTER THIRTEEN
Client assessment lessons learned from the Small Enterprise Education and Promotion (SEEP) Network, USA[1]

Gary Woller

Introduction

This chapter summarizes the primary lessons in client assessment learned by the 17 MFIs that participated in the *Imp-Act* action-research project led by the Client Assessment Working Group (CAWG) of the Small Enterprise Education and Promotion (SEEP) Network. The SEEP Network is an organization of more than 50 North American private and voluntary organizations that support micro and small businesses and microfinance institutions in the developing world. Its mission is to advance the practice of micro and small enterprise development among its members, their international partners and other practitioners. It does this by providing a place for practitioners to come together to share institutional knowledge and establish best practices for the industry.

Background on SEEP and the CAWG

SEEP is a member-driven organization, meaning that its members determine its agenda and activities and produce its outputs. The primary vehicle for member participation in SEEP is the working group, which consists of a group of practitioners and practitioner organizations with a common interest to promote learning and action in a particular area. Members of the working group voluntarily donate their time and efforts to advance the group's action-research agenda, aided by a paid, part-time facilitator. Many of the documents (publications, guidelines, standards) produced by SEEP are products of working group efforts.

Currently SEEP has six working groups: 1) the client assessment working group; 2) the poverty assessment working group; 3) the financial services working group; 4) the consumer protection working group; 5) the business development services working group; and 6) the HIV/AIDS and microfinance development working group. CAWG, originally named the Client Impact Working Group, was formed in 2000 at the request of SEEP members interested in promoting learning and action in impact assessment. It has since evolved to reflect a wider set of interests among member institutions related to client assessment more generally.

The purpose of CAWG is to advance the frontiers of knowledge and practice among MFIs in all areas of client assessment, but especially in the areas of impact assessment, client monitoring and market research. CAWG accomplishes its purpose through: the exchange of ideas, experiences and other information with practitioner organizations; the development, testing and refining of client assessment tools and systems that are practitioner-friendly and that inform management decisions; and the promotion of client-centred practices that enhance social and economic impact.

CAWG study of client assessment processes

Consistent with its purpose, in 2000 CAWG received a grant from the *Imp-Act* programme to conduct a longitudinal study of the client assessment process of 17 MFIs. The purpose of the study was to observe the client assessment process over time at participating MFIs and from this experience to derive key lessons that could inform the client assessment process for other MFIs. The term process here refers to the many steps involved in client assessment beginning with planning and ending with management decision making and action. CAWG and *Imp-Act* were interested in how this process evolved over time, including the organizational structure, the planning and design, the obstacles encountered, the solutions and strategies implemented, the interaction between different levels of the organization and with external stakeholders, the tools and indicators implemented, the successes and failures, and the results.

The research methodology used by CAWG was to administer three in-depth questionnaires – including a baseline – to the 17 MFIs, hereafter referred to as CAWG research partners, at one-year intervals over a two-year period. Baseline questionnaires were completed during October of 2001 at the CAWG Client *Imp-Act* Workshop in Washington, DC. The second and third rounds of data collection took place during October–November 2002 and 2003. The questionnaires covered various topics, including client assessment objectives, primary audiences for client assessment information, feasible approaches to client assessment, client assessment indicators used, analysis of client assessment data, uses of client assessment information, and obstacles and challenges to client assessment.

The 17 CAWG research partners included two from Latin America, five from Africa, two from Central Asia, three from Asia and five from Central and Eastern Europe. The five research partners from Central and Eastern Europe were members of the MicroFinance Centre (MFC), based in Warsaw, Poland. Table 13.1 lists the CAWG research partners by region, country and (where relevant) their North American SEEP partner.

Responses to the three questionnaires were summarized by the CAWG facilitator and sent to CAWG members and research partners for comment and

Table 13.1 CAWG research partners

Research partner	Acronym	Country	SEEP partner
Latin America			
Avance Chalco	–	Mexico	Enterprise Development International
CRECER	–	Bolivia	Freedom from Hunger
Africa			
FOCCAS Uganda	FOCCAS	Uganda	Freedom from Hunger
First Allied Savings and Loan	FASL	Ghana	–
Sinapi Aba Trust	SAT	Ghana	Opportunity International
CRS Benin	–	Benin	Catholic Relief Services
Kenyan Rural Enterprise Programme	K-Rep	K-Rep	Plan
Central Asia			
Asian Credit Fund	ACF	Kazakhstan	Mercy Corps
National Association of Business Women	NABW	Tajikistan	Mercy Corps
Asia			
Activists for Social Alternatives	ASA	India	–
Nirdhan Utthan Bank Limited	Nirdhan	Nepal	Plan
Center for Rural and Agricultural Development	CARD	Philippines	Plan, Freedom from Hunger
Central and Eastern Europe			
Fund for Support of Microentrepreneurship	FORA	Russia	Opportunity International
ICMC–Demos Savings and Loan Cooperative	DEMOS	Croatia	–
The Integra Foundation	Integra	Slovakia	–
Prizma	–	Bosnia & Herzegovina	–
Partner	–	Bosnia & Herzegovina	–

follow-up. In May of 2004 representatives from SEEP, CAWG member organizations and CAWG research partners attended a workshop in Warsaw to review the questionnaire summaries and draft the outline of a book based on the summaries. This chapter presents one output from this process. Before presenting the main lessons learned, however, it will be instructive to define more clearly what is meant in this chapter by client assessment and how it both differs from, and is similar to, the more general framework of social performance management described in this book.

What is client assessment?

Client assessment is the term that refers to the process of gathering information about clients, analyzing the information and acting on the information. There are at least three generic approaches to client assessment: impact assessment, market research and client monitoring. Although distinct in many respects, in practice there is substantial crossover among the three approaches.

Impact assessment is the process of collecting information about clients' well-being and experience with the programme for the purpose of attributing – or proving – the impact of programme participation on clients, clients' enterprises, clients' households or the communities in which clients live. Market Research is the process of gathering information on clients' needs and wants, behaviours and perceptions for the purpose of improving market offerings and targeting effectiveness. Finally, client monitoring is the process of tracking changes in clients' profiles, well-being and behaviour for the purposes of monitoring changes in clients' socio-economic status and trends in market-related information.

As made explicit in the above definitions, client assessment is a process. It involves a number of steps that build on each other in a sequential and continuous manner. This was one of the primary lessons learned by CAWG research partner FOCCAS Uganda, which 'learned that client assessment is a continuous process – that is, one learning point and innovation lead to another and the process continues in a continuous cycle'. The client assessment process includes the following steps:

1. Articulation of the MFI's information needs in the context of its mission and strategic objectives.
2. Assessment of the MFI's resources and technical capacity.
3. Developing the research design, including the selection of indicators and assessment tools.
4. Data collection and quality control.
5. Data analysis.
6. Reporting.
7. Decision-making.
8. Communication of action plans to relevant stakeholders.
9. Implementation of action plans, including pilot-testing.

Comparing client assessment and social performance management

Client assessment is an iterative process that involves communication to and from stakeholders at every step or iteration. At all steps in the process, those responsible for client assessment need to communicate with relevant stakeholders and, where appropriate, make adjustments to the process based on stakeholder feedback. Experience and learning at each step are communicated to stakeholders and fed back into the process leading at the conclusion to a new iteration in which past experience and learning shape and drive the ongoing assessment process.

This definition of client assessment is in many ways remarkably similar to the definition of social performance management advanced in this book. Both refer to a system an organization uses to track, understand and improve social performance. Both include monitoring systems for tracking performance and decision-making systems for making sure that information gathered is used to improve performance. Both, moreover, explicitly link organizational outcomes to social mission and strategic objectives.

The principal difference between the two lies in their conceptual framework, a distinction perhaps of little practical interest to practitioners focused on the day-to-day 'reality' of field work, but of significant practical relevance to system design and function. Social performance management articulates an integrated, coherent and internally consistent framework for managing an organization's progress toward fulfilment of its social mission and social objectives. Whereas the experiences of the CAWG research partners offer practitioners useful lessons for improving the client assessment process, *Imp-Act*'s social performance management framework offers a useful and strategic format for nesting social performance within an organization's core management functions.

Obstacles to client assessment

Lack of technical capacity

CAWG research partners cited the lack of technical capacity as the most significant obstacle to client assessment. Within this category, the research partners cited the lack of data analysis skills as the greatest capacity deficit, followed by selecting/developing client assessment methodologies, learning and integrating qualitative research methods, identifying and selecting assessment indicators, designing sample methodologies, collecting and managing data, and planning and managing assessment logistics.

Doing good client assessment requires training and experience. The more complex the assessment methodology is, the more training and experience that is required. Client assessment, however, need not be complicated. In practice it ranges from the very simple (for example, customer suggestion boxes) to the very complex (for example, longitudinal impact studies). Any MFI can do client assessment and many probably already do it, but just do not think of it as such.

The objection that client assessment is too difficult for the 'typical' MFI is often based on stereotyped beliefs about client assessment. A common misperception, for example, is that client assessment has to involve expensive and complicated large-scale studies. The process can, however, be long or short. It can also be complicated or simple, theoretical or practical, expensive or inexpensive and one-off or routine. In short, client assessment can take any number of forms depending on the needs, resources, capacity and imagination of the MFI.

Citing the lack of technical capacity for not doing client assessment can equally be a statement of organizational priorities. MFIs routinely train credit officers, a clear statement of the importance the MFI attaches to the lending function and to doing it well. If client assessment is important, it is important to do it well. The extent to which management allocates resources to capacity development is likewise a clear statement of the importance it attaches to client assessment.

Lack of staff resources and time

According to CAWG research partners, the opportunity cost of staff time is more often than not the largest cost in client assessment. MFI staff are already stretched thin with barely enough time to perform daily tasks, let alone take on client assessment duties. MFIs often assign client assessment responsibilities to loan officers, who collect data at the loan application or during other routine interaction with clients. Grafting data collection onto loan officers' duties is a pragmatic and cost-effective approach to client assessment. Nonetheless, tasking loan officers with data collection can add significant additional demands on their time. It may only add a minute or two per client, but a minute or two times hundreds of clients adds up quickly and can be substantial in the aggregate.

Because loan officers are already busy, they are understandably resistant to additional demands on their time, particularly when they are not rewarded for doing client assessment work and when client assessment work takes time away from other duties for which they are rewarded. (See the case study in Box 13.1 for an exception to these general principles.) The perception that client assessment is an uncompensated burden is likely to create resistance among staff. Resistance in turn manifests itself through non- or half-hearted compliance and loss of staff morale.

Box 13.1

URWEGO is a Rwandan MFI. In the early stages of its client assessment work, URWEGO attempted to implement client surveys using field staff. To incentivize staff to collect the surveys, management offered them 100 Rwandan franks (approximately US$0.30) for each survey collected. Feedback from field staff, however, suggested that the incentive system was not well-received and failed to elicit the desired response. The field staff felt that if client assessment was important enough to do, it was important enough to include in their regular job duties. Field staff felt as if management was, in effect, bribing them for doing their job. This perception, and the time burden of survey collection, led to resistance toward client assessment among URWEGO field staff.

Solutions to this problem include integrating client assessment into staff incentive systems, more and better training, and involving management and staff earlier in the client assessment process, so as to increase their ownership of the process, or outsourcing. Unfortunately, while the solutions to this problem are reasonably straightforward, the implementation is not and it is a step on which many MFIs stumble.

Lack of funding

MFIs are typically resource constrained and many struggle to achieve financial sustainability. Many do not have substantial financial resources to invest in client assessment. There is no getting around the point that client assessment costs money. Money is needed for every step in the process. Many of the CAWG research partners benefited from generous grants from donors in developing their assessment processes, but most MFIs do not have access to such generous technical capacity or development grants earmarked for client assessment. They must fend for themselves from operational subsidies granted by donors or from financial surpluses created through operations.

The lack of funding for client assessment might also be a statement of organizational priorities. If management does not perceive client assessment as a core function, it will not allocate money to it. The lack of funding might also be explained in part by stereotyped perceptions of client assessment as costly, lengthy and impractical. This situation reinforces the need to demonstrate early on to management the usefulness of client assessment in terms of providing information that leads to management decisions and improved performance, as shown in by the case study in Box 13.2.

Box 13.2

The experience of the ASOMIF network in Nicaragua demonstrates how lingering stereotypes of client assessment can hinder assessment activity. Funded in part through *Imp-Act* money, via the CAWG, ASOMIF carried out several training sessions on client assessment tools for its member institutions. It was noted after the training that a number of the participant MFIs did not follow-up with field implementation of the tools. An inquiry into the reasons found that the lack of follow-up stemmed, among other reasons, from the negative perception of client assessment held by senior MFI managers. The managers equated client assessment with 'academic' research that they saw as having little practical value. To encourage member MFIs to implement the tools, ASOMIF senior staff organized a special half-day workshop with the executive directors of ASOMIF members to discuss post-training tool implementation. On hearing the many ways in which other member MFIs had used client information to make changes in their organizations, a number of executive directors were surprised that the tools could produce such useful information. They subsequently committed to follow-up the training with field implementation.

Lessons learned

Uses of client assessment

A major lesson learned by CAWG research partners is that client assessment is an effective means to improve management decision-making and action. Overall, the 17 research partners made nearly 60 programme changes over three years based directly or indirectly on client assessment information and falling broadly into one of three categories: 1) product and service innovations; 2) modifications to the terms and conditions of products and services; and 3) modifications to institutional policies and practices. Research partners also cited client assessment's use for fundraising and public relations as yet another benefit. Client assessment is useful for informing both small and major programme changes, as illustrated by the case study in Box 13.3.

> **Box 13.3**
>
> CARD, in the Philippines, seeks to expand its programme and services to poor women using a modified Grameen Bank methodology. To achieve this goal, CARD continually examines its systems, policies and procedures so as to identify and redress bottlenecks that hinder the efficient and effective delivery of its financial services. On observing the methodology of ASA, Bangladesh, CARD management and staff were so impressed with its simplicity and cost-effectiveness that management investigated ways to integrate the ASA methodology into CARD's lending programme. To this end, CARD has implemented a number of assessment activities, including staff workshops, focus group discussions assessing clients' perceptions of CARD and satisfaction with CARD's current policies, client participatory discussions assessing CARD's market positioning relative to competitors, and a staff satisfaction survey. Based on assessment findings, CARD pilot-tested the ASA methodology in new branches and started a process of adopting ASA principles in existing branches, where appropriate, with the eventual objective of implementing the changes organization-wide.

Integrating client assessment into organizational planning and strategy

One of the key lessons learned by CAWG research partners is that the usefulness of client assessment depends on the extent to which it is an extension of institutional strategy. Conducted properly, client assessment is a tool to carry out institutional strategy in that it is designed to answer specific, pertinent questions to inform management decision-making and action.

NABW in Tajikistan and ACF in Kasakhstan are two examples of CAWG partners that consciously integrate client assessment into institutional strategy. Prior to implementing a client assessment tool, NABW convenes an orientation meeting with management and the board of directors to discuss the proposed tool, the purpose for implementing it, the specific questions to be addressed and the strategy for implementation. ACF conducts a thorough institutional analysis of its institutional strategy and its business and marketing plans before embarking on client assessment. It then plans client assessment activities so as to answer key questions raised during this vetting process.

Proving versus improving impact

Several CAWG research partners underwent an evolution from a proving approach to client assessment to an improving approach. This was not an accident but a result of lessons learned at different points during the assessment process. Driven by the need to deliver better products and services and staunch the exodus of clients, MFIs are increasingly demanding cost-effective client assessment tools that yield timely and useful information. For the same reasons, the demand for complex impact assessments has fallen.

In the first CAWG *Imp-Act* questionnaire, research partners rated demonstrating the impact of their programmes as the most important client assessment objective. By the second and third questionnaires, however, proving impact had receded in importance, being replaced by a number of objectives that fell broadly under the category of market research. Most frequently-cited objectives within this category were assessing and serving clients' needs and wants, tracking and reducing client dropout and assessing and improving client satisfaction. Box 13.4 illustrates this process for NABW.

Box 13.4

NABW in Tajikistan is a CAWG research partner whose client assessment objectives evolved over time. In the first *Imp-Act* questionnaire, NABW said its primary client assessment objective was 'to assess the nature and extent of change in clients' households and enterprises as a result of programme participation'. By the final questionnaire, it cited the same objectives, but with an important qualifier, 'What has changed is that NABW now explicitly recognizes an "improving" role for client assessment, whereas its original response suggested only a "proving" role. That is, it is now interested in understanding how impact is related to specific programme attributes, such as loan size and terms and types of services offered. This is a subtle, but significant, shift'.

Not one of the 17 CAWG research partners cited statistical validity as a client assessment objective, while all 17 expressed a preference for feasibility over scientific validity. CRECER's (Bolivia) response was typical: 'Management is willing to sacrifice scientific validity for lower cost and is much less interested in the precision of the information than in whether it's useful'. This is not to suggest that rigorous impact assessments are redundant. Impact assessments will continue to be relevant to MFIs, donors and investors for whom understanding and demonstrating the impact of their programmes remains a key strategic objective. However, the emphasis is increasingly on attaining standards of statistical validity that meet the needs of management.

Building internal staff capacity

CAWG research partners consistently cited the need to build internal client assessment as one of the main lessons learned. Responses related to staff capacity generally fell under one of two categories: technical capacity (research design, data collection, data management and data analysis) or resource capacity (staff time).

The lack of staff capacity can pose seemingly insurmountable obstacles to client assessment, but it need not. Keys to overcoming capacity constraints include strategic planning, a realistic assessment of staff resources and technical capacity, adequate training and hiring of staff with the appropriate technical skills. A few simple questions can help the MFI address staff capacity issues:

- What technical skills, resources and time are required to collect, manage, analyze and use the data?
- What is the current level of staff technical skills and resources?
- Is it possible to train staff to acquire the appropriate skills? If so, how, where and at what cost?
- Can client assessment processes be integrated into staff job descriptions and routines without unreasonably burdening staff?

For some MFIs, the preferred approach to staff capacity issues is to assign client assessment duties to a core group of staff. Better yet is to create a separate assessment unit within the MFI. Generally, it is expected that as MFIs move up the learning curve, they will seek to create specialized resources responsible for client assessment. Such approaches, however, are not always feasible, particularly among smaller and inexperienced MFIs. Nor is it necessarily a good idea to cut loan officers or other field staff out of the client assessment process. Field staff have good direct knowledge of clients because they are in constant contact with them. Thus, for many MFIs it makes practical and strategic sense to use field staff as the focal point for data-gathering. It can also be an important component of a strategy to create a customer-oriented organizational culture.

Outsourcing

Conducting all client assessment functions in-house is one way to manage the process, but where MFIs do not have the requisite skills or resources, they may want to consider outsourcing one or more assessment tasks. Outsourcing, however, carries its own set of challenges and risks. It is important to maintain regular communication with external entities to ensure that the mission and goals of the MFI guide assessment activities. The MFI also needs to ensure that the client information is timely and is fed into the organizational feedback loop and internalized. There is also the risk that the external entities may not deliver.

The experiences of SAT in Ghana and Avance Chalco in Mexico illustrate these risks. SAT outsourced data analysis and reporting of its SEEP/AIMS impact assessment to external consultants.[2] The consultants failed to provide timely reports. As a result, the client information was not integrated into SAT's feedback loop and used to inform management decision-making. Avance Chalco outsourced the pilot test of its assessment tools to students from a local university. In the middle of the pilot test, the students pulled out and Avance Chalco was unable to complete the test due to pressing operational demands. Following these experiences, a general recommendation is that MFIs contracting with external stakeholders clearly define in advance what is expected of them and set out feasible timelines for completion of work.

Training

CAWG research partners rated the need for client assessment training as the single most important lessons learned over the three years of the project. According to the partners, training is needed in *all* areas of client assessment, even the apparently simplest of tasks, but particularly in data collection and data analysis.

With only one exception (Avance Chalco), each of the CAWG research partners received some form of client training focused overwhelmingly on market research tools. Overall, the research partners found the training very useful in gaining the necessary skills to conduct client assessment, jump-starting the client assessment process at their institutions or convincing management of the value of client assessment.

Good practice in client assessment

Start small and simple

A recommendation made repeatedly by CAWG research partners was to start with a small and manageable study. They highlighted the need to identify a small set of questions of strategic importance and design a simple methodology to answer the questions based on a realistic assessment of organizational resources and capacities. The case study of FOCCAS in Box 13.5 illustrates this principle.

Box 13.5

To assess the impact of its revised group lending programme, FOCCAS placed client issues on the agenda at all monthly branch meetings so that field officers could raise and discuss client concerns and feedback about loan products. FOCCAS accountants next developed a chart for tracking and monitoring clients' borrowing trends to assess whether or not clients were receiving adequate levels of financing. Findings suggest that the improved group lending product has allowed women to secure reasonable amounts of funding for their enterprises.

To avoid taking on too much at once, it helps to ask the following questions:

1. *What are the most important issues facing the organization?* The first step is to decide on a small set of questions of strategic importance to the organization. This is perhaps the most important step in the assessment process, as the questions to be addressed will in turn drive the assessment process, including the choice of indicators and assessment tools, the data analysis, the reporting and the decision-making.
2. *Is the information already available from an internal source?* Another important initial step in the process is to take a careful look at the client information already being collected by the organization. All MFIs collect information on clients in the regular course of operations, including information on client demographics (such as gender, location, household size), households (income, expenditures), enterprises (sales, profits, employment, sector) and programme participation (loan cycles, repayment record, loan products). Much of this information is valuable for client assessment purposes.
3. *What skills and resources does the organization have and what methods can most effectively build on these?* The MFIs noted the importance of assessing available resources and skills for formulating assessment plans accordingly. There is ample time to increase the cost and complexity of the assessment process in the future as the MFI's skills and resources increase with time and experience. Starting small initially will increase the probability of success, and success will increase the organization's commitment to the process and its willingness to invest time, resources and training in it.

Institutionalizing client assessment

A recurrent theme coming from CAWG research partners was the need to institutionalize client assessment. Institutionalization refers to the integration of client assessment into organizational routines and operations, and to the creation of a customer-oriented culture. The institutionalization of client assessment often entails its integration into the organization's computerized management information system (MIS). When asked what their client assessment objectives were for the coming years, the objective CAWG research partners cited most frequently was to do this, thereby embedding it into organizational systems and procedures and by making possible routine and timely collection, analysis and use of client data. As Nirdhan in Nepal noted: 'embedding client assessment into the MIS is part of incorporating it into core operations. We see the need to adapt the MIS to collect more information. Thus computerizing information collection is a priority – it has to be part of the management system'.

Importance of management and staff 'buy-in'

CAWG research partners repeatedly cited the need for management and staff to 'buy-in' to the client assessment process. To create buy-in among management, it is imperative to involve them from the beginning of the client assessment process. Staff should be involved early on in the process as well. Because staff are closest to the clients, they are in a position to provide unique insights on client assessment design, planning and implementation. The opportune time to involve staff and their degree of involvement will vary depending on the circumstances.

Buy-in requires that management and staff see a direct connection between client assessment and organizational performance. If they do not, they are likely to perceive client assessment as an expense line item or as a burden. Alternatively, involving management and staff in the client assessment development and planning process increases the likelihood that they come to see client assessment as a core activity. Also important to create buy-in is timely feedback on data collection activities, timely reporting of findings and evidence that the MFI uses client information.

A risk of involving management and staff in the different stages of the client assessment process is burn-out. At Prizma in Bosnia and Herzegovina, DEMOS in Croatia and Integra in Slovakia, for example, client assessment work consumed excessive amounts of management and staff time, leading Prizma to suspend certain assessment activities for a time, while at DEMOS it became increasingly difficult to motivate staff to take on the additional work load. Their experience serves as a reminder that it is always necessary to balance client assessment activities with organizational needs and priorities, as shown in Box 13.6.

> **Box 13.6**
>
> DEMOS involved management and staff in all steps of the client assessment process, including setting research objectives, designing client monitoring forms, conducting research and data analysis. This approach proved critical in creating enthusiasm for client assessment, helped make the research more consistent and meant that the findings were immediately applied to a range of products and services.
>
> Prizma's senior managers and branch managers participated in all planning/strategy meetings for client assessment and in tool training sessions. Branch managers also played the key role in organizing and implementing customer satisfaction FGDs. Field staff were not involved in the planning/development stage to the same extent. They were brought into the process later during the implementation phase and are now tasked with implementing client exit monitoring and collecting information for the poverty scorecard via the loan application.

Conclusion

The experience of the CAWG research partners provides valuable insights into the client assessment process. They learned that client assessment is not easy and there are many obstacles to be overcome, particularly related to lack of staff capacity, lack of staff resources and time and lack of funding. However, they also learned that these obstacles are not insurmountable and that the key to overcoming them is careful planning. Planning for client assessment includes, first and foremost, integrating it into the MFI's strategic planning process. It requires asking a few simple questions early in the process about the MFI's information needs, its technical capacity and its available human and financial resources. Technical capacity should not be taken as a given. Building the MFI's capacity to do client assessment is important; so important that it was the lesson learned cited most often by CAWG research partners.

CAWG research partners also learned about the virtues of starting with small and manageable studies. They learned that client assessment includes a wide range of approaches and that different approaches are appropriate for different organizations and that they change over time within an MFI commensurate to the MFI's experience and resources. They learned about the importance of institutionalizing client assessment through creating a supporting organizational culture and through integrating it into organizational systems and processes. They further learned that creating a successful client assessment process requires that management and staff buy-in to the process.

CAWG research partners learned to refine their client assessment priorities and their information needs. They learned that client information needs to be useful; that proving impact, although important in itself, was less important to them than improving impact. Perhaps most importantly, however, CAWG research partners learned that client information does inform management decision-making, that it does lead to organizational change and that it does improve financial and social performance.

The experience of the CAWG research partners demonstrates that while microfinance is unique in many aspects, it is not so unique that client assessment is any less important than it is in other industries. Their experience also shows that client assessment is not just a line item in the expense ledger. It is an investment in improved financial and social returns. Client assessment is a core business activity, and as a core business activity, it is appropriate for all MFIs, regardless of their size, level of sophistication or resources.

Notes

1 From service providers to learning organizations: microfinance practitioners' experiences of social performance management

1. *Imp-Act* started as a five-year action-research programme funded by the Ford Foundation. At the heart of the programme were 30 organizations and networks whose proposals had been accepted during a preliminary phase. A core team of academics from the Institute of Development Studies (IDS) and Bath and Sheffield Universities engaged with the MFIs through workshops and visits. A secretariat coordinated the programme from IDS, while a steering committee of experts in the field and regional representatives met periodically to review progress and provide overall guidance. Copestake *et al* (2005) provide a fuller description.
2. These points are based on the closing remarks of Frank de Giovanni, of the Ford Foundation, at the final *Imp-Act* workshop held in Bath in September 2004.
3. For a list and description of all the organizations participating in *Imp-Act* see Copestake *et al* (2005) and the *Imp-Act* website at www.*Imp-Act*.org
4. See Greeley (2005).
5. A self-help group approach generally means that an MFI helps groups to manage and pool their own savings, rather than distributing loans itself.
6. The AIMS-SEEP tools are five 'practitioner-friendly' client assessment tools developed between SEEP and the 'Assessing the Impact of Microenterprise Services' project under USAID.
7. The CGAP PAT is a standardized tool to measure the relative poverty of microfinance clients.
8. The *MicroSave* Toolkit comprises 18 tools that help practitioners through aspects of market research.
9. See Knotts and Newland (2005).
10. More detailed guidelines are available in *Imp-Act*/MFC (2005).

2 Delivering inclusive microfinance with a poverty focus: the experience of the Bangladesh Rural Advancement Committee (BRAC)

1. This was financed out of the EC's humanitarian assistance component.
2. For example, female-headed household without any adult male support or households where the husband was disabled.

3   BRAC's major development programmes are funded by a donor consortium consisting of the UK Department for International Development (DFID), the Canadian International Development Agency (CIDA), the EC, Novib and the WFP. Currently there are two programmes being funded by this consortium: CFPR/TUP and BRAC's Education Programme. BRAC's microfinance programme has been totally self-financed since 2001.
4   BRAC's Research and Evaluation Division is carrying out various studies on this programme. On the targeting methodology and process see BRAC (2004a) and Matin and Halder (2004).
5   See BRAC (2001).
6   A comprehensive baseline study on the ultra poor was carried out. See BRAC (2004b) and Ahmed *et al* (2004).
7   For a study on how BRAC managed the scaling-up challenges of its IGVGD programme, see Matin and Yasmin (2004).

3 Institutionalizing a social performance management system at Lift Above Poverty Organization (LAPO), Nigeria

1   One study revealed that only 4.4 per cent of disbursement from a government credit fund was given to female farmers between 1979 and 1991 (Omoyon-Ita, 1992).
2   Accurate information on the scale of other MFIs currently operating in Nigeria is not available.
3   LAPO was incorporated in 1993 as a non-profit company limited by guarantee under the Company and Allied Matters Act of 1990.
4   In the beginning only the founder Godwin Ehigiamusoe was involved, but he later hired one female member of staff to follow-up on the collection of repayments from clients.
5   See CGAP (2000) and Omohan and Omorogbe (2004).
6   The client exit survey is tool number 2 of the AIMS-SEEP impact assessment tools manual (Nelson, 2000). The tools represent a mid-range approach to impact assessment that is cost-effective, useful and credible.

4 Cost effective impact management: the case of the Small Enterprise Foundation (SEF), South Africa

1   SEF uses the CGAP and Microcredit Summit definition of the 'very poor' as the bottom 50 per cent of those living below the national poverty line.
2   Data is from *MicroBanking Bulletin* sample of self-reporting MFIs (MicroBanking Bulletin, 2002). These are generally among the top performing in the industry and therefore do not represent an average for Africa overall.
3   In this paper the term 'impact management' is used rather than impact monitoring or impact assessment because SEF's approach incorporates both monitoring and assessment and because SEF's approach is best described this way.
4   See SEF (1999).
5   See McCord (2002); *Imp-Act* (2003).
6   SEF utilizes a system called participatory wealth ranking to identify the poorest households in its target area (see Gibbons *et al*, 1999).
7   See Copestake (2003).

8   A separate paper, Baumann (2004), for the *Imp-Act* programme investigates this issue in detail.

5 Methodological and organizational lessons from impact assessment studies: the case of SHARE, India

1   PRADAN is an Indian NGO that promotes microfinance through an SHG model and works in seven of the poorest states in India.
2   M-CRIL, a microfinance capacity assessment division of EDA Rural Systems, Delhi, conducted capacity assessment of SML. The rating report clearly states that SML has strong organizational, management and financial performance. SIDBI (Small Industries Development Bank of India) has appointed CRISIL, which is recognized by the Reserve Bank of India, and is one of the mainstream rating agencies in India to conduct the rating of SHARE Microfin Ltd. SML was ranked mfR3 on a scale from mfR1 (being the highest rating) to mfR10 (being the lowest rating).

6 The challenge of sustainability in India's poorest state: the case of the Centre for Youth and Social Development (CYSD)

1   As low as Rs15 (US$0.34) a day for women and Rs25 (US$0.57) for men.
2   SGSY is a very large rural poverty alleviation credit programme of the Indian government launched in April 1999. It promotes self-employment. Prior to 1999 the government implemented various rural development programmes, such as the Development of Women and Children in Rural Areas (DWCRA) and Training of Youth for Self-Employment (TRYSEM). These have now been integrated as the SGSY.
3   Although the study showed that there was distrust of moneylenders, new members often did not have any other choice if they needed financial support, and the SHGs of which they were part were still too new to provide a secure source of loans.
4   Response bias, as always, has to be taken into consideration for if someone from the SHG support organization asks you where you go to for loans, politeness requires that you respond 'to the SHG madam'.
5   Indigenous breed of chicken.
6   The ration cards are given by the government to below-poverty line households to enable them to access subsidized products, such as rice, sugar and kerosene. The ration shops are usually located at the *panchayat* headquarters, which may be located as far as 10 km from SHG members' villages. Those coming to the shop need to bring enough money for their full quota of rice, sugar and kerosene to make the journey worthwhile, since it would involve taking time off work. Thus being able to afford to go is a privilege mature members are able to enjoy. One interviewee in Koraput said that he was 'too poor to be poor', meaning that he could not afford the time and bribes required to get the card that certified that he was poor.
7   The *palli sabha* is the general body of a village or hamlet, where every adult in the settlement is a member. The Indian self-governance system provides for a three-tier system. The *gram sabha* is the assembly for a cluster of villages at the lowest level of the *gram panchayat*. Every village has a *palli sabha*, that sends its ward member to the *gram sabha* at the *panchayat*, which is headed by the *sarpanch*. The next level of governance is the *panchayat samitee*, attended by members of the local *gram pan-*

chayats and headed by the *panchayat samitee* chairman. The district level is known as the *zilla parishad* (or district council), represented by the *panchayat samitees* and headed by the *zilla parishad* chairman.

7 Institutionalizing internal learning systems: experiences from Professional Assistance for Development Action (PRADAN), India

1 *Munshi* is the Hindi word for 'accountant'. The Computer Munshi is a relatively better educated, entrepreneurially inclined individual drawn from an area of about 30–40 villages, equipped with a computer and SHG accounting software, and providing accounting and MIS services to 100–200 SHGs for a fee. In PRADAN there are currently 51 Computer Munshis.
2 A SHG cluster is a collective of 10–15 mature SHGs from neighbouring villages, whose selected representatives meet regularly to discuss and deliberate on issues that affect them individually or collectively.

8 Measuring and managing change in Bosnia-Herzegovina: Prizma's steps to deepen outreach and improve impact

1 See www.microsave.com for more details.
2 Between 1 per cent and 2 per cent portfolio-at-risk, 1–180 days.
3 While there is scant evidence across the industry confirming the financial implications of high dropout, Prizma's initial use of activity-based costing confirmed the significant cost of client dropout after the first loan cycle. Dropout is a considerable problem in Bosnia-Herzegovina given significant competition, limited service options for microfinance institutions under the law and relatively high financial literacy among low-income people.
4 For more on exit monitoring, see Matul and Vejzovic (2004).
5 The Living Standards Measurement Study was established by the World Bank in 1980 to explore ways of improving the type and quality of household data collected by government statistical offices in developing countries.
6 Given the very complex nature of inter-household poverty, the scorecard focuses on poverty status at the household level.
7 Developed with assistance from CGAP, activity-based costing has enabled Prizma to understand the more accurate price of its products and its cost structure more generally.
8 Efforts to improve efficiency are focused not on loan balance, which does have a fundamental bearing on efficiency ratios, but on activities associated with targeting, attracting, serving and retaining the poorest clients.
9 There is now significant evidence that credit card companies' use of credit scoring has led to deeper outreach in highly developed financial markets in Europe and North America.
10 PAR 31–180 days, loans disbursed, client caseload (per product) and dropout. Additionally, depth is monitored and rewarded non-financially.
11 Emphasizing write-off as a longer-term measure of portfolio quality allows branch staff (and their supervisors) to manage arrears flexibly, to set priorities and accommodate the special circumstances of poor clients. Administrative efficiency was chosen because it allows comparison of efficiency across all branches without

having to adjust for each branch's cost of funds borrowed internally from headquarters – something that is heavily influenced by age and maturity of a branch.
12 Performance is measured against historic benchmarks rather than targets set by branch teams themselves, to mitigate the risk of 'gaming' – over- or under-targeting – that can result when teams or individuals are rewarded for performance towards targets they have been tasked with setting.
13 Prizma's external auditor confirms performance results at the end of the year to ensure transparency and objectivity before the board of directors approves the bonus.

9 Achieving the double bottom line: a case study of Sinapi Aba Trust's (SAT) client impact monitoring system, Ghana

1 See McCord (2002); see also *Imp-Act* (2003) on feedback loops.
2 See McCord (2002); Cohen (2003); *Imp-Act* (2003).

10 Institutionalizing feedback from clients using credit association meetings: the experience of FOCCAS, Uganda

1 FOCCAS is registered as Company Limited by Guarantee Not Having Share Capital. This legal structure involves subscribers but not shareholders. The two subscribers represent the two founding organizations: the Foundation for Credit and Community Assistance and Freedom from Hunger. Past donor grants form its equity base and in 2003 some 75 per cent of its assets were funded by loans.
2 FFH investigated the costs of adding the education component to four MFIs using the Credit with Education methodology in the mid-1990s. This included the extra costs of training for field agents, time for delivering the sessions at the meetings and extra monitoring and reporting. It also included the additional cost of time for the head office staff (trainers, bookkeepers) to carry out work associated with the education service. New, medium and older MFIs were analyzed to get a sense of the cost variance across a mix of institutions. The cost ranged from 5 per cent to 10 per cent of total operating costs.
3 See www.microlinks.org for more details.

11 Microfinance networks and the evaluation of social performance: the case of FINRURAL, Bolivia

1 The current members of the FINRURAL network are: Asociación Nacional Ecuménica de Desarrollo (ANED); Centro de Investigación y Desarrollo Regional (CIDRE); Crédito con Educación*(CRECER); Fondo Rotativo de Inversión y Fomento (DIACONIA-FRIF); PROMUJER-Bolivia*; Fondo de Desarollo Comunal (FONDECO); Fundación para Alternativas de Desarollo (FADES); Instituto para el Desarollo de la Pequeña Unidad Productiva (IDEPRO); Servicios Financieros Rurales (SARTAWI); Fondo de Credito Solidário (FONCRESOL); Fundación Boliviana para el Desarollo de la Mujer (FUNBODEM)*; Fundación Boliviana para el Desarollo (FUBODE); Incubadora de Microempresas Productivas (IMPRO); Organización de la Mujer em Desarollo (OMED)*. The organizations asterisked are women-only.

2   The MFIs evaluated by means of impact assessment studies were: CRECER, PROMUJER-Bolivia, FADES, DIACONIA-FRIF, FIE*, Ecofuturo*, Trinidad** and Comarapa**. The entities marked * are *fondos financieros privados* (see note 2 above) and those marked ** are credit cooperatives.
3   For more information on what has already been achieved in this direction, and for further discussion of cost-effectiveness, see Marconi and Mosley (2003) and (2004).
4   Two of the most successful institutions in bucking the 1999–2003 recession – CRECER and PROMUJER – are members of the FINRURAL consortium, and a third, FIE, although a FFP (see footnote 2) and thus not a member of the consortium, nonetheless was a participant in the first round of impact assessment surveys.

12 The potential of regional networks to stimulate innovation in microfinance: lessons from the Microfinance Centre (MFC) in Eastern Europe

1   More information on MFC can be found at www.mfc.org.pl
2   Project learning with regard to poverty scoring, cost-effective qualitative research for client assessment, exit monitoring and satisfaction measurement, as well as their use and institutionalization in various regional MFIs, has been summarized in 11 MFC Spotlight Notes available from www.mfc.org and www.imp-act.org
3   More information on regional microfinance can be found in Forster *et al* (2003).
4   The average age of an operationally self-sufficient regional MFI is three to four years as compared to five to seven years for the best performing MFIs worldwide (Foster *et al*, 2003).
5   For more information on the projects, lessons learnt and scope please see www.mfc.org, and in particular Pawlak *et al* (2000) and Matul and Pawlak (2001).
6   An action-research project cycle takes one to three years to complete.
7   More discussion on important factors for networks managing regional-level innovation development can be found in Cohen (2004).
8   The training was pilot-tested in September 2004.

13 Client assessment lessons learned from the Small Enterprise Education and Promotion (SEEP) Network, USA

1   This chapter is based on a version published in *Building Successful Microfinance Institutions through Client Assessment*, 2005, SEEP, Washington.
2   The impact survey is one of the AIMS-SEEP tools. Other than the impact survey, the AIMS-SEEP tools include exit surveys, client satisfaction focus group discussions, empowerment interviews, and loans, savings and profits use over time interviews (see www.microlinks.org).

References

Ahmed, S.M., Hadi, A. and Rana, M. (2004) *Customized Development Intervention for the Ultra Poor: Does it Make Any Difference in their Health, Consumption and Health-Seeking Behaviour? Preliminary Change Assessments 2002 to 2004*, unpublished paper presented at the October BRAC DCM.

Barrès, I. (2002) Bulletin highlights, *MicroBanking Bulletin No. 8*, The MiX, Washington DC.

Baumann, T. (2004) *Imp-Act* cost effectiveness study of the Small Enterprise foundation, South Africa, *Small Enterprise Development Journal*, Vol. 15, No. 3.

Bosogno, M. and Chong, A. (2002) Poverty and inequality in Bosnia and Herzegovina after the Civil War, *World Development Journal*, Vol. 30, No. 1.

BRAC (2001) *Challenging the Frontiers of Poverty Reduction: Targeting the Ultra Poor – Targeting Social Constraints, Proposal Overview*, Research and Evaluation Division, BRAC, Bangladesh.

BRAC (2004a) Stories of targeting: process documentation of selecting the ultra poor, *CFPR/TUP Working Paper Series*, No. 1, Research and Evaluation Division, BRAC, Bangladesh.

BRAC (2004b) *Towards a Profile of the Ultra Poor in Bangladesh: Findings from CFPR/TUP Baseline Survey*, Research and Evaluation Division, BRAC, Bangladesh.

Chambers, R. (1983) *Rural Development: Putting the Last First*, Longman, London.

Chowdhury, N.S. (2000) *Listening to the Extreme Poor: IGVGD Participants Speak on their Success*, Research and Evaluation Division, BRAC, Bangladesh.

Cohen, M. (2002) Making microfinance more client led, *Journal of International Development*, Vol. 14, No. 3.

Cohen, M. (2004) *Review of the Microfinance Centre: Adapting the Feedback Loop to the Assessment of a Network*, unpublished *Imp-Act* report, Brighton.

Consultative Group to Assist the Poor (2000) *Assessing the Relative Poverty of Microfinance Clients: A CGAP Operational Tool*, International Food Policy Research Institute, Washington DC (overview available at www.cgap.org).

Consultative Group to Assist the Poor (2003) *CGAP Phase III Strategy: 2003–2008*, CGAP, Washington DC (available at http://www.cgap.org/docs/CGAP_III_Strategy.pdf).

Copestake, J. (2000) Impact assessment of microfinance and organizational learning: who will survive?, *Journal of Microfinance* Vol. 2, No. 2.

Copestake, J. (2003) Simple standards or burgeoning benchmarks? Institutionalizing social performance monitoring, assessment and auditing of microfinance, *IDS Bulletin* Vol. 34, No. 4.

Copestake, J., Greeley, M., Kabeer, N. and Simanowitz, A. (eds) (2005) *Money with a Mission: Microfinance and Poverty Reduction*, Intermediate Technology Development Publications, Rugby.

Cortijo, M.J.A. and Kabeer, N. (2004) *Wider Impacts of SHARE Microfin Limited (SML), Andhra Pradesh*, unpublished paper, *Imp-Act*, Brighton.

Deaton, A. (2001) *Computing Prices and Poverty Rates in India, 1999–2000*, Research Program in Development Studies Paper, Princeton University.

Dunn, E. and Tvrtkovic, J. (2003) *Microfinance Clients in Bosnia and Herzegovina: Report on Baseline Survey*, Foundation for Sustainable Development of the Federation of Bosnia and Herzegovina (available at http://www.odraz.ba/Documents/LIPII_Report_on_BaselineFindings.pdf).

FINRURAL (2003a) *Impactos Agregados de las Microfinanzas en Bolivia*, FINRURAL, La Paz.

FINRURAL (2003b) *Sistematización Metodológica de Evaluación de Impactos en Microfinanzas*, FINRURAL, La Paz.

Forster S., Greene S. and Pytkowska J. (2003) *The State of Microfinance in CEE and the NIS*, MFC and CGAP, Washington DC.

Gibbons, D., Simanowitz, A. and Nkuna, B. (1999) *Poverty-Targeting Tools: An Operational Manual*, CASHPOR inc., Kuala Lumpar.

Government of India (2002a) *Ministry of Finance Economic Survey 2001–2002*, Ministry of Finance, New Delhi.

Government of India (2002b) *National Human Development Report 2001*, Ministry of Finance Planning Commission, New Delhi.

Greeley, M. (2005) Sustainable poverty outreach, in Copestake, J., Greeley, M., Kabeer, N. and Simanowitz, A. (eds) (2005) *Money with a Mission: Microfinance and Poverty Reduction*, Intermediate Technology Development Publications, Rugby.

Halder, S. and Husain, A.M.M. (2001) *The Extreme Poor and their Development Needs: Results of an Exploratory Study in Bangladesh*, Research and Evaluation Division Paper, BRAC, Bangladesh.

Hashemi, S. (2001) Linking microfinance and safety net programmes to include the poorest, *CGAP Focus Note*, No. 21 (available at http://www.cgap.org/docs/FocusNote_21.pdf).

Hulme, D. (2000) Impact assessment methodologies for microfinance: theory, experience and better practice, *World Development Journal*, Vol. 28, No. 1.

Imp-Act (2003) The feedback loop: responding to client needs, *Practice Note No. 1*, *Imp-Act*, Brighton (available at http://www.imp-act.org).

Imp-Act (2004) QUIP: The qualitative individual in-depth interview protocol, *Practice Note No.2, Imp-Act*, Brighton (available at http://www.imp-act.org).

Imp-Act/Microfinance Centre for Central and Eastern Europe and the New Independent States (MFC) (2005) *Guidelines for Social Performance Management in Microfinance*, *Imp-Act*, Brighton.

International Institute for Population Sciences (IIPS) (2001) *India National Family Health Survey-2*, IIPS, Mumbai.

Khandker, S. (2003) Micro-finance and poverty: evidence using panel data from Bangladesh, *World Bank Policy Research Working Paper 2945*, World Bank, Washington DC.

Kline, S. (2003) Sustaining social performance: institutionalizing organizational learning and poverty outreach at Prizma, *IDS Bulletin*, Vol. 34, No. 4.

Knotts, K. and Newland, J. (2005) From service providers to learning organizations: an examination of the *Imp-Act* action research process, *Occasional Paper No. 4, Imp-Act*, Brighton (available from http://www.imp-act.org).

Kumar, M.U. (1998) *Growing Stronger with our Members: Microfinance at SHARE*, paper presented at Bankers' workshop on 'Kick-starting Microfinance, A Challenge for the Indian Banks', Institute for Rural Development, Lucknow.

Kumar, S. (2001) *Study of Political Systems and Voting Behaviour of the Poor of Orissa*, DFID, New Delhi.

Marconi, R. and Mosley, P. (2003) *Towards a Macroeconomics of Microfinance*, unpublished paper, *Imp-Act*, Brighton.

Marconi, R. and Mosley, P. (2004) The FINRURAL impact assessment service: a cost-effectiveness analysis, *Small Enterprise Development*, Vol. 15, No. 3.

Matin, I. (2002) Targeted development programmes for the extreme poor: experiences from BRAC experiments, *CPRC Working Paper No. 20*, Chronic Poverty Research Centre, University of Manchester (available at http://www.chronicpoverty.org/cp20.htm).

Matin, I. and Begum, S.A. (2002) *Assessing the Extreme poor: Experiences and Lessons from a BRAC Project*, Research and Evaluation Division, BRAC, Bangladesh.

Matin, I. and Halder, S. (2004) Combining methodologies for better targeting of the extreme poor, *CFPR/TUP Working Paper Series No. 2*, Research and Evaluation Division, BRAC, Bangladesh.

Matin, I. and Yasmin, R. (2004) Managing the scaling up challenges of a programme for the poorest: lessons from BRAC's experiences with the IGVGD, in CGAP (2004) *Scaling Up of Poverty Reduction: Case Studies in Microfinance*, CGAP, Washington DC (available at http://www.cgap.org/docs/CaseStudy_scalingup.pdf).

Matul, M. and Kline, S. (2003) Scoring change: Prizma's approach to assessing poverty, *MFC Spotlight Note No. 4*, MFC, Warsaw (available at http://www.mfc.org.pl/doc/Research/ImpAct/SN/MFC_SN04_eng.pdf).

Matul, M. and Pawlak, K. (2001) *Poverty, Microenterprise and Microfinance in the Eyes of the Rural Poor in the Region of Northwest Poland: Implications for Polish Rural Development Foundation Microlending Program*, MFC, Warsaw.

Matul, M. and Vejzovic, S. (2004) Beyond numbers: Prizma's exit monitoring system, *MFC Spotlight Note No.10*, MFC, Warsaw (available at http://www.mfc.org.pl/research).

McCord, M. (2002) *The feedback loop: a process for enhancing responsiveness to clients*, unpublished paper, *MicroSave*, Kenya and *Imp-Act*, Brighton.

Microbanking Bulletin (2002) Data from Microbanking Bulletin of self-reporting MFIs, *Microbanking Bulletin No. 8*, The MiX, Washington DC.

Morduch, J. (1999) The microfinance promise, *Journal of Economic Literature*, Vol. 37, No. 4.

Nègre, A. and Maguire, K. (2002) Comparing apples to oranges: using MFI rating, *MicroBanking Bulletin* No. 8, The MiX, Washington DC.

Nelson, C. (2000) *Learning from clients: assessment tools for microenterprise practitioners*, Small Enterprise Education and Promotion Network, AIMS, Washington DC (available at www.seepnetwork.org).

Nwabuzor, E.J. and Garuba, A.S. (2004) *Findings from the Client Exit Study of Lift Above Poverty Organization, Nigeria 2003*, unpublished report, LAPO, Nigeria.

Omohan, M.E. and Omorogbe, S.K. (2004) *An Assessment of Relative Poverty of Lift Above Poverty Organization's Clients on Behalf of the Consultative Group to Assist the Poorest (CGAP) Sponsored Survey*, unpublished report, CGAP, Washington DC.

Omoyon-Ita (1992) *Access of Women to the Government Promoted Agricultural Credit Guarantee Scheme Fund*, paper presented at the conference organized by Development Finance Department, Central Bank of Nigeria.

Pawlak, K. et al (2000) *Aims and MFC Impact Assessment Project: Tools Testing in the Region of Central and Eastern Europe and the New Independent States*, MFC, Warsaw.

Pritchett, L. (2002) It pays to be ignorant: a simple political economy of rigorous program evaluation, *Journal of Policy Reform*, Vol. 5, No. 4.

Rangacharyulu, S.V. (2004) *A Report on Targeting of and Dropouts Among SML Clients*, unpublished report, National Institute for Rural Development/*Imp-Act*, Brighton.

Rhyne, E. (2001) *Mainstreaming Microfinance: How Lending to the Poor Began, Grew and Came of Age in Bolivia*, Kumarian Press Inc, Bloomfield.

Robinson, M. (2001) *The Microfinance Revolution: Sustainable Finance for the Poor*, The World Bank and Open Society Institute, USA.

Rutherford, S. (1999) *The Poor and Their Money: An Essay About Financial Services for Poor People*, Institute of Development Policy and Management, University of Manchester (available at http://www.undp.org/sum/MicroSave/ftp_downloads/rutherford.pdf).

SAT (2004) *Final Report, Impact Assessment Findings, Using the AIMS-SEEP Tools*, Sinapi Aba Trust.

Sattar, M.G., Chowdhury, N.S. and Hossain, M.A. (1999) *Food Aid and Sustainable Livelihoods: BRAC's Innovations Against Hunger*, Research and Evaluation Division, BRAC, Bangladesh.

Schreiner, M. (2001) Seven aspects of loan size, *Journal of Microfinance*, Vol. 3, No. 2 (available at http://www.microfinance.com/English/Papers/Aspects_of_Loan_Size.pdf.).

Schreiner, M., Michal, M., Pawlak, K. and Kline, S. (2005) *The Power of Prizma's Poverty Scorecard: Lessons for Microfinance*, MFC Spotlight Note, MFC, Warsaw.

Sebstad, J. and Cohen, M. (2001) *Microfinance, Risk Management and Poverty, AIMS Project Report*, Management Systems International, Washington DC (available at www.mip.org).

Sharma, M., Rangacharyulu, S.V., Hanumantha, R.K. and Reddy S. (2000) *Assessing the Relative Poverty Level of MFI Clients: Development of an Operational Tool*, Synthesis report for the case study of SHARE, India, CGAP, Washington DC.

Simanowitz, A. (2001) From event to process: current trends in microfinance impact assessment, *Small Enterprise Development*, Vol. 12, No. 4.

Small Enterprise Education and Promotion Network (2005) *Building Successful Microfinance Institutions Through Client Assessment*, SEEP, Washington DC.

Small Enterprise Foundation (1999) *Understanding Impact: Experiences and Lessons from the Small Enterprise Foundation's Poverty-Alleviation Programme, Tšhomišano*, paper for the Third Virtual Meeting of the CGAP Working Group on Impact Assessment Methodologies.

TATA (2004) *Statistical Outline of India 2003–2004*, Department of Economics and Statistics, TATA Services Ltd, Mumbai.

Todd, H. (2001) *Paths Out of Poverty – The Impact of SHARE Microfin Limited in Andhra Pradesh, India*, unpublished report to SHARE commissioned under *Imp-Act*.

Webb, P., Coates, J., Houser, R., Hassan, Z. and Zobair, M. (2001) *Expectations of Success and Constraints to Participation Among Women*, report to World Population Fund, Bangladesh.

Woller, G. (2004) *Additional Comparative Analysis of LAPO's Participation Form to the CGAP Poverty Assessment Tool*, unpublished report, LAPO, Nigeria.

Woller, G., Simanowitz A. and Copestake, J.G. (2004) Integrating poverty assessment into client assessment, *SEEP Network Progress Note 1* (available at http://www.seepnetwork.org).

World Bank (1999) *Bosnia and Herzegovina (1996–1998) Lessons and Accomplishments: Review of the Priority Reconstruction Program*, World Bank, Washington DC.

World Bank (2002) *Welfare in Bosnia and Herzegovina, 2001: Measurement and Findings*, report prepared by the State Agency for Statistics (BHAS) Republika Srpska, Institute of Statistics (RSIS) Federation of Bosnia-Herzegovina Institute of Statistics (FIS), World Bank, Washington DC.

Zeller, M. and Sharma, M. (2000) Assessing the relative poverty level in clients of microfinance institutions: an operational tool, in *Rural Financial Policies for Food Security of the Poor Policy Brief*, No. 10, IFPRI, Washington DC.

Index

ABC *see* activity-based costing
absolute poverty 59–60, 66, 106
academic impact assessments 49–50
accounts systems 92
ACF, Kasakhstan 164–5
action-research process 150, 155
activity-based costing (ABC) 104
adaption phase, ISM 152
administration 52–3, 136
agriculture 17–18, 69, 71, 75, 78
AIMS *see* Assessing the Impact of Microenterprise Services
AIMS-SEEP *see* Assessing the Impact of Microenterprise Services-Small Enterprise Education and Promotion Network
alcoholism 72, 80–1
Aliaga, Irina 138–46
Andhra Pradesh (AP), India 55–6, 58–60, 66
applications, loans 33, 44–5, 121
arrears 102–3
Assessing the Impact of Microenterprise Services (AIMS) 115–19, 145
Assessing the Impact of Microenterprise Services-Small Enterprise Education and Promotion Network (AIMS-SEEP) 35, 150, 153
asset bases, households 77
asset loans 119, 123
Association of Financial Institutions for Rural Development (FINRURAL) 7–8, 138–46

Avance Chalco microfinance institution 167

Bangladesh Rural Advancement Committee (BRAC) 4, 11, 15–25
  agriculture 17–18
  CFPR/TUP 21–4
  Dabi programme 17–18
  IGVGD programme 17–23
  inclusive microfinance 15–25
  JFRP 20–1
  opportunity ladders 19–22
  poverty alleviation 15–25
  ultra-poor 21–5
Baumann, Ted 40–54
bias, loan approval 125
Bolivia 7, 138–46, 165–6
bonuses 111
Bosnia-Herzegovina 6, 98–113, 149–51, 169–70
BRAC *see* Bangladesh Rural Advancement Committee
branches, Prizma 109
breaking even, SEF 51–2
Brody, Alyson 1–14
business aspects, SEF 45, 52
buyer-driven markets 71

CAMM *see* credit association management meetings
CAs *see* credit associations
case studies, summary 4–8
CAWG *see* Client Impact Working Group
Central and Eastern Europe (CEE) 147–54

184 INDEX

Centre for Youth and Social Development (CYSD) 6, 9, 11, 68–82
CFPR/TUP *see* Challenging the Frontiers of Poverty Reduction: Targeting the Ultra Poor
CGAP *see* Consultative Group to Assist the Poor
CGAP PAT *see* Consultative Group to Assist the Poor: poverty assessment tool
Challenging the Frontiers of Poverty Reduction: Targeting the Ultra Poor (CFPR/TUP) 21–4
change management 98–113
CIMS *see* Client Impact Monitoring System
client assessment
  SEEP 157–71
  see also impact assessment; poverty
client exit
  LAPO 34–6
  monitoring system 13, 34–6, 45–6, 104
  Prizma 104
  rates 65
  SAT 118–19
  SEF 43, 45–6, 51
  SHARE 65
  SPM 12–13
Client Impact Monitoring System (CIMS) 7, 114–26
Client Impact Working Group (CAWG) 157–71
client satisfaction 128–9
client status 12, 14
client well-being 48–9
client/staff learning system, LAPO 33–4
CM *see* Computer Munshi accounts system
communication 133, 136
community organizations 74
community response, PRADAN workbooks 93
composite poverty index 61
Computer Munshi (CM) accounts system 92, 95
confidentiality 152
Consultative Group to Assist the Poor (CGAP) 15–16, 29–30, 58–9, 86–7, 148

Consultative Group to Assist the Poor; poverty assessment tool (CGAP PAT) 29–30, 58–9
Copestake, James 1–14
coping strategies 131
Cortijo, Marie Jo A. 55–67
cost-effectiveness
  CIMS 124–5
  impact management 40–54
  ISM 152–3
  LAPO 37–8
  MFC 152–3, 156
  SEF 40–54
costs 53, 96, 104
credibility 145
credit association management meetings (CAMM) 133–4, 136
credit associations (CAs) 127–46
Credit with Education model 127–8, 135
credit officers, LAPO 33–4
credit scoring 50–1
crises 129–30
culture, organizational 111, 123
customized products 153–5
CYSD *see* Centre for Youth and Social Development

Dabi programme 17–18
Dash, Anup 68–82
data
  analysis 125
  collection 44–5
  qualitative/quantitative 136
  usage 14
decision-making 3, 117–19, 164
dependency burdens 63
design processes
  CIMS 115–23
  ILS 87–92
  microfinance products 24
Development of Women and Children in Rural Areas (DWCRA) 55–6, 63–4, 66–7
dialects 122, 132
disbursement of loans 118–19, 122–3
dropout *see* client exit
DWCRA *see* Development of Women and Children in Rural Areas

INDEX

Eastern Europe 147–56
education 80, 127–9, 135
efficiency 85
enabling the poor 83–4
equity, women 85
exclusion 101–4
exit *see* client exit

feedback
　CYSD 81
　FOCCAS 127–37
　PRADAN 89, 91
　SAT 124
　SEF 44, 50
FFH *see* Freedom from Hunger International
FGDs *see* focus group discussions
field tests 91
fieldworkers 43, 45, 47–8, 51–3
　see also staff
financial performance, FINRURAL 138–40
FINRURAL *see* Association of Financial Institutions for Rural Development
five-indicator poverty assessment tool 30–2
flexible products 131–2, 134
FOCCAS *see* Foundation for Credit and Community Assistance
focus group discussions (FGDs) 116, 134–5, 138
follow-up investigations 36
food security 77–8, 118, 128–31
formal exclusion 103
Foundation for Credit and Community Assistance (FOCCAS) 7, 9–10, 127–37
　CAMM 133–4
　CAWG 160
　client satisfaction 128–9
　flexible products 131–2, 134
　good practice 168
　lessons learned 135–6
　loan product changes 132–4
　loans as coping strategies 131
　seasonal difficulties 129–31
Freedom from Hunger International (FFH) 127–8, 135
funding 163

Garuba, Stanley Aifuwa 26–39
gender research 116
　see also women
Ghana 7, 114–26, 167
good practice 167–70
grain banks 74, 78
grants 19
grass-roots work 84
Greeley, Martin 1–14
growth of MFIs 2

headquarters' team, Prizma 111

IAS *see* impact assessment service
IGVGD *see* Income Generation for Vulnerable Groups Development programme
ILSs *see* internal learning systems
Imp-Act programme 3–14
　CYSD 74–82
　FINRURAL 138, 140, 142
　FOCCAS 128, 135
　LAPO 27, 29, 34
　MFC 147, 150, 153
　PRADAN 86–8
　Prizma 99–100, 102, 105, 110
　SAT 114–15
　SEEP 157–8, 161, 163, 165
　SEF 40, 43, 50
　SHARE 5, 60
impact assessment
　academic assessment 49–50
　AIMS-SEEP 35, 150, 153
　FINRURAL 138–45
　IAS 140–5
　PRADAN 86–8
　Prizma 98–113
　SEEP 160
　SHARE 55–67
　SPM 13–14
impact assessment service (IAS) 140–5
impact management 40–54
impact surveys 37
improving impact, SEEP 165–6
incentives 111–12, 133
inclusive microfinance 15–25
Income Generation for Vulnerable Groups Development (IGVGD) programme 17–23

independent studies, FINRURAL 145
India 5–6, 55–67, 68–82, 83–97
indicators
  ILSs 89–90
  impact management 47
  monitoring systems 116, 120–1
  negative impact 47
  performance 127
  poverty 30–2, 61–2
  scorecards 105–7
industry 149, 154, 156
innovation 147–56
innovation scaling-up model (ISM) 7, 147, 150–4
institutionalization
  PRADAN 83–97
  Prizma 101–3, 107–8
  SEEP 168–9
  SEF 48
  SPM 10–11, 26–39
internal learning systems (ILSs) 6, 11, 48, 83–97
international links, SAT 124
interviewing 116, 122
ISM *see* innovation scaling-up model

Jamalpur Flood Rehabilitation Project (JFRP) 20–1, 24
Johnson, Susan 127–37

Kabeer, Naila 55–67, 68–82
Kasakhstan 164–5
Kline, Sean 98–113
knowledge management 154–5
Koraput, Orissa 70–82
Kumasi branch, SAT 122

LAPO *see* Lift Above Poverty Organization
launching CIMS 123
leadership 110
learning 33–4, 83–97, 155
learning diaries 87–96
Lift Above Poverty Organization (LAPO) 5, 9–10, 26–39
  client exit monitoring system 34–6
  client/staff learning system 33–4
  commitment of the board 38
  cost-effectiveness 37–8
  monitoring systems 27–38
  poverty monitoring systems 27–33
  poverty targeting system 28–30
  social performance management 26–39
Limpopo province, South Africa 41
livelihoods
  Koraput 71, 74–8
  PRADAN 89–90, 93, 95
loans
  applications 33, 44–5, 121
  borrowing patterns 76–7, 80
  coping strategies 131
  disbursements 118–19, 122–3
  flexibility 131–2, 134
  incentives 111
  product changes 132–4
  SHARE products 56–7
  sizes 34–6, 65, 123, 129, 136
  usage 62–3, 72
local knowledge, MFIs 9

management information systems (MIS) 35–7, 46, 121, 169
management issues 1–14, 26–39, 110, 169–70
Marconi, Reynaldo 138–46
marketing aspects
  buyer-driven markets 71
  ISM 154
  MFC 153
  MFIs 2
  research 115, 141–4, 160
  SEF 52
Matin, Imran 15–25
mature clients 61–4, 74–80, 118, 123
MCP *see* Microcredit Programme
means tests 29–33, 37, 117
measurement
  poverty 58–62
  social performance 105–10
MFC *see* Microfinance Centre
MFIs *see* microfinance institutions
Microcredit Programme (MCP) 41, 45
Microfinance Centre (MFC) 7–8, 147–56
  ISM 147, 150–4
  regional innovation 147–56
  SEEP network 158
microfinance institutions (MFIs) 1–14, 114
  CGAP PAT 29

comparisons 58–9
Nigerian women 26–7
sustainability 68, 82
minimalism 65–7
MIS *see* management information systems
mission statement, Prizma 110
modules, PRADAN workbooks 89–91, 93
moneylenders 81
monitoring systems
   CIMS 7, 114–26
   client exit 12–13, 34–6, 45–6, 104
   client status 12
   CYSD 81–2
   LAPO 27–38
   MIS 35–6
   poverty 27–33
   Prizma 104
   SAT 114–26
   SEEP 160
   SEF 44–6
   self-help groups 81–2
   vulnerability 45–6
Mosley, Paul 138–46

NABW, Tajikistan 164–5
Nakayenga, Regina 127–37
Narendranath, D. 83–97
negative impact 47–8, 52–3, 118–19
networking 138–46, 147–56
new clients 61–4, 74–80, 96, 117
New Independent States (NIS) 147–54
Nicaragua case study 163
Nigeria 5, 26–39
NIS *see* New Independent States
Noponen, Helzi 87, 89

official poverty line estimates 60
operational impact management 49–50
Opoku, Lydia 114–26
opportunity ladders 19–22
organizational culture 111, 123
Orissa state, India 68–82
outreach 58–64, 86, 98–113
outsourcing 166–7
ownership, ILSs 88

participation forms, LAPO 28–9, 37
participatory programmes 8–10
partners in research 150, 152, 158–9

Pawlak, Katarzyna 147–57
performance
   indicators 127
   SEEP 51–2
   social performance 96–7, 100–13, 138–46, 160–1
   SPM 1–14, 26–39
Philippines case study 164
pictorial workbooks 87–96
pilot testing, CIMS 121–2, 124–5
Poland 7
political issues 20, 70, 79–80
poorest people
   BRAC 21–5
   CYSD 68–9, 82
   Orissa 68–9, 82
   PRADAN 86–7
   Prizma 99–100
   SEF 50–2
   SHARE 58–62
portfolios 43, 102–3
poverty
   alleviation 15–25
   assessment 29–32, 58–9, 86–7
   means tests 29–33, 37, 117
   measurement 58–62
   monitoring systems 27–33
   poverty line 60
   rates 109
   research 100–1
   scorecards 105–8, 117
   targeting system 28–30
PRADAN *see* Professional Assistance for Development Action
price indices 60
Prizma 6, 11, 98–113
   background/mission 99–100
   exclusion 101–4
   poverty research 100–1
   social performance 100–12
   staff time 169–70
proactive impact management 50
product design 24
Professional Assistance for Development Action (PRADAN) 6, 9–10, 83–97
   background 83–6
   impact assessment 86–8
   institutionalization 83–97
   internal learning systems 83–97

profit sharing 111
protest campaigns 80

qualitative/quantitative data 136
quantitative impact surveys 87
questionnaires 44–5, 158–9

Rangacharyulu, S.V. 58–9
regional aspects 55–6, 147–56
relative poverty 59–60, 66, 106
repayments 57, 65–6, 131–2, 134
research
  gender research 116
  market 115, 141–4, 160
  partners 158–9
  poverty 100–1
Rwanda case study 162

SAT *see* Sinapi Aba Trust
satisfaction, clients 118–19, 128–9
savings 64, 76–7, 80–1, 124
scaling-up phase, ISM 153–4
scorecards 105–8, 117
seasonal difficulties 129–31
SEEP *see* Small Enterprise Education and Promotion Network
SEF *see* Small Enterprise Foundation
self-exclusion 103–4
self-help groups (SHGs) 6, 72–82, 84–96
sensitive issues 93–4
service providers, MFIs 1–14
SHARE *see* Society for Helping Awaken Rural Poor through Education
SHGs *see* self-help groups
simple approach, SEEP 167–8
Sinapi Aba Trust (SAT) 7, 9–10, 114–26, 167
Small Enterprise Education and Promotion (SEEP) Network 7–8, 11, 157–71
  CAWG 157–71
  client assessment 157–71
  good practice 167–70
  lessons learnt 164–7
Small Enterprise Foundation (SEF) 5, 11, 40–54
  cost effectiveness 40–54
  impact management 40–54
  key components 42–6

  lessons learnt 46–53
  performance problems 51–2
  philosophy 41–2
social context, Orissa 69–70
social impact assessment studies 143
social performance 96–7, 100–13, 138–46, 160–1
social performance management (SPM) 1–14, 26–39
Society for Helping Awaken Rural Poor through Education (SHARE) 5, 9, 55–67
  historical details 56
  impact assessment 55–67
  methodology 55–67
  operations 56–8
  poverty measurement 58–62
South Africa 5, 40–54
SPM *see* social performance management
staff issues
  fieldworkers 43, 45, 47–8, 51–3
  FOCCAS 132–6
  PRADAN 88–9, 91–2, 95, 97
  SAT 125
  SEEP 162–3, 166, 169–70
staff/client learning system, LAPO 33–4
standardized products 153–5
start-up enterprises 103
strategy
  SEEP 164–5
  SPM 12
studies
  CAWG 158–9
  FINRURAL 143–5
  impact management 42–3
  SEF 42–3
  SHARE 55–67
subsidies 19
surveys 37, 87
sustainability 48–9, 68–82
systems improvements, SPM 14

Tajikistan 164–5
targeting system, poverty 28–30
TCP *see* Tšhomišano Credit Programme
technical capacity 161–2, 166
testing phase, ISM 151–2
Todd, H. 60–5

training, SEEP 167
Tšhomišano Credit Programme (TCP) 40–5, 50–1

Uganda 7, 127–37
ultra-poor 21–5
United States of America (USA) 157–71
urban clients 35
USA *see* United States of America

vertical learning 155
VGD *see* Vulnerable Group Development programme
village banks 138
voting 70, 79
vulnerability 17–23, 45–6, 72
Vulnerable Group Development (VGD) programme 19–22

war, Bosnia-Herzegovina 98
well-being of clients 48–9
Woller, Gary 157–71
women
  CAs 127
  CFPR/TUP 21
  CYSD 73–4
  DWCRA 55–6, 63–4, 66–7
  FOCCAS 127, 131
  IGVGD programme 19–20, 23
  Nigeria 26–7
  PRADAN 85–6
  Prizma 99
  SEF 40–1
  SHARE 55–8, 62
workbooks 87–96
working groups, SEEP 157–8

zero tolerance policy 102, 104

More Books on Microfinance from

ITDG PUBLISHING

Small Customers, Big Market
Commercial Banks in Microfinance

Malcolm Harper & Sukhwinder Singh Arora

- **First comprehensive look at commercial bank experience in microfinance**

- **Shows commercial opportunities for banks in a new market**

- **Worldwide case studies and applicability**

This book shows commercial bankers that they can profitably provide microfinance services to the poor. It illustrates, through the experience of particular banks, why banks have become involved and how they have made a success of their involvement.

The 18 case studies all show that banks can earn good profits at the same time as serving the needs of people who previously lacked access to financial services. The book also demonstrates that it is often quicker, less expensive and more effective for microfinance services to be provided by commercial banks than by specialist microfinance institutions.

Paperback•ISBN 1-85339-608-7•320pp•£24.95•US$44.95•€37.95
Not available from ITDG Publishing in India.

To order this and other leading books for development visit www.developmentbookshop.com or contact us:
☎ + 44 (0)1926 634501 or ✉ orders@itpubs.org.uk